Enterprise Application Integration With XML and Java

D1082363

ISBN 0-13-085135-3

90000

9 780130 851352

⟨!CFG/OIM⟩ Charles F. Goldfarb Series on Open Information Management

"Open Information Management" (OIM) means managing information so that it is open to processing by any program, not just the program that created it. That extends even to application programs not conceived of at the time the information was created.

OIM is based on the principle of data independence: data should be stored in computers in non-proprietary, genuinely standardized representations. And that applies even when the data is the content of a document. Its representation should distinguish the innate information from the proprietary codes of document processing programs and the artifacts of particular presentation styles.

Business data bases—which rigorously separate the real data from the input forms and output reports—achieved data independence decades ago. But documents, unlike business data, have historically been created in the context of a particular output presentation style. So for document data, independence was largely unachievable until recently.

That is doubly unfortunate. It is unfortunate because documents are a far more significant repository of humanity's information. And documents can contain significantly richer information structures than data bases.

It is also unfortunate because the need for OIM of documents is greater now than ever. The demands of "repurposing" require that information be deliverable in multiple formats: paper-based, online, multimedia, hypermedia. And information must now be delivered through multiple channels: traditional bookstores and libraries, the World Wide Web, corporate intranets and extranets. In the latter modes, what starts as data base data may become a document for browsing, but then may need to be reused by the reader as data.

Fortunately, in the past ten years a technology has emerged that extends to documents the data base's capacity for data independence. And it does so without the data base's restrictions on structural freedom. That technology is the "Standard Generalized Markup

Language" (SGML), an official International Standard (ISO 8879) that has been adopted by the world's largest producers of documents and by the World Wide Web.

With SGML, organizations in government, aerospace, airlines, automotive, electronics, computers, and publishing (to name a few) have freed their documents from hostage relationships to processing software. SGML coexists with graphics, multimedia, and other data standards needed for OIM and acts as the framework that relates objects in the other formats to one another and to SGML documents.

The World Wide Web's HTML and XML are both based on SGML. HTML is a particular, though very general, application of SGML, like those for the above industries. There is a limited set of markup tags that can be used with HTML. XML, in contrast, is a simplified subset of SGML facilities that, like full SGML, can be used with any set of tags. You can literally create your own markup language with XML.

As the enabling standard for OIM of documents, the SGML family of standards necessarily plays a leading role in this series. We provide tutorials on SGML, XML, and other key standards and the techniques for applying them. Our books vary in technical intensity from programming techniques for software developers to the business justification of OIM for enterprise executives. We share the practical experience of organizations and individuals who have applied the techniques of OIM in environments ranging from immense industrial publishing projects to websites of all sizes.

Our authors are expert practitioners in their subject matter, not writers hired to cover a "hot" topic. They bring insight and understanding that can only come from real-world experience. Moreover, they practice what they preach about standardization. Their books share a common standards-based vocabulary. In this way, knowledge gained from one book in the series is directly applicable when reading another, or the standards themselves. This is just one of the ways in which we strive for the utmost technical accuracy and consistency with the OIM standards.

And we also strive for a sense of excitement and fun. After all, the challenge of OIM—preserving information from the ravages of technology while exploiting its benefits—is one of the great intellectual adventures of our age. I'm sure you'll find this series to be a knowledgeable and reliable guide on that adventure.

About the Series Editor

Dr. Charles F. Goldfarb is the father of markup languages, a term that he coined in 1970. He invented the SGML language in 1974 and later led the team that developed it into the International Standard on which both HTML and XML are based. He serves as editor of the Standard (ISO 8879) and as a consultant to developers of SGML and XML applications and products. He is based in Saratoga, CA.

About the Series Logo

The rebus is an ancient literary tradition, dating from 16th century Picardy, and is especially appropriate to a series involving fine distinctions between things and the words that describe them. For the logo, Andrew Goldfarb incorporated a rebus of the series name within a stylized SGML/XML comment declaration.

The Charles F. Goldfarb Series on Open Information Management

As XML is a subset of SGML, the Series List is categorized to show the degree to which a title applies to XML. "XML Titles" are those that discuss XML explicitly and may also cover full SGML. "SGML Titles" do not mention XML per se, but the principles covered may apply to XML.

XML Titles

Goldfarb, Pepper, and Ensign
- SGML Buyer's Guide™: Choosing the Right XML and SGML Products and Services

Megginson
- Structuring XML Documents

Leventhal, Lewis, and Fuchs
- Designing XML Internet Applications

DuCharme
- XML: The Annotated Specification

Jelliffe
- The XML and SGML Cookbook: Recipes for Structured Information

McGrath
- XML by Example: Building E-commerce Applications

Goldfarb and Prescod
- The XML Handbook™ Second Edition

Floyd
- Building Web Sites with XML

Morgenthal and la Forge
- Enterprise Application Integration with XML and Java

McGrath
- XML Processing with Python

SGML Titles

Ensign
- $GML: The Billion Dollar Secret

Rubinsky and Maloney
- SGML on the Web: Small Steps Beyond HTML

McGrath
- ParseMe.1st: SGML for Software Developers

DuCharme
- SGML CD

General Titles

Martin
- TOP SECRET Intranet: How U.S. Intelligence Built Intelink—The World's Largest, Most Secure Network

Enterprise Application Integration With XML and Java

■ JP Morgenthal with Bill la Forge

Prentice Hall PTR, Upper Saddle River, NJ 07458
www.phptr.com

Library of Congress Cataloging-in-Publication Data

Morgenthal, JP
  Enterprise application integration with XML and Java / JP Morgenthal, with Bill la Forge.
    p. cm. -- (The definitive XML series from Charles F. Goldfarb)
    ISBN 0-13-085135-3 (alk. paper)
      1. XML (Computer program language)   2. Java (Computer program language)   3. Application
  software. I. la Forge, Bill. II. Title. III. Series.

  QA76.76.H94 M6 2000
  005.7'2--dc21   99-058839

Editorial/Production Supervision: *Wil Mara*
Acquisitions Editor: *Mark L. Taub*
Editorial Assistant: *Sarah Hand*
Series Editor: *Dr. Charles F. Goldfarb*
Technical Editor: *David McGoveran*
Marketing Manager: *Kate Hargett*
Manufacturing Manager: *Alexis R. Heydt*
Cover Design Director: *Jerry Votta*
Cover Designer: *Anthony Gemmellaro*
Art Director: *Gail Cocker-Bogusz*

© 2001 Prentice Hall PTR
Prentice-Hall, Inc.
Upper Saddle River, New Jersey 07458

Prentice Hall books are widely used by corporations and government agencies for training, marketing, and resale. The publisher offers discounts on this book when ordered in bulk quantities. For more information, contact Prentice Hall's Corporate Sales Department—phone: 1-800-382-3419; fax: 1-201-236-7141; email: corpsales@prenhall.com; address: Corp. Sales Dept., Prentice Hall PTR, 1 Lake Street, Upper Saddle River, NJ 07458.

Printed in the United States of America
10   9   8   7   6   5   4   3   2

ISBN 0-13-085135-3

Prentice-Hall International (UK) Limited, *London*
Prentice-Hall of Australia Pty. Limited, *Sydney*
Prentice-Hall Canada Inc., *Toronto*
Prentice-Hall Hispanoamericana, S.A., *Mexico*
Prentice-Hall of India Private Limited, *New Delhi*
Prentice-Hall of Japan, Inc., *Tokyo*
Pearson Education Asia P.T.E., Ltd.
Editora Prentice-Hall do Brasil, Ltda., *Rio de Janeiro*

Names such as company names, trade names, font names, service names, and product names appearing in this book may be registered or unregistered trademarks or service marks, whether or not identified as such. All such names and all registered and unregistered trademarks, service marks, and logos appearing in this book or on its cover are used for identification purposes only and are the property of their respective owners.

Series logo by Andrew Goldfarb for EyeTech Graphics, copyright © 1998, 2000 Andrew Goldfarb.

Series Foreword and book Foreword copyright © 1998, 2000 Charles F. Goldfarb.

Opinions expressed in this book are those of the Author and are not necessarily those of the Publisher or Series Editor.

The Author of this book has included a diskette or CD-ROM of related materials as a convenience to the reader. The Series Editor did not participate in the preparation, testing, or review of the materials and is not responsible for their content.

This book is dedicated to my family: Amy Lynn, Amanda, and Daniel. Through their love and support, I am able to accomplish any goal.
– JP Morgenthal

I would like to dedicate this work to my parents, who have been there for me when times were tough.
– Bill la Forge

Acknowledgements

First, I would like to thank Charles Goldfarb, who was able to convince me to write another book after swearing off book writing for good. I would also like to thank the staff at Prentice-Hall: Mark Taub, Wil Mara, and Kathleen Caren for their assistance in getting this book published. Thank you also goes to the following people: David McGoveran, who provided excellent insight through his technical editing; Steve-Ross Talbot for getting me a working copy of a JMS implementation against which I could develop code and for allowing us to distribute it with this book; and Nam Lamore, the hardest-working PR man in the computer industry and who really helped me navigate the rough waters of Sun Microsystems in the days of Java's youth. We'd aso like to thank Lee Buck of Extensibility and Andy Roberts of Bow Street for their literary contributions to this book. We also acknowledge the following companies for providing software to go on the associated CD-ROM: Bluestone Software, IBM, Extensibility, and WDDX.org. - JP

Contents

▌ Part Two
Sharing and Exchanging Data   **89**

Introduction

Enterprise Application Integration (EAI) is rapidly emerging as one of the leading initiatives for the computing industry in the early half of the new century. With the Y2K scare behind us, 2000 looks to be a year of rebirth for new computing initiatives with a strong focus on the use of technology for establishing tighter relationships with an organization's consumers and suppliers.

These relationships will be forged in many ways; for example, providing customized information for customers tailored to their specific interests and buying patterns, or including supply-chain in the automation of the overall procurement cycle. To accomplish these missions, developers are going to need a broad experience with many tools, products, operating systems, and hardware platforms. Experienced EAI development teams will include members with skills in networking, administration, project management, and software development for multiple platforms, all focused with the single goal of providing seamless integration of business systems.

The goal of EAI is not new; we have been doing it since we started distributing data away from the mainframe and onto front-end processors. However, with so much data trapped in so many different systems and data formats, companies are finding it extremely difficult and very expensive to open up and share this data with their trading partners.

Fundamentally, EAI is about developing systems that provide seamless business functionality. A key requirement for integration of systems to provide this seamless functionality is an ability to share and exchange data. Furthermore, this sharing and exchange occurs between systems that have little to no knowledge about each other's storage locations or formats.

For example, an accounting system may not have knowledge of the schema used for a sales system, thereby making it difficult for the accounting system to update sales order information after an invoice has been paid. Or, perhaps, a company needs to update its shipping and inventory systems simultaneously based upon the receipt of a new order. The data needs to be input into each of the existing systems in a manner that they understand. Due to the fact that many of these systems were departmentally chosen or developed without forethought of integrating with other departments within or external to the company, this is a significantly difficult task.

1.1 | About this Book

As we already mentioned, a key requirement of EAI is moving data from one system in one particular format, transforming it to be used by one or more other systems, and delivering the data to those other systems. It includes communications, data management, and business processing under the single, umbrella task of making disparate systems work as one.

The primary purpose of this book is to discuss the techniques and methodologies for integrating systems. Secondly, this book will illustrate how to build solutions based on these methodologies using Java and XML. Throughout this book, we will address and discuss the needs of

EAI and discuss how XML can be used to solve some of the more complex issues surrounding EAI. Each of these solutions will be examined in technical depth by exercising the capabilities of the Java platform.

XML and Java are clearly the two most intriguing developments of the computer industry within the last ten years. Java is a programming language and a specification for a virtual machine that can execute binary modules by compiling the programming language. It also defines a consistent set of services that is available to all Java programs. This is a significant change from applications developed using traditional third-generation programming languages, which most often do not offer a consistent set of services, such as networking, file I/O, windowing, etc.

XML, on the other hand, is a specification that allows users to define their own markup languages. No fancy tricks or computer voodoo; XML is a simple definition that was forged by a group of industry leaders that recognized the importance of a truly open and well-defined, neutral data format.

Together these two bodies of work allow users to write applications that can process dynamically structured and unstructured data anywhere on a network where there is a Java virtual machine. In addition, for those places where a Java virtual machine is not available, such as when dealing with C++ or legacy applications, XML provides a method of moving data outside of the virtual machine in a way that is highly reusable by non-Java platforms. In effect, we end up with a ubiquitous programming environment and a ubiquitous data representation.

This book is the melding of these two technologies in a way that is not often examined. True, most of the early XML parsers and tools were written in Java, but this book goes beyond processing XML using the Java programming language.

This book is about integrating disparate systems using XML with advanced Java capabilities, such as:

- Java Reflection
- Java Serialization

- The Java Naming & Directory Interface (JNDI)

- The Java Messaging Service (JMS)

- Java Database Connectivity (JDBC)

When you finish this book, you will have a better understanding of how to build powerful Java applications to automate business processes, conduct electronic commerce, and share information effortlessly.

1.2 | XML Basics

The Extensible Markup Language (XML) has received a lot of attention since the W3C officially blessed it in early 1998. If you ask knowledgeable people involved with the XML community about its popularity, you will get a diverse set of opinions concerning XML's quick climb to success. For example, one response would be that XML isn't really a new technology, just a new name for a subset of a proven technology called "SGML" (Standard Generalized Markup Language). The XML subset is optimized for the unmanaged heterogeneous networked environment of the Web.

The answer we like best, however, is that it is simple! HTML (Hypertext Markup Language)—another derivative of SGML—was extremely successful as the presentation language for the World Wide Web because it was simple and because most people could learn to use it with ease. That does not necessarily mean that what people created was beautiful to look at, but it conveyed information that was important to its author and that is the most important part of the Web.

XML lives because those closest to the Web soon realized that forcing users to tie their presentation to their content was defeating. The Web is about presentation, but most times, the look changes without a corresponding change in the underlying messages being presented. XML provides a way to design content such that any presentation can be applied post-authoring and the messages are preserved in reusable documents.

For some, the last paragraph has significant importance, but when we attempted to use XML for this purpose, we soon found ourselves creating a vocabulary that very closely mimicked HTML. That is, we had to include too many visual hints in the markup language to get the effect we wanted in our presentation.

Still, XML had hit a nerve with us—it represented a way to encapsulate variable-length, free-form text with highly structured data under a single context. The start of real electronic knowledge-capture was ours to be had with a set of initiatives for simple processing.

Since our introduction to XML, we have put a significant amount of time and effort into analyzing this phenomenon. We know that XML is more than just a fad that became popular because it had an Internet label. The real benefit that XML provides to the industry is data interoperability. After all, we have been working on the problem of process interoperability for over ten years, but only in recent years has real data interoperability become a concern for the reasons we mentioned earlier in the introduction. Between the industry's advancement in distributed computing and the addition of XML to the toolkit, we finally had the ability to build complete solutions for exchanging and sharing data without requiring months of design and development for a single point-to-point exchange.

1.3 | XML in the Business World

Before jumping into the technical end of the pool, let's take a brief moment to explore the business requirements that are driving XML's popularity and success. In this section, we will explore how XML is being used to solve complex, real-world business problems today.

Computers have been mostly helpful to companies for automating data processing and providing near instantaneous access to information about the business. We use the qualifier "near" here because it is theoretically possible, but hindered due to poor system and application designs. There is a certain instant gratification that can be brought about by the use of computers. They provide a sense of immediate feedback for any stimuli we provide them—including bad stimuli.

Companies are just starting to realize that they will never be finished building systems to run their businesses, because business is always changing. Therefore, the systems that support business need to change rapidly as well. This was not a widely held belief before the mid-1990s when many companies viewed their Information Systems (IS) departments as nasty expenses that were less expensive than using humans to perform the same tasks.

However, finally there has been a revolution within the last five years. Companies have realized that they can use the talent in their IS departments to provide them with systems that proactively watch market trends and conditions and help the business react in a positive direction. With this change comes a major paradigm shift. No longer will businesses need monolithic systems that perform a single task, such as accounting, human resources, or sales, but they will need modular components that can talk to each other and be aggregated into a larger component that understands the goals of the business. *The more of these components that become available, the more intelligent the system becomes.*

So it goes; we reached the end of a century and the end of a millennium. Companies were faced with the possibility of widespread system failure if they underestimated their risk from potential Y2K problems, and at the same time were forced to enter into a growing global electronic economy. The choices were minimal; take what we have and make it work with new applications. There were neither time nor resources available for rebuilding legacy systems, even if that were the preferred option. This alone has had sweeping consequences for the computer industry.

EAI exists today as a means of freeing the data trapped inside existing legacy systems for use by many other applications. EAI encompasses many fine-grained technologies, such as supply-chain integration, automated procurement, sales, customer service, distribution, routing, etc. Underlying each of these areas are technologies for data exchange and data sharing, such as file systems, distributed objects, Web, application servers, etc.

As we go deeper and deeper under the covers, it soon becomes clear that woven into this intricate tapestry is the need to move data from point A to point B in a secure and transacted manner with no guarantee that points A and B know anything about each other. Until now, most of the work of moving data from A to B was accomplished by having two teams of developers that were intimate with A and B get together and hash out a middle ground. Then each team would walk away to create its half of an application portal that would connect these two disparate systems. Some weeks later, when each team was finished, they would put the two halves together and run a test. All this cost between $30,000 and $250,000. *Imagine the costs of making all production applications in the enterprise communicate this way!*

It did not take long, based on the financial requirements cited above, to realize there had to be a better way. Some software companies began to provide software that simplified the process of building the portals between applications. These portal development tools, however, did not come cheaply, but they did lower the cost of each additional system being integrated. And, even with this software, developers intimate with the system being integrated were required to spend time making the innards of their application known to those trained in using the portal development tools.

We are now entering the next phase of this process. With agreement by the industry on XML as a language for representing hierarchically structured information, there is now a way for system experts who are intimate with the structures of their applications to describe their data without having to spend hours communicating how their application works and what their internal structures mean. XML can even be leveraged by portal development tools for help in speeding integration between systems.

Here are some simple scenarios that illustrate how XML can enhance this process significantly:

Integrating Internal Applications

Company A has two systems—sales and customer service—handling various aspects of business processing, but they do not communicate. Due to the nature of business, a customer in the sales system will eventually become a user in the customer service system. This usually happens the first time a customer calls in with a particular problem with regard to the products sold to them.

There's nothing wrong with this process from the perspective of Company A except that customers are a bit irate that information on the product they purchased, such as the serial number, date, and cost, is not accessible to the customer service representative. Just having this information on file could change the whole experience of some calls from negative to positive.

Company A explores the option of purchasing a new integrated system that links customer service and sales, but decides that the costs are too high when training and data migrating are incorporated into the picture. The simple solution, and less costly one, is to provide a link between these two systems, such that all sales information is transferred to the customer service system when an order is shipped. This includes issuing compensating transactions when items are returned.

Clearly, there is never to be a direct communication between the sales and customer service systems. Instead, some business logic must be developed that takes all completed invoices and all authorized returns at day's end and packages them up in a single XML message to be delivered to a process running in customer service. The grammar for this document must be dictated by the customer service system because only it can decide what is the minimal set of information needed by other systems. Because they used XML, Company A was able to leverage the large body of tools now available on the market and did not have to spend time building a parser for a proprietary data format.

Dynamic Data Publishing

All companies have terabytes of data trapped inside their legacy applications. Even when the data is stored inside database management systems, it is not readily available because one must understand the schema and table relationships to make use of the data stored there. Unfortunately, it is this base of information that we now wish to use to foster decision support systems within the enterprise.

Luckily, all applications have a way to get at their data, even if it means reading the data right out of the screen memory buffer—a process known as "screen scraping." The question is, how can all this data be brought together in a way that is intelligible and manageable? That is, if new data types are continually being introduced, is there some way to organize the data for maximum reuse? The answer to these questions is yes!

The most likely reason for bringing these data types together is to provide a singular view of some business object; for example, the complete history of information for a customer or product. Inside most large organizations, this data can be found across many systems and stored in many different formats and data sources. XML provides an excellent vehicle for representing these new interim data objects.

If Company A wants to view the entire history of a product, inclusive of its sales since inception and broken down by geography and consumer; the sales plan for the product; and the biographies of the management team for the product, they would need a format that could support both structured data and free-form text. In addition, they would need a way to identify the information inside this new aggregate data object and some context for the information contained within it. Context is what allows Company A to differentiate between total sales figures in the Northeast and total sales figures for men between the ages of 25 and 34.

It is clear to see how XML could be used to represent the aggregate data set, but the simplicity of the big picture is that if the data source where this data is extracted from generates XML, that data only needs to be grafted into the document as a child element of the root. Thus, XML simplifies the collection of data and provides a container for representing it.

These two examples quickly illustrate what can be accomplished by learning how to integrate XML into your systems today. This book will show you how to do it using Java, but the principles can be applied to other programming environments just as easily.

 ***Note*** *The book assumes a basic knowledge of Java programming and of XML. There are many books available on both subjects that can supply that knowledge. In this series, there are two books with XML tutorials:* The XML Handbook™ *by Goldfarb and Prescod, and* XML by Example *by Sean McGrath. The second edition of* The XML Handbook *also includes tutorials on namespaces, XLink, and other XML-based technologies discussed in this book.*

1.4 | Getting Started

The book begins with Part One, which covers basics of Enterprise Application Integration (EAI) and processing XML. It lays a very important foundation that will be used throughout the rest of the book. The part includes:

- Why XML and Java are useful to EAI.

- The difference between point-to-point and many-to-many application integration.

- The requirements for sharing and exchanging data.

- How XML is processed programmatically.

Part One

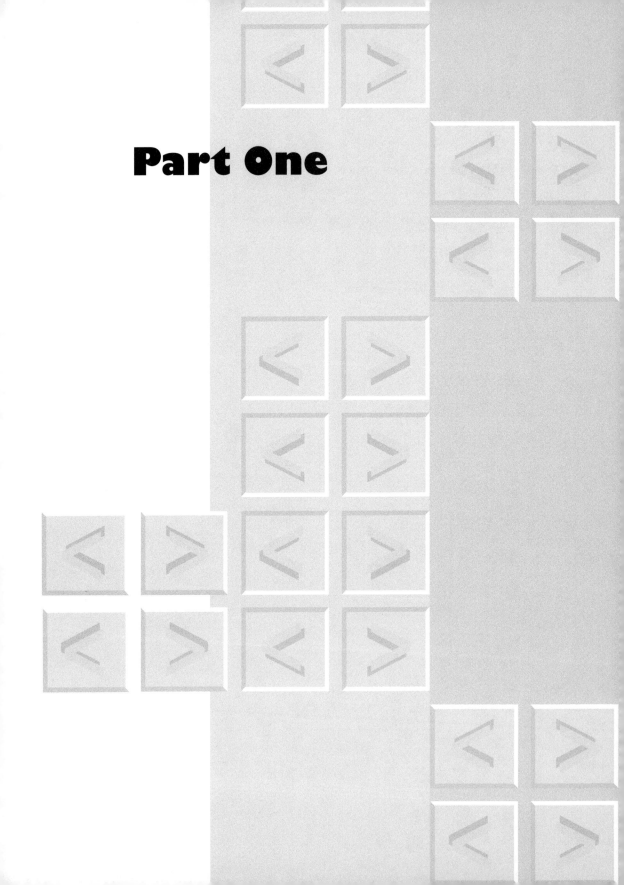

Basics of EAI

Building an EAI
Infrastructure

2

2.1 | Introduction

In this chapter, we will examine the requirements for building an EAI. There are many methods of integrating applications, such as using shared data sources like databases and memory, and developing programming interfaces that communicating applications understand. Each of these methods has positive and negative aspects to consider when scaling across departments and companies. These aspects need to be explored during the design phase of integration projects.

This chapter provides the reader with one particular view of implementing an EAI infrastructure. The design is based on years of application integration experience gained across multiple industries, including telecommunications, finance and banking, insurance, and entertainment. This view was first presented in the XML Solutions report entitled *Lowering Total Cost of Change for Enterprise Application Integrations*, which was published in March 1999 and has since been reproduced in the May/June 1999 issue of *EAI Journal*.

The aforementioned report based its assumptions on the following definitions for EAI:

> *"The seamless integration of business processes for the purposes of conducting business electronically" – JP Morgenthal*

> *"The sharing and/or exchange of data between systems for the purpose of providing a unified interface" – JP Morgenthal*

In each of these cases, the driving factors for the integration will change with respect to the requirements of the business. Because the requirements change often, tightly bound integrations will cost more to change than integrations that are loosely coupled. For many, this is already a widely understood principle; however, building loosely coupled systems is a complex task that requires resources with a significant amount of integration experience. The XML Solutions report provides a framework for companies to use to design their loosely coupled systems and to compare products that assist in this goal.

2.2 | Building Virtual Applications

A virtual application is best defined as a set of loosely coupled systems integrated in such a manner that data from any of these systems is available to any other system that belongs to the virtual application.

Due to the nature of business, systems are often integrated only on a need-to-know basis. That is, operational systems are integrated when there is a business imperative to do so. There is nothing inherently wrong with this method. However, if every integration is implemented in a tightly bound, point-to-point manner—systems bound together over one particular business task—then there will be a high probability that the maintenance and development of these integrations will be at a premium.

Instead, companies can integrate applications using a many-to-many integration methodology. In this methodology, the same business impetus acts as a driving factor; however, each application undergoes its own separate and distinct integration process. These separate integration processes require examination of existing systems for the data and processes it represents and extract this metadata to create a centralized definition of a business element.

Upon completion of this process, other systems will be able to request this system's data as named entities and will be able to send the system data for processing (if this is pertinent to the function of the system). In this way, the data, and the processes that produce that data, are made accessible, but in a way that is abstract and hides implementation details from other systems. The results of this process are that implementations can change without affecting systems that rely on other system data.

In addition, an integration must allow only pure data objects to enter and leave the system. The reason for this is simple: Applications that are integrated using Application Programming Interfaces (APIs) can be broken if one application makes a change that is not immediately recognized across all applications that communicate with the one that has changed. To ensure that invalid or changed code modules that operate over APIs cannot break the system, we simply send pure data that can be acknowledged or ignored by the receiving system. This is a critical point for integrating systems across and within enterprises, and not just single departments. The following illustrates the impact of a change in both interface- and data-centric environments.

Interface-Centric	*Data-Centric*
Interface-centric systems communicate over agreed-upon protocols. These protocols have typed input	Data-centric systems communicate through agreement of data format. Agreement in data format allows receiving

(continued)

Interface-Centric	*Data-Centric*
and output parameters and typed return values. If the interface definition—including its parameter types, return value type, or number of parameters—should change, the system would be in an indeterminate state.	systems to validate the source data prior to processing. Any changes from what is expected will result in an exception being thrown. This results in providing a system that is always in a known state at all times, even if that state is an exception.

This requirement to move only pure data objects in and out of the system boundary results in declarative processing environments. Declarative processing environments have clear advantages over procedural environments in the areas of scalability and maintenance. The following section details this more clearly and defines declarative and procedural environments.

2.2.1   *Procedural vs. Declarative*

The best argument for using a declarative approach over a procedural approach is illustrated by the following true story:

A young man was told by his superiors to calculate a very large set of numbers by adding them together in a very precise manner. The set was so large, and took so long to calculate, that he and his superiors missed a key deadline they were shooting for. When the young man moved on to his next task, which was to calculate yet another large set of numbers, he quickly remarked that the two sets had the same conclusion. Indeed, the response to this feat of computation was one of disbelief by his peers and superior. However, upon further investigation, it was found that the young man was not only correct, but a lightning-fast calculator.

The moral of the story is this: Had his superior just asked him to calculate the first set of numbers and not dictated how he wanted them calculated, he would have had his answer as quickly as the young man completed the second set.

In this story, the approach taken for the first task is a procedural approach, while the approach taken for the second task is declarative. In the first task, the young man was told how to accomplish the goal, while for the second task, the young man was just asked to accomplish the goal, thus yielding a very different outcome.

A declarative environment is one in which requests are oriented toward identifying the goal rather than dictating the steps. Many systems accomplish this by deciphering the type of a data element that it has been given. This implies that a declarative environment has logic and enough internal information to recognize a piece of data as a known type. Based upon its analysis, the declarative environment can then take appropriate action. Declarative environments make no assumptions about the data they are given to process and require no agreements with the environment that created the data. Therefore, new data types can be introduced into the environment at any time with the stipulation that descriptive information about the data and a unique identifier are given to the declarative environment.

Changing or adding a data type in a declarative environment does not require the source application and the receiving application to be changed synchronously.

The opposite of a declarative environment is a procedural environment. A procedural environment attempts to complete a goal by dictating the steps necessary. This means that the sending and receiving parties must agree along many boundaries. For example, the receiving party needs to allow itself to be manipulated by the sender, thus requiring rigid agreement over input and output mechanisms.

> **Changing or adding a data type in a procedural environment requires the source application and receiving application to be changed and tested at the same time.**

Changes in business usually require the addition of a new data type or changes to the way existing data types are processed. Therefore, as one can clearly deduce from the above descriptions, changes to procedural environments take more time, are more expensive, and require significantly more testing, whereas changes to a declarative environment can be accomplished and tested in isolation from the rest of the system. Attempting to use a procedural environment at enterprise-scale, such as distributed object computing models and remote procedure calls, makes the enterprise vulnerable to breakdown and excessive maintenance.

2.3 | EAI Infrastructures

Based upon the requirements laid out in the previous section, it is clear that an important part of a company's overall EAI infrastructure is a declarative processing environment. To this end, we have devised a logical architecture that illustrates for companies the key components for designing such an infrastructure and how products that satisfy this need fit into the overall "big picture" of EAI.

Figure 2–1 depicts a multi-layered approach toward integrating applications in a many-to-many scenario, as discussed earlier in this chapter. There are three major horizontal components that are tied

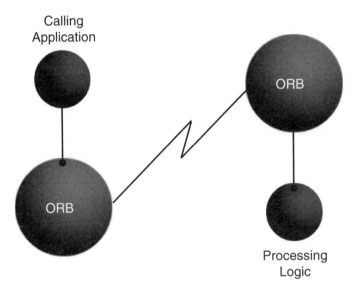

Figure 2–1   The EAI Infrastructure.

together by four vertical components. Each of these is discussed in further detail below.

2.3.1   *Communications Layer*

However, because of the nature of network computing, many products and tools that implement integration functions will seemingly overlap multiple horizontal layers. Here are some examples that will act as guidelines for understanding how to break out this functionality.

Open Database Connectivity (ODBC)
ODBC is middleware that presents an abstract interface for interacting with SQL-based databases. It will be used by either Business Intelligence or Routing & Brokering layers to execute SQL operations against a database, but it does not implement business logic itself.

Message-Oriented Middleware Services

Message-Oriented Middleware (MOM) services allow many applications to register for the delivery of messages published by a single source. MOM functionality needs to be broken across both the Communications and Routing & Brokering layers. The physical transportation of a message via TCP/IP, asynchronous messaging, or an equivalent transport facility is represented in the Communications layer. The queues and subscriber lists are stored in the Routing & Brokering layer.

Legacy Application Mining

Integrating existing 3270 terminal (mainframe) and 5250 terminal (AS/400) screen-based applications requires tools and products that can cross the Routing & Brokering and Communications layers. Typically, these legacy applications operate by filtering the 3270 and 5250 data streams, picking out the relevant fields. These fields are then transformed into a data structure that can be used by newly developed applications. The transformation processes are part of the Routing & Brokering layer, while the physical communications with the data streams occur in the Communications layer.

Object Request Brokering

Object Request Brokers (ORBs) are identified as part of the Routing & Brokering layer (and will be discussed further below); however, ORBs also play a part in the communications middleware function. They work by routing local function calls to functionality located inside another module. This other module can be located locally or on a remote machine. It is the role of the ORB to coordinate the location of this component, pass along the request for execution, and deliver the results back to the calling application. Therefore, ORBs have a communications component that is separate and distinct from the brokering process.

The primary role of this layer is to isolate business functions from the physical requirements of moving data between applications. This allows data to enter and to be sent from the other layers of the EAI Infrastructure, regardless of the transport necessary to complete the task.

2.3.2 *Routing & Brokering Layer*

This horizontal layer represents the real work associated with application integration. Whether exchanging or sharing data, this layer will use its intimate knowledge of each integrated system to aggregate and transform data for maximum reusability.

As illustrated in Figure 2–1, there are many functions that belong in this layer, such as aggregation, transformation, metadata brokering, object request brokering, message routing, and event handling. While each of these functions plays a separate and distinct role, which we will discuss shortly, they do so with the focus of allowing applications to view the collective body of data in a way that it can best be understood. Below is a brief discussion of the types of functions that can be found in this layer.

Aggregation
Aggregation is the process of culling together data from multiple, disparate sources into a single structure that better represents a single business notion, such as a customer or order. Typically, this information is broken out across systems within the enterprise based upon the operational requirements of the business. However, there is a growing need to bring this data back together as a single entity at a later point in time to satisfy requirements for other systems, such as Customer Relationship Management (CRM) and decision support.

Transformation
Many production systems were developed or purchased with the requirement of meeting the business needs of a single department. Most of these systems have some method of importing data from other systems, but enforce their own data formats and protocols. The transformation function within the EAI Infrastructure is responsible for formatting data and messages based upon the needs of these systems.

Metadata Brokering

As the EAI Infrastructure matures and applications are made aware of its existence, it is hoped that some of the manual labor associated with integration will be automated; this will most likely take place during the development phase. Enabling this functionality will be a metadata broker that provides the various integration development environments with information about the types of data already available through the EAI Infrastructure.

Object Request Broker (ORB)

As discussed in the Communications layer overview above, the ORB is a form of message brokering that specializes in executing processing logic in a location-transparent manner. It works by exposing a distinct set of application functionality via an API. This interface is then used by a calling application to execute this functionality, regardless of its locality.

To accomplish this task, the ORB provides the calling application with a function proxy that packages up the function's parameters into a message, which is sent to the ORB. The ORB then locates the logic to be executed and uses the information contained in the message to invoke the method locally. The results of that function, whether exception or success, are packaged up and sent back to the calling application via the same mechanism (see Figure 2–2).

The ORB plays a major role in abstracting the execution of business logic from the calling application. As a result, the EAI Infrastructure can incorporate this functionality easily.

Routing Tables

As a part of an entire integration scenario, it is often necessary to send messages to other systems to either update them or to trigger a processing response necessary to complete an overall integration task. This component allows the EAI Infrastructure to manage the flows between applications in a system-independent manner that can be explored and used by all integrated applications. Additionally, these tables can be updated easily, dynamically changing the flow of data as needed by the business.

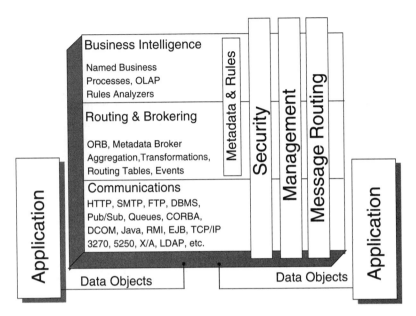

Figure 2–2   ORB Functionality.

Event Handling

A key part of being a declarative environment is reacting to information as it arrives. This is implemented through the event handling system. Events can be driven from a number of different mechanisms, for example, by changes in a directory of a file system or a trigger within a database upon completion of an operation. This component of the EAI Infrastructure is responsible for associating an event with a particular set of processing tasks.

2.3.3   *Business Intelligence Layer*

The Business Intelligence layer is responsible for creating an abstract notion of corporate data. This can be done in two ways:

1. Extrapolation of information by analyzing large sets of existing data.

2. Association of the information with the steps necessary to retrieve it.

For example, the Business Intelligence layer could respond to a request for the current total balance for all accounts by asking the Routing & Brokering layer to create an aggregate composite of all the customer account information and then computing the answer. Moreover, the name "total account balance" might reference a field in a database, in which case, the Business Intelligence layer would simply ask the Routing & Brokering layer to fetch that information on its behalf.

Responses to queries are created by the Business Intelligence layer. They are then handed to the Routing & Brokering layer for transformation and delivered via the Communications layer.

Each of the horizontal layers of the EAI Infrastructure may be provided by a single product on a single machine, many products on a single machine, or comprised of many products working cooperatively over a network. For this reason, the following vertical components were selected as being the most important to the development of an EAI Infrastructure.

2.3.4   *Security*

Security is an encompassing and ambiguous term that, in general, defines a constraint against public access. In some cases, security means encrypting the data on the wire so that it cannot be easily interpreted by those who would spy on data at this level. Security also represents the need for a user to authenticate him- or herself to a system—to prove in the most plausible manner that they are who they claim to be.

For purposes of building an EAI Infrastructure, all of these types of security are important. For the Communications layer, security ensures that those snooping on the wire cannot view the data. For the Routing & Brokering layer, only those applications and users with proper access should be able to invoke certain transformations or receive certain messages. And, for the Business Intelligence layer, security controls access to the available data.

2.3.5   *Management*

Since we're talking about enterprise-level integration here, the ability to remotely manage any deployed integration software is a must. Many home-grown solutions often leave this major component out, forcing severe problems with troubleshooting and maintenance over time. Additionally, it is critical for administrators to be able to evaluate the performance of each layer individually. The administrator of a well-managed integration should be able to answer the following questions about the EAI Infrastructure:

■ How many transformations are occurring per hour?

■ What are the 25 most heavily requested pieces of data?

■ How many messages are entering the system between 9 AM and 6 PM?

■ What was the original request message for the transformation that was marked at 11:00:22 AM EST Mar 29, 1999?

Without proper auditing, logging, and alert management, it would be impossible to deploy and maintain an enterprise-level EAI Infrastructure.

2.3.6   *Message Routing*

Message routing is required to move data between the individual layers. There is no specification for how this message routing should be carried out, only that any layer can communicate and use the services provided by the other two layers. Examples of how different products implement this message routing capability include:

- Windows Message System for Win32 applications.

- Java Method Calls for pure Java applications.

- Asynchronous messaging.

- Interprocess communications (pipes, queues, Microsoft COM).

- Distributed object computing (Microsoft DCOM and CORBA).

2.3.7   *Metadata & Rules Repository*

This repository contains the definitions, data flows, event associations, and other assorted information that allow the EAI Infrastructure to decide intelligently how to react in a declarative manner. Logically, the metadata & rules repository must be centralized and unique; otherwise, it is possible to introduce ambiguity. For example, if two copies of the repository existed and each had a different definition for account balance, then the overall virtual application would respond differently based upon which repository it was talking to. Indeed, this might cause an exception if the two pieces of information were incompatible.

However, physically, the metadata & rules repository can be distributed using replication, thus ensuring that the necessary information is available locally. This means there must be a singular repository against which all maintenance is executed.

The EAI Infrastructure that is presented in this section has proven extremely helpful to many customers in understanding the EAI product market. It can also act to focus the integration efforts within companies so that future projects are carried out with the goal of many-to-many integration in mind.

This architecture provides a framework for overall EAI. However, there still remains a need for understanding the requirements of sharing and exchanging data that are carried out by this infrastructure. The next two sections focus on these goals.

2.4 | Requirements for Data Sharing

The act of sharing data implies that two or more applications will be working from the same conceptual data model. This means that these applications must all have a common agreement about the data format or programming interface that will be used to read and write data. In addition to the common agreement over what is being shared, there are a number of other characteristics common to shared data environments. These include:

- *Concurrency.* Concurrency ensures that multiple applications, or users, accessing and updating the same set of data will not introduce corruption when overlapping these operations. That is, only one application, or user, may modify a particular segment of the data at a time. Usually, this segment is defined as a record, but may be as atomic as a field, or as coarse as an entire page consisting of many records. Until the application has completed its operation, these segments will remain locked, and therefore cannot be corrupted by the actions of other applications or users.

- *Security.* If multiple applications are all sharing the same physical data, then there needs to be a way to ensure that access over segments of this information is provided on a need-to-know basis. Traditionally, this is accomplished through the use of access control lists, which identify a user or role as being able to access a particular table or set of records.

■ *Extensibility.* There needs to be a method of adding new data and datatypes without changing the underlying data representation and, consequently, the applications that are sharing data. As illustrated in Table 2–1, we are using a single field containing self-describing data to store information that is pertinent to the main record, but contains differing data based upon who a person is dealing with. This methodology allows new applications to be integrated into the conceptual model without affecting those applications that are already running.

 Note   One of the ways that shared data implementations can be extensible is by storing XML documents within a binary large object (BLOB) field inside an RDBMS. We will explore this further later on.

Table 2–1   Representation of multiple party data interests.

Name	Age	Partner Data
JP Morgenthal	34	`<X INFO>`
		`<COMPANY A DATA>`
		`<LOCATION>NY</LOCATION>`
		`<EMAIL>jpm@xmls.com</EMAIL>`
		`</COMPANY A DATA>`
		`<COMPANY B DATA>`
		`<ORDER NUMBER>0139482</ORDER NUMBER>`
		`</COMPANY B DATA>`
		`</X INFO>`

Through the use of a secured programming interface, it becomes easy to control viewing and updating this record for a large number of companies while only allowing them to see the portion of the partner data that is pertinent to them.

2.5 | Requirements for Exchanging Data

The act of exchanging data implies that one application will provide another application with a set of data in some format. This exchange can occur as part of a conversational protocol between these two systems or simply a one-way transfer. Regardless of how it is accomplished, the greater implication here is that the first application cannot control what the second application will do with the data.

At least in a shared data model, there is some central facility that can invoke security procedures over the physical data store, but this is not necessarily so for data exchange. Therefore, data exchange has a very different set of requirements from data sharing. The following provides an overview of these requirements:

- *Agreements.* The most important part of successful data exchange is the agreement. This occurs outside the integration task and has more to do with a social agreement between people than between computers. That is, before we can implement data exchange, human resources that represent the applications exchanging data must agree on the data format and conversational protocol for exchange.

- *Eliminate Assumptions.* Long-term, successful data exchange applications eliminate the need for the receiving application to make assumptions about the data format.

This is done by introducing a namespace for processing instead of relying on positional or absolute addressing characteristics. For example, a comma-delimited file provides fields of data separated by commas. If the first line of this file provides the names of the fields, following the same ordering as will be encountered in the file, then each line can be associated with a set of field names. Without the field names, the processing application must make assumptions about the file that could be incorrect and therefore could produce erroneous results.

XML has become a popular format for data exchange in contrast to formats like comma-delimited because it provides even more information about the data and adds the dimension of scope. Comma-delimited and other like formats could only represent hierarchical data if the processing application makes assumptions about the meaning of a line relative to a line that preceded it. These assumptions are not necessary with XML since it can explicitly represent hierarchical data. XML also provides a namespace using tags to indicate the start and end of data segments.

2.6 | Summary

In this chapter, we discussed the requirements for building a virtual application, which is an application that can access all corporate data from a single point. To accomplish this task, we employed a declarative environment that provided us with the ability to integrate individual applications in an isolated manner, but resulted in making each application's data available to the enterprise at large.

One decision that needs to be made when developing an EAI Infrastructure that will power a declarative environment is whether to use the data sharing or data exchange technique. Each has different requirements and offers different benefits. Data sharing is more complex and has a high degree of maintenance, but it allows the data's owner to keep more control over how the data is accessed and used. Data exchange is more complex initially, since it requires agreement on exchange protocols and formats, but is virtually maintenance-free once this is completed.

In the next chapter, we will more deeply examine the relationship between XML, Java, and EAI. Initially, this will be presented by illustrating how to programmatically manipulate XML documents using Java.

Methods of
Processing XML

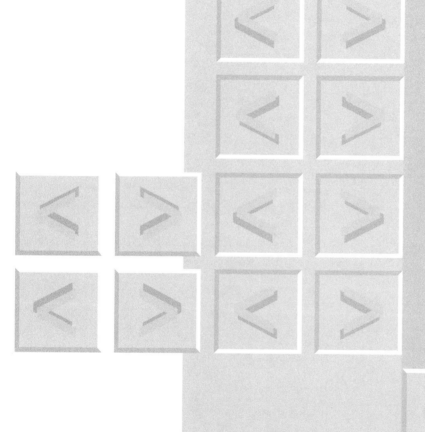

Chapter 3

3.1 | Introduction

In this chapter, we will examine the methods of processing XML documents. This foundation will be used throughout the book to assist us in developing higher-level XML processing functions for Enterprise Application Integration (EAI). It is also the most logical place to start a discussion on XML. Without understanding the following concepts, it will be difficult to exercise XML inside more complex business processes.

This chapter starts with an overview of the requirements for parsing XML documents. From there, we will explore some of the programmatic ways that parsed XML data can be accessed. At the end of this chapter, you will have an excellent understanding of how to build higher-level processes based on data formatted in XML.

3.2 | Parsing XML

A *parser* is executable processing logic that ensures that a particular document conforms to a specific grammar. Consequently, an XML parser is responsible for ensuring that XML documents conform to the XML grammar. This section examines the details regarding how to parse an XML document.

XML is a specification for a grammar that defines a set of tokens and the sequential ordering of these tokens that allow it to represent data hierarchically. The results of this specification are the following:

1. Documents have a set of rules to be followed for their creation.

2. The grammar defines how to build a process to verify that a document has followed the rules of the grammar, and thus is valid.

This is true of any computer language, whether it is a markup language or a programming language. This is accomplished by means of "production rules." The rules define the "nonterminal symbols" composed of both tokens and/or nonterminal symbols.

There are many ways to define a grammar, but the most popular one in use today is the Extended Backus-Naur Form (EBNF). The grammar defines the set of acceptable token sequences, which in turn defines the syntactic correctness of a statement in a language.

Example 3.1 below is a production rule for a `First` symbol. It states that the `First` is a nonterminal of a single `Name` symbol.

Example 3.1: Sample EBNF production rule.

```
First ::= Name
```

As the grammar has no production for `Name`, it is a token, or terminal symbol. Every machine-language definition has at least one root production, called a "starting nonterminal," that breaks down into a set of productions for statements that can be formed by that language. When reconstructing tokens from a character stream, a parser needs to assume that the starting nonterminal will be satisfied, and attempts to verify that the resulting tokens do indeed match that assumption.

Interestingly, an EBNF grammar is very similar in design to an XML Document Type Definition (DTD) content model; this is by design. In essence, XML with DTDs provides a way to build a generic parser for tag-based notations. This is why XML is called a meta-language. It is a language for creating other languages, just as EBNF is a language for creating other languages.

EBNF nonterminal symbols keep expanding into other nonterminals until a terminal token is eventually reached.

Example 3.2: An EBNF grammar.

```
Person ::= First Middle Last
First ::= Name
Middle ::= Name
Last ::= Name
```

In Example 3.2, the starting nonterminal `Person` is comprised of three other nonterminals: `First`, `Middle`, and `Last`. Each of these nonterminals is comprised of a single token called `Name`, which is eventually is composed of a sequence of characters.

Notice also that grammars are designed using a component-like philosophy. The declarations define a set of types. `First`, `Middle`, and `Last` symbols could easily have been declared as nonterminal tokens, but this would make the grammar difficult to change if necessary in the future. Using this current definition, a change to the `Name` token will be propagated all the way back to `Person`.

Once you understand how grammars work, you can read and understand the definitions within the XML 1.0 grammar. Grammars also serve another useful purpose: They are directly convertible to state diagrams, which are then used to code the parsing logic. That is, to simplify the development of the parser code, it is best if the developer first builds a state diagram from the EBNF in the XML specification.

These state diagrams then become the logical statements that eventually identify a particular symbol.

Parsing is traditionally a two-phase process. First, the lexical analyzer parses the document and turns raw character streams into a series of tokens. These tokens are then processed by the syntactic checker and compared against the original EBNF rules to ensure that the document is syntactically correct. Sometimes, with simple and lightweight languages, such as XML, it is possible to compress these two steps into a single function.

Let's explore how the parser will ensure that an XML document is well-formed. Again, a well-formed XML document is one that follows the rules of the 1.0 grammar, but may or may not follow the rules of a DTD. For the rest of this discussion, we will refer to the following XML document (Example 3.3):

Example 3.3: XML Document for Parsing.

```
<?xml version="1.0"?>
<ROOT>
   <ELEMENT_1>Some Text</ELEMENT_1>
   <ELEMENT_2 attribute="1">
      <ELEMENT_3>Some More Text</ELEMENT_3>
   <ELEMENT_2>
   <?PI_1?>
   <ELEMENT_4/>
   <!- Comment ->
</ROOT>
```

Example 3.4: The first rule of the XML Grammar.

```
[1] Document ::= prolog element Misc*
```

The rule in Example 3.4 tells the parser that it needs to break the entire document up into two or three major symbols (there may be zero `Misc` symbols). The goal of parsing is to ensure that the XML document meets the criteria for being a `Document`. To do this the parser will start with the first symbol and attempt to locate that symbol within the document. If the first symbol is optional (indicated by the *), then it will look for the first and second symbols, whichever comes first, and so on until it can make a suitable match, or it fails because no matches occur.

In Example 3.3, the prolog consists of the XML declaration processing instruction. If we had defined a DTD, that too would be considered part of the prolog. Thus, our parser starts reading in characters. It finds the less than (<), question mark (?), x, m, and l, which tell it that this is the XML processing instruction. The parser will continue scanning characters until the greater than (>) character is found. Along the way, the processor will find pseudo-attributes pertinent to parsing, such as the XML version and language encoding. The parser is responsible for extracting these pseudo-attributes and using them to prepare the parser for forthcoming text.

When the parser comes across the > character in the XML declaration processing instruction, it knows it has a complete XMLDecl (Declaration 23 as illustrated in Example 3.5). The next step is a bit more tricky for the parser as the next symbol could be a Misc, a doctypedecl, or an element.

Example 3.5: Prolog rule.

```
[22]  prolog ::=  XMLDecl? Misc* (doctypedecl Misc*)?
[23]  XMLDecl ::=  '<?xml' VersionInfo EncodingDecl? SDDecl? S? '?>'
[24]  VersionInfo ::=  S 'version' Eq (' VersionNum ' |
         " VersionNum ")
[25]  Eq ::=  S? '=' S?
[26]  VersionNum ::=  ([a-zA-Z0-9_.:] | '-')+
[27]  Misc ::=  Comment | PI | S
```

As the parser examines the stream of characters in the XML document from start to finish, it continually manages a stack of symbols. When a token is found, the stack is evaluated to see if the current set of symbols matches a valid XML rule. If it does, those symbols are removed from the stack and replaced with the name of the matched symbol. Eventually, the stack should look just like the rule in Example 3.4.

We mentioned earlier in this chapter that besides helping to identify if a document is syntactically correct, grammars can also assist us in developing the actual code necessary to build the lexical analyzer (the piece that turns character streams into tokens). To move from EBNF to building the lexical analyzer, we must first build a set of state diagrams. State diagrams visually identify the states that the parser can be in at any one time and the legal states that can be achieved from the current state.

Figure 3–1 below illustrates the state changes that can occur once we've detected the start of an element by the < character. It shows us that the next character must be a legal element type name start character (Namechar), an exclamation mark (!), or a forward slash(/). In turn, states 2, 3, and 4 will be expanded to illustrate the valid states that they support.

As long as the character stream continues along a path of legal states, the lexical analyzer will keep spitting out tokens. However, if a character should force the parser to attempt to create an illegal state,

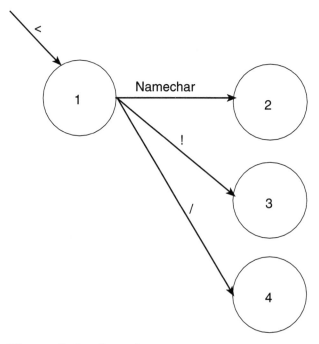

Figure 3–1 State diagram.

then the parser will immediately know that the XML document is not well-formed. This should result in a fatal parsing error.

Converting the XML 1.0 grammar to a state diagram is a tedious chore. This is because states operate differently from a grammar. For example, the XML 1.0 grammar breaks down the `prolog` rule into its component symbols and defines rules for them within close proximity (see Example 3.5). However, the developer of a lexical analyzer would rather see all the rules with exclamation points (!) following a less than sign (<) grouped together. That is, grammar represents the syntactic correctness, but the lexical analyzer is interested in lexical—sequences of lexicons—correctness.

3.2.1 *Parsing XML in Java*

This section will explore building a syntactical parser in Java. Its job will be to ensure an XML document follows the 1.0 recommendation. Once a token is found, there are a number of different things that can be done with it. Some of these will be explored later in this chapter when we cover the Simple API for XML and the Document Object Model (DOM).

The first step in building a syntax checker for XML is to define a way to ensure that the characters are within the scope of legal characters as defined by the XML 1.0 grammar. There are many algorithms that one could choose to accomplish this. For this book, we will use a Boolean array, where the value of a character acts as an index into the array; legal characters are set to true.

 Note   *The code for parsing shown in this book, though illustrative of the logic and algorithms derived from a state diagram, is not optimized for business solutions. For professional software development we recommend downloading one of the freely available Java-based XML parsers on the Internet; one is supplied with this book.*

```
class CharacterSet {
   boolean [] setarray = new boolean[0x10000];
```

- *Creates an array of 10000 booleans. Each location represents one Unicode character value.*

```
CharacterSet() {
```

- `CharacterSet()` *constructor initializes the array.*

```
    for (int i=0; i<0x10000; i++)
      setarray[i]=false;
  }
  CharacterSet(CharacterSet original) {
```

- *This version of the constructor uses a previously defined* `CharacterSet` *object. This is because some character sets share some properties.*

```
    for (int i=0; i<0x10000; i++)
      setarray[i] = original.setarray[i];
  }
  void SetRange(int start, int stop) {
```

- *The* `SetRange` *function sets a sequential range of character values to true.*

```
    for (int i=start; i<=stop; i++)
      setarray[i] = true;
  }
  void SetRange(CharacterSet base) {
```

- *Updates a range using an alternate* `CharacterSet` *object. If the value of the supplied set is not true, it uses the current* `CharacterSet` *value.*

```
    for (int i=0; i<0x10000; i++)
      setarray[i] = base.setarray[i] ? true : setarray[i];
  }
  void SetChar(int location) {
```

- `SetChar` *sets the value of one character location to true.*

```
    setarray[location] = true;
  }

  boolean inSet(char chkChar) {
```

■   inSet *tests whether a character is valid by testing to see if it is in the character set.*

```
    return setarray[chkChar];
  }
}
class CharacterSets {
```

■   *The* CharacterSets *class builds specific character sets based upon the XML 1.0 specification.*

```
  CharacterSet setLegalChars = CreateLegalCharSet();
  CharacterSet setLetter = CreateLetterSet();
  CharacterSet setNameStartChar = CreateNameStartCharSet();
  CharacterSet setDigit = CreateDigitSet();
  CharacterSet setNameChars = CreateNameCharSet();

  private CharacterSet CreateLegalCharSet() {
    CharacterSet cs = new CharacterSet();

    cs.SetChar(0x0009);
    cs.SetChar(0x000A);
    cs.SetChar(0x000D);
    cs.SetRange(0x0020, 0xD7FF);
    cs.SetRange(0xE000, 0xFFFD);

    return cs;
  }

  private CharacterSet CreateLetterSet() {
    CharacterSet cs = new CharacterSet();
    . . .
    return cs;
  }

  private CharacterSet CreateNameStartCharSet() {
    CharacterSet cs = new CharacterSet(setLetter);
```

```
      cs.SetChar('_');
      cs.SetChar(':');
      return cs;
    }

  private CharacterSet CreateDigitSet() {
    CharacterSet cs = new CharacterSet();
    . . .
    return cs;
  }

  private CharacterSet CreateNameCharSet() {
    CharacterSet cs = new CharacterSet (setNameStartChar);
    cs.SetRange(setDigit);
    cs.SetChar('-');
    cs.SetChar('.');
    return cs;
  }
}
```

The lexical analyzer requires five separate character set arrays: LegalChar set, Letter set, NameStartChar set, Digit set, and the NameChar set, which are defined above to illustrate their configuration. The sets that are missing detail are extremely large and use the character set definitions that can be found at the end of the XML 1.0 specification.

In addition to developing a class to handle validating characters, we have also created a class to represent the XML document being parsed and to keep track of the context. The Element class implements java.util.Vector, which essentially provides us with dynamic array functionality and allows us to add child elements more easily.

```
import java.util.Vector;
import java.util.Enumeration;
import java.util.Hashtable;

class Element extends Vector {

    private Element parent=null;
```

■ parent *Represents the current parent element.*

```
private String name = null;
```

■ name *represents the element type name of the XML element.*

```
boolean collecting = false;
```

■ collecting *tells us we're collecting characters that belong to the element's content. When we hit a new element start-tag or this element's end-tag, we will convert the collected characters into a string and add it to the current element's content buffer.*

```
private StringBuffer text = new StringBuffer(10);
```

■ text *is the buffer for storing the characters until they can be converted into a string.*

```
private Hashtable attrs = new Hashtable();
```

■ attrs *holds the attributes as key/value pairs in a* hashtable.

```
Element() {
```

■ The Element *constructor calls the constructor for Vector.*

```
    super();
}

void setName(String s) {
```

■ *Allows the parser to name the element type of the* Element *object once it is created.*

```
    name = s;
}

String getName() {
```

■ *Allows the parser to retrieve the element type name of an* Element *object.*

```
    return name;
  }

  void addElement(Element n) {
```

■ *Adds a child element to the current element. This builds the graph of objects that represents the XML document hierarchy.*

```
    CheckCollecting();
    super.addElement(n);
  }

  void setParent(Element p) {
```

■ *Sets the parent attribute within the* Element *object. Doing so creates a bi-directional parse tree.*

```
    parent = p;
  }
  Element getParent() {
```

■ getParent *provides the parser with a method of moving up and down the tree.*

```
    return parent;
  }
  void addPCDATA(char p) throws Exception {
```

■ *While adding characters, we set* collecting *to true and append to the internal text buffer. If* collecting *is false, we first create a new text buffer.*

```
    if (!collecting) {
     text = new StringBuffer(10);
     collecting = true;
    }
    text.append(p);
```

```
}

    void setComplete() {
```

■ *This method is called by the parser on the current* `Element` *when its end-tag is found. It is unnecessary to call this method for an empty* `Element` *since it will have no PCDATA.*

```
        CheckCollecting();
    }

    void addAttribute(Object key, Object value) {
```

■ `addAttribute` *stores a new attribute in the table. If one of that name exists already, it will change the value to that of the new one.*

```
        attrs.put(key, value);
    }

    Object getAttribute(Object key) {
```

■ *Gets an attribute value from the set based upon the supplied key.*

```
        return (attrs.get(value));
    }

    void CheckCollecting() {
```

■ *This function will take all data text collected so far and convert it into a* `String` *object to add to the vector.*

```
        if (collecting) {
            collecting=false;
            String value = new String(text);
            super.addElement(value);
        }
    }
}
```

The next stage of parsing is to read characters from a stream and determine if they are legal XML characters. If they are then they imply some construct that must be determined based upon where they appear. For example, a less than symbol (<) signals the parser that some XML-specific construct is coming. Likewise, a greater than symbol (>) will signal that that construct has terminated.

The following Java source code simplifies parsing by combining syntactic identification with the tokenizing process. This requires that we keep some additional state around so we can identify the context of any character. Of note, we use the design of the application itself to keep state. For example, when a < is found we delegate to the HandleTag function. The HandleTag function has the job of either finding a valid XML tag or throwing an exception. Therefore, the fact that HandleTag function was called represents a state within the parser.

```java
import java.io.*;
import java.net.*;
import java.util.Enumeration;
import com.ncfocus.xmlparse.CharacterSets;
import com.ncfocus.xmlparse.Element;

class XMLParse {

    static char EOF = (char) -1;

    CharacterSets sets = null;
    InputStream stmXML = null;
    Element current = null;
```

■ *The parser must always point to the current* Element *object being evaluated.*

```java
    boolean emptyElement = false;
```

■ emptyElement *allows the parser to know that it does not need to wait for an end tag.*

```java
    public static void main (String args[]) {
```

■ `main` *is the root function that will create a parser object and determine if the document is well-formed.*

```
XMLParse xp = new XMLParse();
try {
 URL ptrXMLFile = new URL(args[0]);
 xp.stmXML = ptrXMLFile.openStream();
 xp.Parse();
} catch (Exception e) {
 System.err.println("ptrXMLFile:
   "+e.toString());
}
}

void Parse() throws Exception {
```

■ *The* `Parse` *function will handle top-level identification of the XML grammar and call out to special handling functions based upon the E-BNF grammar rules in the XML specification.*

```
sets = new CharacterSets();

try {
 boolean doneParsing=false;
```

■ `doneParsing` *identifies when the end of file has been reached.*

```
boolean whitespaceon=false;
```

■ `Whitespaceon` *tells the parser that sequential whitespace characters have been found within parsed character data.*

```
while (!doneParsing){
   char parseChar = (char)stmXML.read();
```

■ *Reads a character from the XML document.*

```
switch (parseChar) {

    case (char)-1:
```

■ *If it is the end of file character, the parser must stop.*

```
        doneParsing=true;
        break;
    case '<':
```

■ *If it is a <, then it is a tag and will be delegated to the* HandleTag *function. If a tag is not found, then this case catches the exception and terminates the parsing.*

```
        try {
            HandleTag();
        } catch (Exception e) {
        System.err.println(e.toString());
        doneParsing=true;
        }
        break;

    case ' ':
    case '\t':
    case 0:
```

■ *Identifies legal* whitespace *characters. The block of them will be turned into a single whitespace.*

```
        whitespaceon=true;
        break;

    case 0x0A:
```

■ *Line feeds are ignored.*

```
        break;

    case 0x0D:
```

■ · *Carriage returns must be propagated into the Element's content.*

```
if (current != null)
    current.addPCDATA((char)0x0D);
break;

case '&':
```

■ *Ampersands signal the start of an entity reference.*

```
HandleEntityReference();
break;

default:
```

■ *Otherwise, adds the character to the current Element's content.*

```
if (whitespaceon) {
    whitespaceon=false;
    if (current != null)
        current.addPCDATA(' ');
```

■ *Adds characters to the current Element's data text buffer.*

```
}
if (current == null)
```

■ *This check identifies that there is a single root element, which is a required part of the XML specification.*

```
throw new
    Exception("XMLParse:" +
        "Expecting Tag");

if (sets.setLegalChars.inSet
    (parseChar) && current != null)
```

■ *Checks to see that the character is a legal XML character.*

```
                        current.addPCDATA(parseChar);
                    else throw new
                        Exception("XMLParse: Invalid" +
                            "Character");
        }
      }
    } catch (Exception e) {
      System.err.println("XMLParse: "+e.toString());
    }
  }

  void HandleTag() throws Exception {
```

■ `HandleTag` *looks at the first character after a < and decides what the markup represents.*

```
  try {
    char parseChar = (char)stmXML.read();

    switch (parseChar) {
    case '!':
```

■ *An exclamation point indicates that it is a comment, not a tag.*

```
      HandleExclaim();
      break;

    case '?':
```

■ *A question mark indicates a processing instruction.*

```
      HandlePI();
      break;

    case '/':
```

■ *A forward slash indicates that it is an end-tag.*

```
        HandleEndTag();
        break;

    default:
```

■ *Otherwise, it should be the Element type name, as long as it follows the rules for naming.*

```
        if (sets.setNameStartChar.inSet(parseChar))
                    HandleStartTag(parseChar);
        else {
                    throw new Exception("HandleTag:" +
                        "Malformed Tag");
        }
        break;
    }
    System.out.println();
  } catch (Exception e) {
    throw new Exception(e.toString());
  }
}

void HandleStartTag(char first) throws Exception {
```

■ `HandleStartTag` *determines if the preceding characters indeed represent a start-tag. Otherwise, it is invalid.*

```
    char parseChar;
    StringBuffer text = new StringBuffer(64);
```

■ *This buffer will be used to store the Element type name.*

```
    text.append(first);
```

■ *Because* `HandleTag` *pulled the first character out, we needed to add it to the* `text` *buffer here to ensure the name was completely recorded.*

```
    while ((parseChar = (char)stmXML.read()) != '>') {
```

■ *We will not stop building the name unless the character is illegal or the > character is found.*

```
if (parseChar == EOF)
  throw new Exception("HandleStartTag: Malformed" +
    "Tag");

if (parseChar == '/') {
```

■ *A / indicates that it is an empty element. We simply need to retain that state, but not act on it here.*

```
  emptyElement=true;
  continue;
}

if (sets.setNameChars.inSet(parseChar))
```

■ *Here we check to see that the current character falls within the legal limits of an element type name.*

```
  text.append(parseChar);
else if (parseChar == ' ') {
```

■ *If a space is found after the name, then we might have attributes. These attributes will be collected by the* HandleAttributes *function.*

```
  HandleAttributes();
  break;
}
else
  throw new Exception("HandleStartTag: Invalid" +
    "Tag Name" +
      "Character '"+parseChar+"'");
}
Element em = new Element();
```

■ *When we find a legal start-tag, we need to create a new* `Element` *object to represent it in memory.*

```
em.setName (new String(text));
em.setParent(current);

if (current != null)
  current.addElement(em);
```

■ *We need to add the* `Element` *we just created into the hierarchical memory representation of the XML document as long as there is already a root* `Element`.

```
if (!emptyElement)
  current = em;
```

■ *If the* `Element` *is not empty, we need to set it as the current* `Element` *so all future PCDATA is directed to its vector until we find the end-tag for this* `Element`.

```
else {
  emptyElement=false;
}
}

...
}
```

We'll leave it as an exercise for the reader to expand this parser further, but the important concepts are contained within the above code. These are:

1. XML parsers must make sure that characters fall within the acceptable character sets for a particular token designation.

2. XML parsers must first identify a particular token by examining the sequence of characters that represents it.

3. XML parsers must check that a sequence of tokens and nonterminal symbols matches a valid nonterminal symbol within the XML grammar.

4. XML parsers must maintain context within a document to make sure there are matching start- and end-tags for each element and that they do not overlap.

In the next sections, we will further explore how a parser can be extended to offer application-level functionality.

3.3 | The Simple API for XML

The Simple API for XML (SAX) is an interface for event-based XML parsing, developed collaboratively by the members of the XML-DEV mailing list, xml-dev@ic.ac.uk. Widespread adoption of SAX by many parser developers has made it a de facto industry standard.

SAX arose out of the need to reuse XML parsers as software components, but to extend them for application-specific use. For example, if you wanted to develop an application that processed INVOICE documents represented in XML, then you would need to use an XML parser to read and extract the data. All applications that process XML must encounter this step. However, not all applications process the INVOICE document identically. SAX allows an application to receive the extracted data directly from the parser, which it can then use accordingly.

SAX is an event-based parser, which means that it notifies the applications every time it identifies a "parse event" within the XML document. This includes element starts and ends, data content, attributes, processing instructions, whitespace, etc. The next section explains how event parsing works in detail.

3.3.1 *Event Parsing*

One output of an XML parser could be a document model. This is an in-memory representation of an XML document as a tree of connected nodes. It is constructed from the parse event information. We will explore this type of output further when we look at the W3C DOM.

A parser does not always construct a document model; instead, it can limit itself to reporting a series of parse events while it processes a document (see Figure 3–2). This places a greater processing bur-

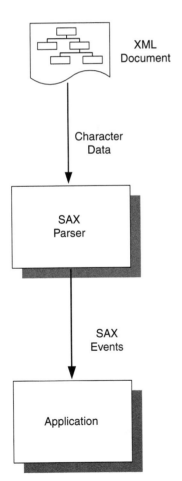

Figure 3–2 Event Parsing.

den on the application, which must now create the document model from parse events. There is also no assurance that a document is valid or even well-formed until the parser finishes processing the document. But, there are a number of advantages to this approach:

1. **Small memory footprint**. A document model is often not an efficient means of representing a document. And, when constructed by the parser, the entire model must fit in memory, limiting the size of a document that can be processed. By using an event interface, the application may be able to process very large documents.

2. **Single mapping to internal structures**. The generic document model constructed by a parser also may not be usable directly by an application, with the application constructing a second model at additional costs in time and memory. This application-specific model can often be constructed directly from parser events, eliminating the cost of constructing two models.

3. **Non-standard validations**. An event interface also gives an application the means of participating in the validation of a document—application-specific validation that would be difficult to define in a general schema, though this could be done after the document had been parsed. The real advantage here is in being able to clearly identify the place in the text where an error occurred, using information that is not available once the parse is complete.

The use of a standard interface for parse events makes it easy to change an application to use a different parser. One such interface that has become widely supported is SAX.

3.3.2 *SAX Interfaces*

SAX defines interfaces for each of the following four different types of parse events, as well as a top-level interface for the parser itself. Table 3–1 explains these interfaces.

The `Parser` and `DocumentHandler` interfaces are central to understanding SAX-based applications. They are also a good place to begin, as they are used to connect the components of an application with the parser itself.

Table 3–1   SAX interfaces.

Parser Interface	*Description*
DocumentHandler Interface	Most SAX applications implement this interface. Once the application registers its document handler, the parser uses this interface to report basic document-related events like the start and end of elements and character data.
EntityResolver Interface	This interface is implemented by an application to override a parser's default method for retrieving entities. It is especially useful for applications that build XML documents from databases and for applications that use URI types other than URLs.
DTDHandler Interface	This interface is implemented by an application to receive information about notations and unparsed entities.
ErrorHandler Interface	By default, a parse error results in a SAXParseException being thrown on the parse method. This exception carries details about which document contained the parse error and where in that document the error occurred. When this default behavior is insufficient, the application can register its own error handler with the parser. Note that a custom error handler is needed if warnings and recoverable errors are to be reported.

There are seven methods included in the `Parser` interface. They are outlined in Table 3–2.

Table 3–2   Parser interface.

Function Name	*Description*
`void setLocale( java. util.Locale locale)`	This method allows an application to request a locale for errors and warnings. Parsers are not required to support this capability and may simply throw a `SAXException` when the method is called.
`void setEntityResolver ( EntityResolver resolver)`	An application can use this method to register its own implementation of `EntityResolver`, which is then used by the parser to retrieve any documents or other entities needed by the parser.
`void setDTDHandler ( DTDHandler handler)`	An application can use this method to register its own implementation of `DTDHandler`. The registered `DTDHandler` object then receives information about notations and unparsed entities.
`void setDocumentHandler ( DocumentHandler handler)`	An application uses this method to register its own implementation of `DocumentHandler`, to which the parser then passes all document-related events.
`void setErrorHandler ( ErrorHandler handler)`	By default, errors and warnings are ignored by a parser, with only fatal errors throwing a `SAXException`. By registering its own `ErrorHandler`, an application has the option of reporting errors and warnings, as well as being able to abort a parse when an error or warning occurs.
`void parse( String systemID)`	This method is used by the application to start the parse of a document. The `systemID` is typically the fully resolved URL of the document.
`void parse( InputSource source)`	This is an alternative method for starting the parse of a document. The `source` object may specify a system ID, an `InputStream` or `Reader` object. Character encoding and a public ID can be specified in the `source` object as well.

All document-related events reported by the parser are passed to the application document handler using the `DocumentHandler` interface. There are eight methods included in this interface for passing these events. They are discussed in Table 3–3.

Table 3–3   DocumentHandler interface.

Function Name	*Description*
`void setDocumentLocator` `( Locator locator)`	The parser uses this method to share its `Locator` object with the application. The `Locator` object identifies the document being parsed and the current position in a document being processed. Other methods in the `DocumentHandler` interface can all throw `SAXParseExceptions` when the document does not conform to the application's requirements. The `Locator` object can be used to construct this exception, which will then identify where in the document the error occurred.
`void startDocument()`	This method signals the start of a new document and can be used to reinitialize the document handler, an important consideration when more than one document is being processed.
`void endDocument()`	This method signals the end of a document and should be used to clear references to any objects no longer in use.
`void startElement(` `String name,` `Attribute List atts)`	This method signals the discovery of a start-tag, and consequently, the start of an XML element. Elements can be nested, with each start element event being paired with an end element event.
`void endElement)` `(String name`	This method signals the discovery of an XML end-tag.
`void characters(` `char ch[],` `int start,` `int length)`	The data text held by an element is passed to the document handler via one or more calls to this method.

(continued)

Table 3–3   DocumentHandler interface. (*continued*)

Function Name	Description

void ignorable
   Whitespace(
     char ch[],
     int start,
     int length)
	Validating parsers will use this method instead of the characters method for whitespace. This event can be ignored.

void processing
   Instruction(
     String target,
     String data)
	This method is used to pass a processing instruction to the document handler.

Using the SAX interface is described in the following steps. Let's say we have an application that implements the DocumentHandler interface. To parse a document, the application must do the following:

1. Create a Parser object. There are various ways to do this, but the most direct approach is simply to create the object using the Java operator new. The catch to this direct approach is that we need to know the class name of the parser.

    Let's say that we are using the IBM parser. The class in IBM that implements the SAX parser interface is SAX-Driver, so we can create a parser object with the following line:

    ```
    org.xml.sax.Parser parser = new
    com.ibm.xml.parser.SAXDriver();
    ```

2. Register the application's DocumentHandler object by calling the setDocumentHandler method on the parser object.

    For example, say we have an object, referenced by the variable myDocumentHandler, which is an instance of a class that implements the SAX `DocumentHandler` interface. The following line will register the object with the parser so that the object will receive all the document events during a parse:

```
parser.setDocumentHandler(myDocumentHandler);
```

We'll examine the `DocumentHandler` interface in more detail shortly.

3. Parse the document by calling the `parse` method on the `parser` object.

For example, say we have a file, `"a.xml"`, in the directory where the program is running (the current working directory). The URL for this file is `"file:a.xml"`. We can now parse this document with the following line of code:

```
parser.parse("file:a.xml");
```

Once a parse is begun, a series of callbacks are made to the application's `DocumentHandler` object. Example 3.6 shows a trace of the events for a very simple document:

Example 3.6: Sample XML for SAX test.

```
<helloWorld><greeting>Hi!</greeting></helloWorld>
```

The expected results of parsing Example 3.6 are indicated below:

1. Event `setDocumentLocator`—Passes the parser's locator object to the application.

2. Event `startDocument`—The document is begun.

3. Event `startElement`—The start-tag for `helloWorld` is processed.

4. Event `startElement`—The start-tag for greeting is processed.

5. Event characters—The characters "Hi!" are processed.

6. Event endElement—The end-tag for greeting is processed.

7. Event endElement—The end-tag for helloWorld is processed.

8. Event endDocument—The document is finished.

Taking this one step further, we will now explore the program that reports these various SAX events that occur when parsing a document. Next, we'll examine the output that this program produces when parsing the above helloWorld document. First, here's the Java source code:

```
import com.ibm.xml.parser.*;
import org.xml.sax.*;

public class SAXTest implements DocumentHandler {

    public static void main(String args[])
    {
      try
      {
        org.xml.sax.Parser parser = new
com.ibm.xml.parsers.SAXParser();
```

■ *Create a new instance of a parser.*

```
        DocumentHandler myDocumentHandler = new
          SAXTest("IBM");
```

■ *Creates an instance of the* DocumentHandler *object that will respond to parser events.*

```
        parser.setDocumentHandler(myDocumentHandler);
```

■ *Register the* `DocumentHandler` *object with the parser to facilitate callbacks.*

```
parser.parse("file:a.xml");
```

■ *Tells the parser to start parsing the file.*

```
  } catch (Exception e) {
    e.printStackTrace();
  }
}

protected String prefix;
```

■ `prefix` *will hold the name of the parser we're using for illustrative purposes.*

```
public SAXTest(String prefix){
  this.prefix=prefix;
}

public void setDocumentLocator(Locator locator) {
  System.out.println(prefix+": setDocumentLocator");
}

public void startDocument() throws SAXException {
  System.out.println(prefix+": startDocument");
}

public void endDocument() throws SAXException {
  System.out.println(prefix+": endDocument");
}

public void startElement(String name, AttributeList atts)
  throws SAXException {
  String attsOut=new String();
  for (int attIndex=0; attIndex<atts.getLength();
    attIndex++) {
  attsOut=attsOut.concat("[" + atts.getName(attIndex) +
    "=" + atts.getValue(attIndex) + "]");
```

■ *Here we build a list of all the attributes on the start element using the associ-ated* AttributeList.

```
    }
    System.out.println(prefix+": startElement
      "+name+attsOut);
  }

  public void  endElement(String name) throws SAXException {
    System.out.println(prefix+": endElement "+name);
  }

  public void  characters(char ch[], int start, int length)
      throws SAXException {
    String cs = new String(ch, start, length);
    System.out.println(prefix+": characters["+cs+"]");
  }

  public void ignorableWhitespace(char ch[], int start, int
    length) throws SAXException {
    String iws = new String(ch, start, length);
    System.out.println(prefix+": ignorableWhitespace
      ["+iws+"]");
  }

  public void  processingInstruction(String name, String
    remainder) throws SAXException {
    System.out.println(prefix+":
      processingInstruction["+name+"]["+remainder+"]");
  }
```

■ *The above methods implement the* DocumentHandler *interface. All methods must be implemented.*

```
}
```

Here are the results of running the above code using the XML4J Java parser version 2.0.6. Notice that it matches our previously expected results.

```
IBM: setDocumentLocator
IBM: startDocument
IBM: startElement helloWorld
IBM: startElement greeting
IBM: characters[Hi!]
IBM: endElement greeting
IBM: endElement helloWorld
IBM: endDocument
```

Using the SAX interfaces, an application can now participate in the validation of a document. It can also create an output stream based on those events or create some application-specific document model, which it can use once the parse of the document is complete. Moreover, by using the SAX interfaces, an application can work closely with a parser without being tied to any particular parser. Should the requirements of an application change, it is still quite easy to replace the parser with a more appropriate selection.

As you can see with this example, when we are done parsing the file, our application terminates because application processing is concurrant with parsing. This programming model is in contrast to the W3C Document Object Model that we are going to look at next. In that programming model, we parse first and process second.

3.4 | W3C Document Object Model

Like SAX, the Document Object Model (DOM) is another way that applications can access the data found inside an XML document. However, instead of the application getting the data directly with event handlers, DOM creates an in-memory tree of objects that the applications can traverse to extract the information at will.

As you may remember from our parsing example at the beginning of this chapter, as part of parsing an XML document, we can create a hierarchical representation in memory of that document consisting of Java objects. The W3C Document Object Model, or DOM, uses this hierarchical representation to allow developers to further manipulate an XML document.

The DOM has three core functions to XML: 1) it represents the document in memory; 2) it acts as the factory for creating new XML elements; and 3) it offers the necessary functions for manipulating the in-memory representation, also known as the parse tree. With these functions, developers can identify the elements of an XML document, but in contrast to SAX, which we discussed earlier, they will not be able to do this until the parser has completely finished parsing the document.

The benefit gained from using this programming model is that the developer will be able to perform multiple transformations on the XML document in memory, as well as iterate over the elements within the tree and pull information out.

The W3C DOM is designed for use by many programming languages and facilities. Some of these do not have the rich data type support that Java and C++ have. Instead, these environments can simply view the object model as one big array that can contain other arrays. For these impaired facilities, the DOM has a basic "flat" definition (see Figure 3–3).

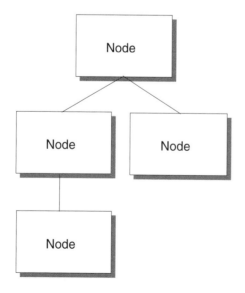

Figure 3–3   DOM flat model.

Notice how these implementations of the DOM look at the XML world as if it were a nail and the DOM a hammer. That is, to the flat view, the DOM is just a set of node structures that contain other node structures. This makes it far more difficult to compare and identify these elements. Additionally, these node structures must be associated with all the functions that might ever be performed on an XML element as illustrated by the Node interface depicted in Table 3–4 below.

Table 3–4 Node interface.

```
Public interface Document extends Node {

    public DocumentType       getDoctype();

    public DOMImplementation  getImplementation();

    public Element            getDocumentElement();

    public Element            createElement(String tagName)

        throws DOMException;

    public DocumentFragment   createDocumentFragment();

    public Text               createTextNode(String data);

    public Comment            createComment(String data);

    public CDATASection       createCDATASection(String data)

        throws DOMException;

    public ProcessingInstruction createProcessingInstruction
        (String target, String data) throws DOMException;

    public Attr               createAttribute(String name)

        throws DOMException;

    public EntityReference    createEntityReference(String name)

        throws DOMException;

    public NodeList           getElementsByTagName(String tagname);

}
```

Most developers building EAI solutions, however, use the typed model, also known as the object-oriented model. The typed model provides a separate class definition for each object represented in the tree.

The best way to approach learning the DOM is to start with a visualization of a DOM object tree (see Figure 3–4).

Let's explore some of the more important objects in the typed view as depicted in Figure 3–5. In particular, we will be looking at the `Node`, `Document`, `Element` and `Attr` object classes.

3.4.1 *The Node Object*

The `Node` object is the base class that is used to define all other DOM objects. All possible manipulations on the tree can be performed on the `Node` object, and subsequently on all inherited object types.

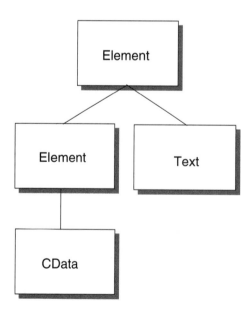

Figure 3–4 DOM typed object model.

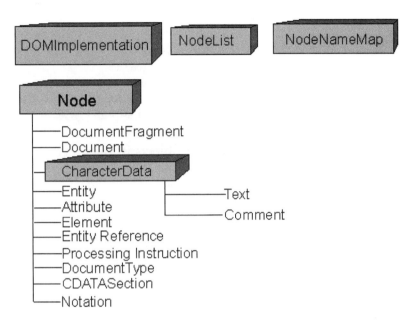

Figure 3–5   DOM interfaces.

Table 3–4 depicts the Java Language Binding for the `Node` object. The binding represents the mapping from the abstract definition in the DOM specification to a specific programming language; in this case, Java. The W3C also offers bindings for other programming languages and object models, such as COM and CORBA.

Figure 3–6, which is an illustration of an XML document represented as a DOM, is helpful in understanding the relationship between the DOM and an XML document.

Table 3–5 and Table 3–6 provide a more detailed look at the `Node` interface, with Table 3–6 outlining the return values that could be obtained from the `getNodeName` method. It is important to understand the implications of viewing each object in the DOM as a node, and Table 3–6 outlines this best. The `getNodeName` method is overloaded to provide different return values based on the XML object the `Node` represents.

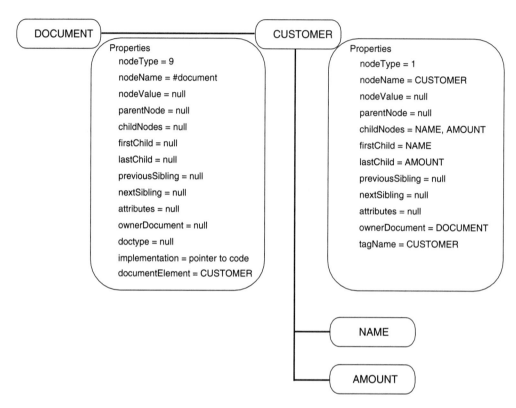

Figure 3–6   DOM memory representation.

Table 3–5   The DOM node interface explained.

Function Name	*Description*

```public static final short ELEMENT_NODE = 1;```
```public static final short ATTRIBUTE_NODE```
``` = 2;```
```public static final short TEXT_NODE = 3;```
```public static final short CDATA_SECTION_```
``` NODE = 4;```
```public static final short ENTITY_```
``` REFERENCE_NODE = 5;```
```public static final short ENTITY_NODE = 6;```
	These definitions are used by the flat view to determine what XML object the Node represents. This value can be found and compared against the getNodeType method.

(continued)

Table 3–5   The DOM node interface explained. (*continued*)

Function Name	Description
| ```
public static final short PROCESSING_
  INSTRUCTION_NODE = 7;
public static final short COMMENT_NODE = 8;
public static final short DOCUMENT_NODE
  = 9;
public static final short DOCUMENT_TYPE_
  NODE = 10;
public static final short DOCUMENT_
  FRAGMENT_NODE = 11;
public static final short NOTATION_NODE
  = 12;
``` | |
| ```
public String getNodeValue() throws
  DOMException;
``` | Per Table 3–6 |
| ```
public NamedNodeMap getAttributes();
``` | Per Table 3–6 |
| ```
public void setNodeValue(String node
  Value) throws DOMException;
``` | Attempts to set the value of the Node based upon acceptable values in Table 3–6. Illegal values force the DOMException to be thrown. |
| ```
public short getNodeType();
``` | Returns one of the static node types defined above. |
| ```
public Node getParentNode();
``` | If the current node is not the root element, this method will return the element's parent node. |
| ```
public NodeList getChildNodes();
``` | Returns a NodeList object that contains all the children of the current element. |
| ```
public Node getFirstChild();
public Node getLastChild();
public Node getPreviousSibling();
public Node getNextSibling();
``` | These methods allow the developer to traverse the tree quickly by moving between the child elements and to the element's siblings. |

(*continued*)

Table 3–5   The DOM node interface explained. (*continued*)

Function Name	Description
`public Document getOwnerDocument();`	Returns the Document object that is associated with the current Node. This document can be used to create additional nodes.

`public Node insertBefore(Node newChild,`
`   Node refChild) throws DOMException;`
`public Node replaceChild(Node newChild,`
`   Node oldChild) throws DOMException;`
`public Node removeChild(Node oldChild)`
`   throws DOMException;`
`public Node appendChild(Node newChild)`
`   throws DOMException;`
	These methods provide the developer with a way to transform the tree by adding, changing, and removing nodes. Removal of a node will automatically remove all of its children as well.

`public boolean hasChildNodes();`	This method allows developers to see if a particular node has children.
`public Node cloneNode(boolean deep);`	This method creates a separate and distinct copy of the current Node, including all of its children if the parameter deep is true. The DOM does not allow developers to move Node objects between Document objects. The only way to accomplish this is to clone the Node object and insert it into the another Document object.

Sidebar: Is DOM Too Heavyweight For EAI?

JP Morgenthal

I want this book to be more than a slavish recitation of what you might be able to learn from the W3C specifications. I also want you to think about the applicability of those specifications to your needs. I'll keep these critical insights inside these well-defined sections to differentiate the opinions from the factual content. It is my hope that both will be useful to you.

Table 3–6 Return Values for getNodeName.

NodeType	NodeName	nodeValue	attributes
Element	TagName	Null	NamedNodeMap
Attr	Name of attribute	Value of attribute	Null
Text	#text	Content of the text node	Null
CDATASection	#cdata-section	Content of the CDATA Section	Null
EntityReference	Name of entity referenced	Null	Null
Entity	Entity name	Null	Null
ProcessingInstruction	Target	Entire content excluding the target	Null
Comment	#comment	Content of the comment	Null
Document	#document	Null	Null
DocumentType	Document type name	Null	Null
DocumentFragment	#document-fragment	Null	Null
Notation	Notation name	Null	Null

I believe there are a number of problems with the DOM's design that make it unnecessarily heavy for all applications, and some that make it overkill for specific applications of XML, such as messaging and other rudimentary data exchange operations. The following are the reasons behind these conclusions:

1. While both the flat and typed views of an XML document are necessary for the reasons described earlier, the decision to make the `Node` the base class for other DOM objects in the typed view results in a heavyweight object. Because of this decision, every `Comment` object could be treated the same as an `Element` object. That is,

(continued)

Sidebar: Is DOM Too Heavyweight For EAI? (continued)

you could call the function `hasChildNodes` *on either one. The problem with this in the typed model is that you do not expect this behavior to be on the* `Comment` *object, but only on the* `Element` *object. The result of this is undefined behaviors from legal method (functions in an object) calls. Again, this is understandable in the flat view, where it is up to the developer to first check for a* `Node`'s *type before deciding what functions can be executed on a particular* `Node`, *but should not be possible in the typed view.*

2. *The* `Element` *object has a function called* `normalize` *that combines adjacent* `Text` *objects in the hierarchy. That is, if there are two child objects that are both* `Text` *objects and follow each other in the tree, then they can be made into one single* `Text` *object. Moreover, the* `Text` *object has a* `splitText` *function that takes a single* `Text` *object and makes two adjacent* `Text` *objects out of it by splitting the* `Text` *object's value at a certain offset within the text string. Clearly, these functions are needed in document-centric processing, but they only further weigh down the DOM in areas where lightweight data processing mechanisms are needed.*

3. *XML is tedious to build with the DOM. It takes three distinct operations to add a new DOM object to the tree. First, you have to ask the* `Document` *object to create a new instance of the object type. Second, you have to prepare that object by setting its value, attributes, and children. Finally, you must add the object to the tree using an insert operation. These steps are far too arduous when attempting to build a dynamic XML document in a high-volume environment. It's easier to just hard code the XML creation directly into the program.*

4. *The DOM provides a simple lookup function to retrieve all the elements that share a particular element type name. However, it retrieves them as a list of objects that have lost their context. For example, requesting the CUSTOMER elements from an invoice will give both the CUSTOMER element within the BILLING element and the CUSTOMER element within the SHIPPING element. As the application iterates over the returned list of nodes, it is its responsibility to get the parent of each CUSTOMER element and look to see what the parent's context is. Clearly, this is functionality that could be added to the DOM and is being examined by the XML-Query Working Group, but as provided, the lookup facilities within the DOM are not overly helpful.*

For some applications, these points may seem trivial, but when building XML into a high-volume, server-based data processing environment, these points may have significant implications. I would welcome a W3C activity focused on providing a standard XML programming model optimized for the needs of high performance applications.

3.4.2   *The Document Object*

The `Document` object has two roles within the DOM. First, the `Document` object is the object factory for creating other DOM objects. Second, the `Document` object is the container for the document's hierarchical representation and therefore holds the root element. Table 3–7 illustrates and describes the functionality of the `Document` object class.

Table 3–7   The Document interface.

Function Name	*Description*
`Public DocumentType getDoctype();`	Returns the `DocumentType` object, which contains Document Type Definition (DTD) information, such as entity and notation declarations.
`Public DOMImplementation get` `  Implementation();`	This method allows developers to check if the current version of the parser will support the features they need, such as XML 1.0 and HTML 4.0.
`Public Element getDocumentElement();`	Returns the root element of the document. For XML, this is the root element and for HTML, it is "HTML".

`public Element createElement(String`
`  tagName) throws DOMException;`
`public DocumentFragment`
`  createDocumentFragment();`
`public Text createTextNode(String`
`  data);`
`public Comment createComment`
`  (String data);`
`public CDATASection createCDATA`
`  Section(String data) throws`
`  DOMException;`
	These methods create new DOM objects that are not associated with the current `Document` object.

(continued)

Table 3–7   The Document interface. (*continued*)

Function Name	Description
`public ProcessingInstruction createProcessingInstruction(String target, String data) throws DOMException;` `public Attr createAttribute(String name) throws DOMException;` `public EntityReference createEntityReference(String name) throws DOMException;`	
`public NodeList getElementsByTagName (String tagname);`	Executes a preorder traversal of the parse tree and returns all elements that match the `tagname` parameter. A preorder traversal is defined as a visiting of the root node and then the child nodes. A supplied value of `'*'` will return all nodes.

3.4.3   *The Element Object*

The `Element` object contains a deep representation of an XML element. That is, it contains the nodes corresponding to all the text between a start-tag and an end-tag. If that text should contain additional elements, or if the element should contain attributes, those would be captured as well. Table 3–8 illustrates and describes the functionality of the `Element` object class.

3.4.4   *The Attr Object*

The `Attr` object represents a single attribute on an element. `Attr` objects are only operated on within the context of an element. Table 3–9 illustrates and describes the functionality of the `Attr` object class.

Table 3–8 The Element interface.

Function Name	Description
`Public String getTagName();`	Returns the element type name of the current `Element`.
`Public String getAttribute(String name);`	Returns the value of the attribute named by the parameter, or null if it does not exist.
`Public void setAttribute(String name, String value) throws DOMException;`	Adds the attribute named by the `name` parameter and sets it to the value defined by the `value` parameter. If the attribute already exists, then it simply changes the value.
`Public void removeAttribute(String name) throws DOMException;`	Deletes the attribute from the current element. In contrast to `removeChild`, this is a permanent deletion.
`Public Attr getAttributeNode(String name);`	Returns the attribute object that has the name defined by the `name` parameter.
`Public Attr setAttributeNode(Attr newAttr) throws DOMException;`	Adds the attribute defined by the attribute object parameter to the current element. If the attribute already exists, the value is copied from the parameter and set on the existing attribute object of the same name.
`Public Attr removeAttributeNode(Attr oldAttr) throws DOMException;`	Permanently deletes the attribute that is defined by the attribute object parameter `oldAttr`.
`Public NodeList getElementsByTagName (String name);`	Executes a pre-order traversal of the current element's descendants and returns all elements that match the `tagname` parameter. A pre-order traversal is defined as a visiting of the root node and then the child nodes. A supplied value of `'*'` will return all nodes.
`Public void normalize();`	Combines adjacent text nodes into a single text node.

Table 3–9   The Attr interface.

Function Name	Description
`Public String getName();`	Retrieves the name of the current `Attr` object.
`Public Boolean getSpecified();`	If this attribute was given a specific value in the original XML document, this field will be set to true.
`public String getValue();`	Retrieves the value of the current attribute as a character string.
`public void setValue(String value);`	Sets the value of the current attribute object. Values are stored as unpaved `Text` nodes that are children of the attributes.

3.4.5   *An Example Of Using DOM from Java*

The following example uses the IBM XML4J parser to read a document from an input stream and create a `Document` object. It takes as input an XML document that represents a list of pages and displays it as a Web page.

Here is a sample of the XML document that it would process:

```
<?xml version="1.0"?>
<PageDB>
<Page ID="pagenotfound"
      title="Sorry, Page Could Not Be Located"
      bgcolor="#ffffff"
      bgimage="BLANK"
      URL="nopage.xml"/>

<Page ID="root"
      URL="pages/root.xml"
      title="NC.Focus Root Page"
      noshow="pages/signup.xml">
    <Description>Contains the default descriptions for all
other pages</Description>
</Page>
```

```
<Page ID="home"
      bgimage="ncftile.gif"
      public="true"
      title="NC.Focus Home Page">
      <Description>Home Page</Description>
</Page>

<Page ID="sitemaptop"
      public="true"
      URL="sitemaptop.xml"
      title="sitemapheader">
      <Description>Site Map Header</Description>
</Page>

<Page ID="sitemapbottom"
      public="true"
      URL="sitemapbottom.xml"
      title="sitemapbottom">
      <Description>Site Map Footer</Description>
</Page>
</PageDB>
```

The following code will generate a table of links automatically from the XML document below. Included in this code is the ability to filter what is displayed by using the attributes.

```
import com.ibm.xml.parser.*;
import org.w3c.dom.*;

public class sitemap {

    public static void main (String args[]) {
      String stype = null;

      try {
        if (args.length < 1) {
          System.out.println("Usage: sitemap URL [filter]");
          return;
        }
        System.out.println("<HTML><HEAD><TITLE>NC.Focus Site" +
          "Map</TITLE></HEAD>");

        NonValidatingDOMParser parser = new
          NonValidatingDOMParser();
```

■ *We create an instance of the IBM XML4J Java parser.*

```
parser.parse(args[0]);
```

■ *We tell the parser to parse the XML file indicated by the URL passed as the first argument on the command line.*

```
Document doc = parser.getDocument();
```

■ *If the document was successfully parsed, we ask the parser to return to us the DOM Document object.*

```
NodeList pages = doc.getElementsByTagName("Page");
```

■ pages *obtains a list of pages by asking the Document object for all elements of type "Page".*

```
System.out.println("<TABLE WIDTH=\"602\"" +
  "BORDER=\"1\"><TR><TD>");
System.out.println("<TABLE WIDTH=\"600\">\r\n");
System.out.println("<TR><TD WIDTH=\"200\"><B>" +
  "<CENTER><FONT" +
  FACE=\"Arial\">Page Title</FONT></CENTER></B>" +
    "</TD>");
System.out.println("<TD WIDTH=\"300\"><B><CENTER><FONT" +
  "FACE=\"Arial\">Description</FONT></CENTER></B>" +
    "</TD>");
int ctr = 0;
for (int i=0; i<pages.getLength(); i++) {
```

■ *We then iterate over the list of pages, creating one row per Page node.*

```
String colorStr = null;
```

■ colorStr *defines the color of the row background.*

```
if ((ctr%2) == 0)
  colorStr = " BGCOLOR=\"#00FFFF\" ";
else
  colorStr = " BGCOLOR=\"#FFFF80\" ";
Node x = pages.item(i);
```

■ *Individual nodes within the* NodeList *are accessed using the item method. Here we set the variable* node *to be the current* Node *object we are processing.*

```
NamedNodeMap nnp = node.getAttributes();
```

■ *We ask the element we are currently processing for its list of attributes.*

```
if (args.length < 2)
  stype = "public";
else
  stype = (String) args[1];
```

■ stype *is the attribute for which we will filter. If it exists on a page, then the page will be included. If no* stype *was supplied, we will default to the value "public".*

```
Node isPublic = nnp.getNamedItem(stype);
```

■ *Once we have* stype *set, we ask the* NamedNodeMap, *which contains our attributes, if the attribute exists. If it does, it is returned as a* Node *object. We could decide to manipulate this object as a* Node *as we have done here, or cast the object to an* Attr *object.*

```
if (isPublic == null)
  continue;
```

■ *If the attribute we are filtering for does not exist, then we move to the next node.*

```
ctr++;
Node title = nnp.getNamedItem("title");
```

■ *Retrieves the title of the page from the list of attributes.*

```
if (title != null) {
  System.out.println("<TR><TD"+colorStr+">");
  Node url = nnp.getNamedItem("ID");
  System.out.print("<A HREF=\"");
System.out.print(System.getProperty("pageurl")+"?" +
          cmd=page&page="+url.getNodeValue());
  System.out.print("\">");
  System.out.println(title.getNodeValue()+"</A>" +
    "</TD>");
```

■ *Prints the title of the page into the table. The string we wish to print can be re-trieved from a Node object using the* getNodeValue *method.*

```
NodeList children = node.getChildNodes();
```

■ *If there's a description, it is stored as a child element of Page, as can be seen in the page called "root" in the XML document above.*

```
System.out.println("<TD"+colorStr+">");
if (children != null) {
```

■ *The string we wish to display from the description is actually stored as a* Text *object that is a child to the Description element. This statement extracts the* Text *node.*

```
Node desc = children.item(1).getFirstChild();
System.out.println("<CENTER>"+
    desc.getNodeValue() + "</CENTER>");
```

■ *In this statement, we simply print the value of the* Text *object, which is the de-scription string.*

```
    }
  }
  System.out.println("</TABLE></TD></TR></TABLE>");
  System.out.println("</BODY></HTML>");
```

```
    } catch (Exception e) {
      System.out.println(e.getMessage());
    }
    }
}
```

In this example, we use the capabilities of the DOM to create an in-memory representation of a page database. We then use the DOM to extract all the elements that have the name "Page" and we access the attributes on each of those elements to see if they pertain to our filter. It's also an example of how we might use the DOM to perform a transformation of the data stored in our XML document for another purpose—in this case, to create a Web page. In future chapters, we will use the DOM to provide a model that we can serialize for data exchange.

3.5 | Summary

This chapter introduced you to the key methods of dealing with XML documents programmatically. All processing of XML documents starts with a parser, which ensures that the document is well-formed. Some XML parsers are also validating, which means that they can confirm that the document follows the rules specified in the Document Type Definition (DTD).

One method of acting upon the content of an XML document is to integrate document handlers with the parser. This method produces lightweight XML document processing solutions, such as when using the Simple API for XML (SAX). SAX is an event-driven processing model that will call methods inside the developer's application to process specific parts of an XML document that have been found.

Another method of processing XML documents is to manipulate them as a tree of objects called the Document Object Model (DOM).

The DOM represents a specific set of object classes that represents the XML document in memory as a set of related nodes. The DOM requires more memory and time for processing, but allows the developer to operate directly on the document as a "live" object.

3.6 | Looking Ahead

This part outlined the fundamentals of EAI, XML and Java. We also discussed some of the ways XML and Java are providing answers to complex EAI issues today. But, most importantly, we covered the basic methods for processing XML documents—SAX and DOM. The next part delves into using XML in tandem with Enterprise Java APIs for the purpose of building EAI solutions.

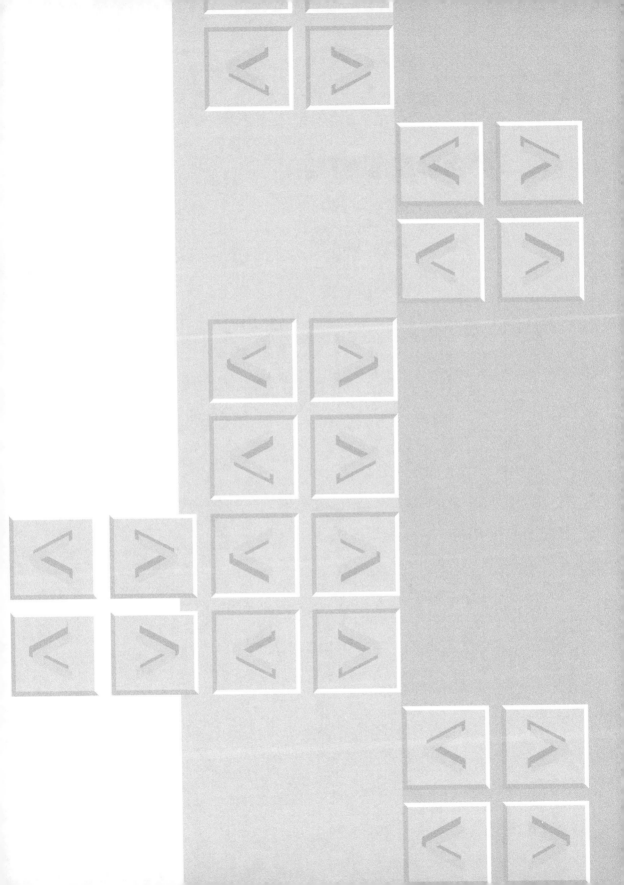

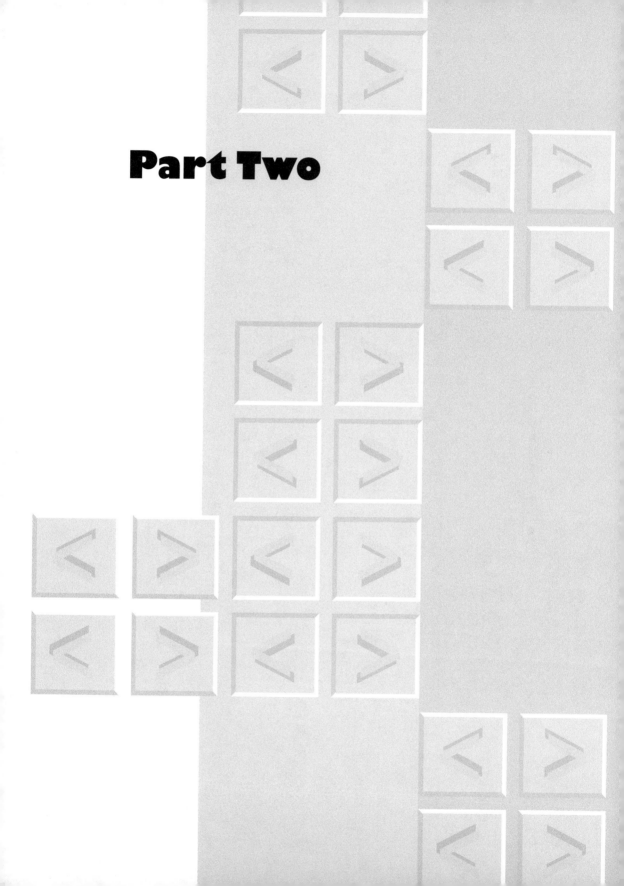

Part Two

EAI and Data

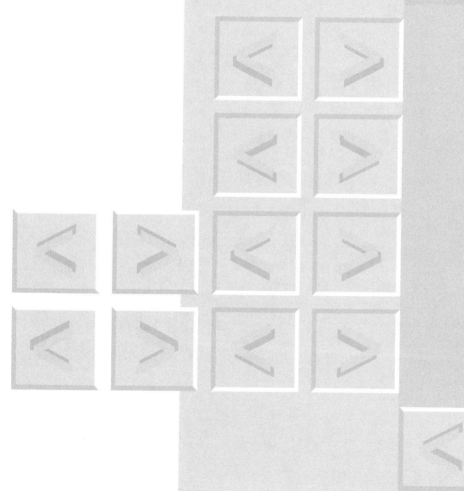

Sharing and Exchanging Data

A majority of the work completed as part of an integration is moving data between two disparate systems that have no knowledge about each other. Sometimes, due to the nature of the applications, this integration must happen over a shared resource, such as a database. Other times, applications simply send their data to each other using networking and inter-process communication mechanisms.

Examples of shared resources that might be used for integration purposes include databases, file systems, networks, and memory. In each of these cases, all integrated applications are working with the same consistent view of the data. These types of integrations reduce redundancy of information and provide for concurrency and security. As a result, these integrations use a consistent view of the data across multiple applications. For example, providing access to financial and sales data from within a customer service system may require all three applications to use a single database. This implies that the customer service application understands the schema and relationships for its own tables, as well as the tables for sales and financial information—a method most commonly used by today's leading Enterprise Resource Planning (ERP) packages. The downside of using shared resources is that applications become highly dependent upon each other and therefore do not work well independently. This phenomenon is now starting to be realized by both ERP vendors and customers alike as they attempt to make their implementations Web-enabled.

On the other hand, integration through data exchange creates a loosely coupled relationship between applications and introduces fewer dependencies than when using a shared resource. That is, the relationship between these applications only exists when preparing and sending data. After that point, the processing application operates in an isolated environment, using the data as it sees fit. To enable these types of integrations, there is a need for more up-front design and agreement over the format for the data, as well as an agreed-upon method of transfer. However, their nature ensures modularity and independent behavior.

Java provides us with a flexible, homogenous mechanism for sharing and exchanging data, but it is critical to understand that most EAI projects will require integration across heterogeneous systems. This means that we can use Java virtual machines to assist us in the routing, transformation, and delivery of data between systems that are being integrated. This approach provides us a consistent development and deployment platform, but those Java virtual machines are going to be communicating with non-Java environments.

Successful integration projects start with data interoperability, which means there is a set of tools and an infrastructure for sharing and exchanging data like the one we saw in Chapter 2. However, when Java is used to integrate non-Java-based applications, there is an added requirement to also move data in and out of the Java virtual machine. We can accomplish this task in the following ways:

1. We can use a Java-based CORBA (Common Object Request Broker Architecture) ORB, which allows any CORBA-compliant application to send data to Java applications through a programming interface.

2. The Java and non-Java applications could use a language-independent shared resource, such as a database or file system.

3. We can use Message-Oriented Middleware (MOM) as an asynchronous inter-process communication mechanism that operates by publishing and consuming messages over a messaging service.

Shared resources and MOM have a requirement for sharing parties to agree on a data format, or schema, and exchange mechanisms. But CORBA provides its own facility, called the Internet Inter-ORB Protocol (IIOP), which defines the data formats and mechanisms for exchange as part of the CORBA standard. Because CORBA takes care of these issues for us, it has a significant amount of baggage and overhead that sometimes makes it too heavyweight for simple data exchange solutions. However, by using one of the non-CORBA solutions in tandem with XML data formats, Java and non-Java environments can seamlessly exchange and share data in a lightweight fashion.

This part will examine using XML and Enterprise Java APIs as a solution for EAI needs. In this regard, we will examine four specific APIs: the Java Reflection API, Java Database Connectivity (JDBC), Java Messaging Services (JMS) and the Java Directory and Naming Interface (JNDI).

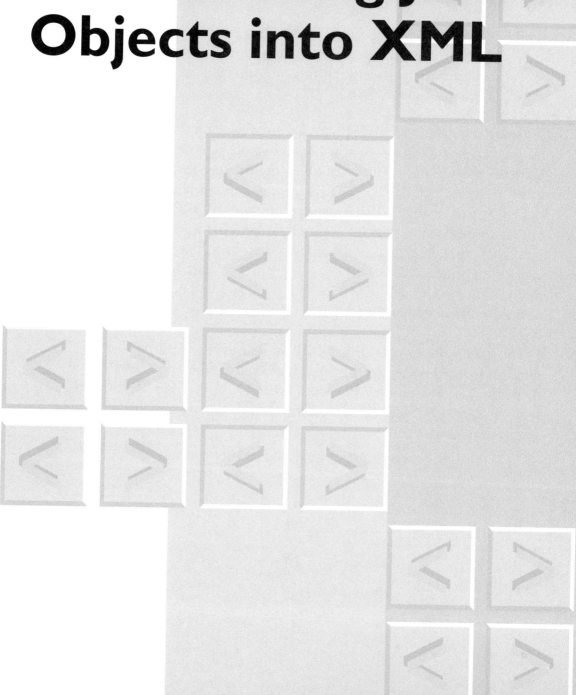

Transforming Java
Objects into XML

5.1 | Introduction

Serializing objects is the process of taking the state portion of the in-memory representation of an object and turning it into a stream of bytes that can be used for moving into the address space of other applications, as well as storing it persistently for use at a later point in time.

Serializing objects, and consequently reverse serialization, can be a complex operation when objects contain other objects as part of their design. For example, a Bank object might contain Customer objects, which in turn contain Account objects. This sequence of objects containing other objects creates what is termed an "object graph." Figure 5–1 illustrates what the object graph looks like in memory. Serializing this tree-like structure requires the developer to make a conscious decision to perform all operations on a deep (recursively include all branches starting from a single node) or shallow (just a single node of the tree) basis.

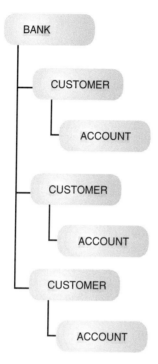

Figure 5–1   Object graph.

Note that object graphs can become very deep and have many layers of nesting. Once these graphs are serialized, there may be no way to determine how much memory is necessary to represent the graph in memory. If retrieving the graph on a different machine from the one on which it was created, there may be problems due to insufficient memory. Additionally, the retrieving machine needs some mechanism for turning the stream back into in-memory data structures again.

Currently, there is no standard for object serialization, but there are a few standards for object model interoperability. This means that object models can communicate using a function call facility, but they often have a data interoperability problem. And, due to the lack of a consistent format for representing a graph of objects in the form of a stream of characters, object models cannot share their state as pure data; this can only be accomplished by calling individual functions (methods) on an object.

These last few paragraphs illustrate just some of the problems associated with serializing graphs of objects. The Java virtual machine has a native capability for serializing objects that can be understood by any Java virtual machine, which relieves the developer of the need to manually write code to read and write the state for each individual object. But the resulting stream is only usable to Java. To overcome this limitation and allow Java to share the state of its objects across multiple platforms and multiple programming languages, we can use XML.

There are two ways to serialize Java objects into XML. The first way is to code a special function on each object that knows how to read and write its own state, using its own set of element types; this is a tedious and time-consuming process. Alternatively, a function can be written generically that can serialize any Java object graph using the Java reflection API. The rest of this section will introduce the reader to the reflection API and then illustrate how it can be used to serialize a graph of Java objects in XML.

5.1.1 Reflection Overview

The reflection API gives developers the ability to inspect the structure of a Java object, access its internal variables, and even execute its functionality dynamically. Because of the power that this facility has for operating over internal Java virtual machine structures, it is limited by the virtual machine security model. This means that these functions, by default, do not have the ability to see everything. Usually, private field values are not visible through the reflection API.

To access the reflection capabilities within Java, a developer needs to use the `java.lang.Class` object. This is a special object that all Java objects have, and it is obtained from the `getClass` function on the `java.lang.Object` object, from which all Java objects are descended. With the `Class` object, the developer has the necessary functions to start exploring the internals of the Java class from which the `Class` object was obtained.

A Java class is comprised of the following components:

- **Constructors.** These special methods are called when the object is first created.

- **Interfaces.** Define a set of methods that other Java class definitions will adhere to. Interfaces usually represent abstract notions that do not have any associated code.

- **Methods.** Define the behavior of a Java class. Methods have signatures that define the input parameters and return values.

- **Fields.** These are variables that maintain state for individual instances of the class.

Figure 5–2 below depicts the internal structure of a Java object inside the Java virtual machine.

Table 5–1 illustrates the types of functions on the `Class` object that support reflection.

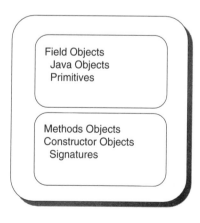

> Field Objects
> Java Objects
> Primitives

> Methods Objects
> Constructor Objects
> Signatures

Figure 5–2   Java object architecture.

Table 5–1 `java.lang.Class` functions for reflection.

Function Name	Description

`Public native boolean isInstance`
`  (Object obj);`
`parameter obj.`
	Checks to see if the current class is an instance of the same type of object represented by the

`Public native boolean isAssignable` `  From(Class cls);`	Determines if the current class or interface is either the same as, or is a superclass or super-interface of, the class or interface represented by the specified parameter `cls`.
`Public native boolean isInterface();`	Determines if the current `Class` object represents a Java interface.
`Public native boolean isArray();`	Determines if the current `Class` object represents a Java array.
`public native boolean isPrimitive();`	Determines if the current `Class` object represents the primitive type set, which includes: ■ `java.lang.Boolean` ■ `java.lang.Character` ■ `java.lang.Byte` ■ `java.lang.Short` ■ `java.lang.Integer` ■ `java.lang.Long` ■ `java.lang.Float` ■ `java.lang.Double` ■ `java.lang.Void`
`public native String getName();`	Returns the fully qualified name of the object represented by this Class.
`public Package getPackage();`	Returns a `Package` object that is associated with the current `Class` object. `Package` objects contain version information about the object represented by this `Class` object.

(continued)

Table 5–1   `java.lang.Class` functions for reflection. (*continued*)

Function Name	Description
`public native Class[] get Interfaces();`	Returns an array of `java.lang.Class` objects of all public interfaces, including the inherited ones, which are supported on this `Class` object.
`public native Class getDeclaring Class();`	If the object represented by this `Class` object is a member of another class, this function returns the `Class` object that represents the object in which it was declared.
`public Class[] getClasses();`	Returns an array of `java.lang.Class` objects of all public classes, including the inherited ones, which are supported on this `Class` object.
`public Field[] getFields();`	Returns an array of `java.lang.reflect.Field` objects of all public fields (members), including the inherited ones, which are supported on this `Class` object.
`public Method[] getMethods();`	Returns an array of `Method` objects for all public method signatures, including the inherited ones, which are supported on this `Class` object.
`public Constructor[] getConstructors()`	Returns an array of public `Constructor` objects for the current Java class.
`public Field getField(String name)`	Returns a public `Field` object as named by the parameter `name`. `Field` objects allow examination of field data.
`public Method getMethod(String name, Class[] parameterTypes)`	Retrieves the `Method` object representation of a public method whose signature matches the parameters `name` and `parameterTypes`. The `parameterTypes` parameter is an ordered array of `Class` objects that identifies the parameter list for the method being queried.

(continued)

Table 5–1 `java.lang.Class` functions for reflection. (*continued*)

Function Name	Description
`public Constructor getConstructor (Class[] parameterTypes)`	Retrieves the `Constructor` object representation of a constructor whose signature matches the parameter `parameterTypes`. The `parameterTypes` parameter is an ordered array of `Class` objects that identifies the parameter list for the constructor being queried.
`public Class[] getDeclaredClasses();`	Returns an array of all `Class` objects declared on the current Java class. These include private, public, and default classes and interfaces, but not inherited ones.
`public Field[] getDeclaredFields() ;`	Returns an array of all `Field` objects declared on the current Java class. These include private, public, and default field members, but not inherited ones.
`public Method[] getDeclared Methods();`	Returns an array of all `Method` objects declared on the current Java class. These include private, public, and default methods, but not inherited ones.
`public Constructor[] getDeclared Constructors();`	Returns an array of all `Constructor` objects declared on the current Java class. These include private, public, and default constructors, but not inherited ones.
`public Field getDeclaredField (String name)`	Returns a `Field` object that represents the declared field identified by the parameter `name` for the current Java class. Declared fields include those that are public and private.
`public Method getDeclaredMethod (String name, Class[] parameterTypes);`	Returns a `Method` object that represents the declared method identified by the parameter `name` and that has the matching signature as identified by the `parameterTypes` parameter for the current Java class. Declared methods include those that are public and private.

(continued)

Table 5–1   `java.lang.Class` functions for reflection. (*continued*)

Function Name	Description

`public Constructor getDeclared`
   `Constructor(Class[]`
   `parameterTypes);`
	Returns a `Constructor` object that represents the declared constructor that has the matching signature as identified by the `parameter-Types` parameter for the current Java class. Declared constructors include those that are public and private.

From the `Class` object, there are other Java objects that we can obtain, such as lists of fields, methods, constructors, and interfaces that are available for the Java class being examined. For purposes of serialization, we are only interested in the fields that contain the state that we wish to distribute to a non-Java application or to represent the object persistently.

We obtain the list of `Field` objects defined for any Java object by using one of the following `Class` methods: `getFields` or `getDeclaredFields`. These two methods could very easily return a different set of Field objects as denoted by Table 5–1 above. Once we have the list of `Field` objects, we can iterate over the list using common array operations, such as `Array.getLength` and the [ ] operator.

The `Field` object provides us the ability to evaluate individual characteristics of a field, such as if it is a primitive, array, or a Java `Class` object. Since a `Field` object can represent these various characteristics, it has special methods that allow us to access and change the data stored in these fields. We identify the type of a particular field by using the `Field` object's `getType` method. This method returns a `Class` object that represents the class for the field. We can then use the `Class` object to check if the object is of type primitive or array using the method identified in Table 5–1 above. The flow of this exploration goes as follows:

```
Class being reflected → Array of Field objects → 1 Field
    object → Class object representing this field
```

Since the Field object is itself a Java object, it has a Class object that we can use to reflect its properties.

Once we have the type of an object, we can then act on it more knowledgeably. In the case of primitives, the type will tell us the exact type of primitive that the field represents. In these cases, the class returned from getType will be equivalent to one of the following statically defined Class objects: Boolean.TYPE, Character. TYPE, Byte.TYPE, Short.TYPE, Integer.TYPE, Long.TYPE, Float.TYPE, Double.TYPE, and Void.TYPE. Alternatively, we can also ask each of these objects for its Class name, which will return to us a String object that contains text, such as "boolean", "int", or "long".

For each primitive type that is supported by the Java virtual machine, the Field object has a matching get/set method—for example, getLong and setLong. Each get/set pair takes the object being examined as a parameter, for example:

```
Class theClass = theObject.getClass();
Field theField = theClass.getField("key");
long aLong = theField.getLong(theObject);
```

The Class object can also provide us with lists of an object's methods, interfaces, and constructors. However, this capability is less useful to us in our approach to simply move states between Java and non-Java applications, and therefore will not be explored in depth in this book.

The key thing to remember when using the reflection capabilities of the Class object is that some methods only include public and inherited information, while others include public, private, and default information, but only for the local class. For developers just learning reflection for the first time, we recommend writing your own Java program that will print out the results of these methods over a user-defined class. Try to include as many different types within the user-defined class as possible.

Once we understand how to use the Class object to provide us with the internal structure of a Java object, we can then use those principles to serialize the public state of a Java object graph as an XML document. The code in the following section illustrates how to accomplish this goal.

```
class Object2XML {
   static int ERR_NO_FIELDS = 0;
   static int ERR_NONE = 255;
```

■ *Defines static error numbers for exception handling.*

```
int writeObjectXML(Object o, String name) throws
   Exception{
```

■ `writeObjectXML` *is the function that takes any Java object and the name of an output file and serializes the object and all of its children into an XML representation.*

```
Class cls = o.getClass();
```

■ `cls` *is the Class object for the current Java object to be serialized.*

```
Field [] publics;
```

■ `publics` *will be used to hold the list of all declared fields.*

```
RandomAccessFile raf = null;
try {
  publics = cls.getDeclaredFields();
```

■ `publics` *is initialized with the results of* `getDeclaredFields` *on the Class object that represents the Java object passed to us on invocation.*

```
if (Array.getLength(publics) == 0)
   return ERR_NO_FIELDS;
```

■   *If a class has no fields, then there's nothing to serialize and the program terminates gracefully. Some may desire to have a file generated regardless, in which case, they should remove this line.*

```
    } catch (SecurityException e) {
      System.out.println("writeObjectXML: Access Denied");
      throw (e);
```

■   `SecurityExceptions` *are thrown by the virtual machine when reflection methods are attempted on certain private data.*

```
    }
    try {
      raf = new RandomAccessFile(name, "rw");
      raf.writeBytes("<?xml version=\"1.0\"?>\r\n");
      raf.writeBytes("<CLASS name=\"");
      raf.writeBytes(o.getClass().getName());
      raf.writeBytes("\">\r\n");
```

■   *The previous few lines open up the file for writing, and they write the header, which includes the XML prolog and the root class, which is based on the name of the Class object.*

```
      DumpClass(o, raf, "");
```

■   `DumpClass` *is a recursive procedure that will serialize the current object's children and subsequently all of their children.*

```
      raf.writeBytes("</CLASS>\r\n");
      raf.close();
```

■   *Writes out the end-tag for the serialized Java object graph and closes the file.*

```
    } catch (IOException e) {
      System.out.println("writeObjectXML: Error Opening" +
        "File");
    }
    return ERR_NONE;
```

```
}

void DumpClass(Object o, RandomAccessFile raf, String
   stIndent) throws Exception {
```

■ `DumpClass` *is the recursive procedure that will "walk" the Java object graph and write out the values of each object. It takes as parameters a Java object, the output file object, and a string that will be used for indentation purposes in the output file.*

```
String aIndent = stIndent + "   ";
```

■ `aIndent` *represents the indentation string locally and adds three spaces to the value passed in.*

```
Field [] publics = o.getClass().getDeclaredFields();
```

■ *For each object that we will be investigating, we will need to extract the declared fields. Since publics is declared locally within* `DumpClass`, *a new instance of it will be created for each recursive call.*

```
try {
  //set root object to be class name
  for (int i=0; i < Array.getLength(publics); i++) {
```

■ *This loop will be called for each member of the current object.*

```
if (publics[i].getDeclaringClass().getName().startsWith
   ("java."))
   return;
```

■ *If the object is part of the core Java libraries, don't explore further.*

```
raf.writeBytes(aIndent+"<FIELD name=\""+publics[i]." +
   "getName()+"\" parent=\"");
raf.writeBytes(publics[i].getDeclaringClass()
   .getName());
```

```
raf.writeBytes("\"");
raf.writeBytes(" type=\"");
```

■ FIELD *is the element type used to represent all members of the root object. This includes inherited members as well.*

```
Class toEval = publics[i].getType();
```

■ toEval *returns the Class object associated with the field being analyzed.*

```
// We won't be handling arrays
if (toEval.isArray()) {
```

■ *Checks to see that the current field is of type array.*

```
raf.writeBytes("array\">");
```

■ *Writes the type of the field as an array to the output file.*

```
try {
  for (int j=0; i<Array.getLength(publics[i].
    get(o)); j++) {
    DumpClass(Array.get(publics[i].get(o), j),
      raf, aIndent);
```

■ *If the field is an array, then each index could possibly be an object. Therefore, we need to call* DumpClass() *for each array index.*

```
  }
} catch (IllegalAccessException e) {
  raf.writeBytes("No Access");
}
}
else if (toEval.isPrimitive())
  EvaluatePrimitive(publics[i], o, raf, aIndent);
```

■ *If the field is one of the primitives, then we need to call a special routine to retrieve the value.*

```
//We won't be handling interfaces
else if (toEval.isInterface())
  raf.writeBytes("interface\"/>\r\n");
```

■   *If the field represents an interface, then we just want to identify it as such.*

```
else {
  raf.writeBytes(publics[i].getType().getName()+
    "\">\r\n");
  raf.writeBytes(aIndent+publics[i].get(o).
    toString()+"\r\n");
  DumpClass(publics[i].get(o), raf, aIndent);
```

■   *This code assumes that the current field is a Java object. It prints out the value and then serializes its own fields.*

```
  }
  raf.writeBytes("\r\n"+aIndent+"</FIELD>\r\n");
  }
  //end tag for element CLASS
} catch (IOException e) {
  System.out.println("writeObjectXML: Error Writing To" +
    "File");
  }
}
void EvaluatePrimitive(Field i, Object o, RandomAccessFile
  raf, String aIndent) throws Exception{
```

■   *This function will use the special primitive access functions to extract the value from the current field.*

```
Class type = i.getType();

try {
  if (Boolean.TYPE == type) {
    raf.writeBytes("boolean\">");
    Boolean b = new Boolean(i.getBoolean(o));
    raf.writeBytes(b.toString());
  } else if (Integer.TYPE == type) {
    raf.writeBytes("int\">");
    Integer b = new Integer(i.getInt(o));
```

```
    raf.writeBytes(b.toString());
} else if (Long.TYPE == type) {
    raf.writeBytes("long\">");
    Long b = new Long(i.getLong(o));
    raf.writeBytes(b.toString());
}else
    raf.writeBytes("N/A\">");
```

■ *The above functions will print out the actual value of a primitive as long as it is not defined as private.* **Not all types have been programmed into this function.**

```
} catch (IllegalAccessException e) {
    raf.writeBytes("No Access");
```

■ *If the field is declared private, an* IllegalAccessException *will be thrown when this application attempts to read it. Here we catch that exception and write out "No Access".*

```
        }
    }
            }
```

We will now use this code to serialize out the following Java object.

```
class SerialTestClass {
    private long keynum = 0xF23ac32;
    String theString= "This is a string!";
    boolean active = true;
    long theLong = 0x00001111; // hexadecimal 4369
    int theInt = 0x0011; // hexadecimal 17
    SerialTestClass(int setActive) { active=setActive; }
            }
```

The result of this exercise yields the following:

```
<?xml version="1.0"?>
<CLASS name="com.ncfocus.XML.Serialize.SerialTestClass">
    <FIELD name="keynum"
        parent="com.ncfocus.XML.Serialize.SerialTestClass"
        type="long">No Access
    </FIELD>
```

```
<FIELD name="theString"
  parent="com.ncfocus.XML.Serialize.SerialTestClass"
  type="java.lang.String">
This is a string!

</FIELD>
<FIELD name="active"
  parent="com.ncfocus.XML.Serialize.SerialTestClass"
  type="boolean">true
</FIELD>
<FIELD name="theLong"
  parent="com.ncfocus.XML.Serialize.SerialTestClass"
  type="long">4369
</FIELD>
<FIELD name="theInt"
  parent="com.ncfocus.XML.Serialize.SerialTestClass"
  type="int">17
</FIELD>
        </CLASS>
```

Now that we have the Java object graph serialized as an XML document, we could provide access to the state of this object by simply parsing the XML into a DOM representation. This representation would then properly depict the parent-child hierarchy of the original Java object graph, along with its state, but the original structure and method information will be lost. If sharing state is our only intention, then we can simply access the values of the objects directly from the DOM; otherwise, we must develop a mapping from the original Java objects into new structures that we can operate over in our non-Java application.

For example, to use the results of serializing `SerialTestClass` into XML inside a C++ application, we could simply examine the state based upon the element FIELD and its attribute `name`. However, if it were important to also have the behavior of the `setActive` method, then we would have to develop a C++ class with this functionality and map the DOM representation into the new C++ class structure.

In the example above, we used an arbitrary XML document type just to illustrate the code working, but you could use this example to make your Java objects relate directly to a business-oriented element type name. Therefore, your in-memory representation of a data item as a set of Java objects could also be represented by an equivalent XML document. Of course, to maintain the level of generality provided by this code, you may want to create the mappings from Java object types to element type names in a separate repository that would be called by this code. For example, the repository might have a mapping that was used by this program that states for every `SerialTestClass` object, map the field `active` to the element type name `ACTIVE_FLAG`.

5.2 | Summary

Reflection is a very powerful API within the Java virtual machine. It allows us to look at and manipulate structures directly. In the next chapter, we will examine a method of sharing data with Java and non-Java applications using relational database technology.

Using XML with Relational Databases

6

6.1 | Introduction

Chapter 5 examined ways to move data between Java and non-Java environments using a data exchange methodology. This chapter examines using relational database technology to share data between Java and non-Java applications.

Because we are concentrating on integrating multiple applications, the notion of creating a master schema to represent all corporate data is unacceptable. Clearly, some of the data we're sharing between these applications will have common fields—it makes sense to provide direct access for these fields. However, sometimes there is a requirement to share non-relational and semi-relational (relational but requires extensible schema) data. In this section, we examine a possible solution using XML as a method of solving these problems.

6.1.1 *JDBC Overview*

The key to working with relational databases from within the Java environment is to understand the Java Database Connectivity (JDBC) library. Essentially, this library creates abstract notions of the connection with a database, the Structured Query Language (SQL) statements that will be used to execute operations, and the result set of any operation. SQL is a standardized language that implements database verbs, such as insert, update, select, and delete, and allows users to interact with a database using ASCII/UNICODE strings.

JDBC is divided across two key components: the `java.sql` API and the JDBC driver. We're going to explore the `java.sql` API in detail throughout this section, but first let's briefly examine the role of the JDBC driver. The JDBC driver provides a Java interface into a Relational Database Management System (RDBMS). Four types of JDBC drivers exist and are identified as follows:

- Type 4 is a pure Java driver that communicates with the database directly using TCP/IP and a proprietary database messaging protocol.

- Type 3 is considered a net protocol, all-Java driver, and it translates JDBC into a neutral messaging protocol and is converted to a proprietary DMBS protocol by the database server.

- Type 2 drivers are partly native and partly Java. They convert JDBC calls directly into direct DBMS API calls.

- A Type 1 driver is a JDBC/ODBC bridge.

It is important to know which type of JDBC driver you are working with if performance is essential to your project.

Drivers are accessed through a special URI (Uniform Resource Indicator) that uses the JDBC protocol type. Each driver will interpret the URI for itself, requiring the developer to understand how to formulate the URI to connect to each individual JDBC driver in use.

Example 6.1 shows two examples of URI for two different JDBC drivers.

Example 6.1: URI to connect to a MYSQL database and a JDBC/ODBC database.

```
jdbc:mysql://localhost:3306/mysql
jdbc:odbc:ClientBase
```

There are two ways to load JDBC drivers into an application's address space. The first is to use the `jdbc.drivers` system property. This would be specified in the `hotjava.properties` files as follows:

```
jdbc.drivers=gwe.sql.gweMysqlDriver, sun.jdbc.odbc.
   JdbcOdbcDriver
```

An application can also dynamically load and unload drivers at run-time. To load a driver, the developer would use the `forName` method on the `java.lang.Class` object. This function takes a fully qualified Java object path name and loads the class files into memory. In the case of the JDBC driver, it makes the driver available for use to the `java.sql.DriverManager` class. The following shows two examples of how to dynamically load a JDBC driver:

```
Class.forName("gwe.sql.gweMysqlDriver");
Class.forName("sun.jdbc.odbc.JdbcOdbcDriver");
```

Likewise, the developer can remove a driver from memory using the `deregisterDriver` method on the `java.sql.DriverManager` object.

Once the driver is loaded into memory, we can then execute SQL operations against the driver, which return `java.sql.ResultSet` objects that allow the developer to use, analyze, and extract information using a row/column metaphor.

At a minimum, there are three steps to executing an SQL operation against a JDBC driver:

1. Obtain a connection to the database via the JDBC driver.

2. Create a `java.sql.Statement` object that will be used to represent the SQL statement to the driver.

3. Execute the SQL statement.

The following code further illustrates how to program these operations:

```
con = DriverManager.getConnection("jdbc:mysql://" +
"localhost:3306/mysql",    "root", "");
Statement stmt = con.createStatement();
ResultSet rs = stmt.execute("SELECT * FROM booktest WHERE" +
   "booktest.doctype='book.xml'");
```

This provides enough background on the JDBC driver to start developing Java-based database applications. Once a query is executed, all the work will center on working with the `ResultSet` object. In the next section, we will explore the `ResultSet` object in-depth and look at treating XML as a special data type from within the JDBC environment.

6.1.2   *The XML Column*

As previously mentioned, the value returned from the execution of an SQL operation on a JDBC driver is a `ResultSet` object. A `ResultSet` object is an abstract entity that allows users to move between the rows that are returned and to view columns within those rows. It is up to each individual JDBC driver to define how that data will be made available. Some JDBC drivers use the *cursor*—a database-specific entity that keeps track of the row being evaluated inside a result set stored on the server—capability of the database, which requires many calls to the DBMS system. Meanwhile, others use *caching* to keep more of the results in the local machine's memory. For developers, it is important that you understand how your JDBC driver is implemented before deploying your application to a large number of users. For example, cursors allow the DBMS to ensure consistency and concurrency through locking. However, these mechanisms may not be maintained when using the caching method since that same record can exist in many caches simultaneously.

The `ResultSet` object contains a number of methods that allow the developer to extract data from columns in a typed manner. That is, the developer can retrieve integers from integer columns, floats from decimal columns, and strings from text columns. Likewise, developers can set the values of these columns using an alternate version of these methods geared toward writing instead of reading.

Traditionally, XML is stored in a Binary Large Object (BLOB) or text field within the database. However, this makes it very cumbersome to work with from the developer's point of view. To simplify the task of reading and writing XML to a relational database column, we can extend the `ResultSet` object to support XML as one of the native data types that it reads and writes. But, before we look into implementing the XML column, let's first review how to use the `ResultSet` data to process the results of our SQL operation.

 **Note**   *Not all JDBC drivers properly implement the update capabilities of the* `ResultSet` *object. For drivers that don't, the only way to do updates and inserts is by building SQL* UPDATE *and* INSERT *statements and executing them using the* `java.sql.Statement` *object.*

Here are two basics for working with the `ResultSet` object:

1. Initially, the cursor is positioned before the first row. Therefore, it is necessary to execute a `next` method on the `ResultSet` before you can process any data. The `next` method returns a Boolean value that can be used to determine if the current row is valid or not. An SQL operation that returns zero rows will return false on the first call to `next`.

2. Columns can be addressed by name or position. That is, the `getXXX` and `updateXXX` (XXX represents a specific

data type) methods are overloaded to accept either an integer (position) or string (name).

Because each driver embeds its own `ResultSet` object implementation, it is difficult to enforce our implementation of `ResultSet`. Therefore, our `ResultSet` is designed to aggregate an existing `ResultSet` object, but adds a few extra functions to operate specifically with XML data.

Note: Since the `ResultSet` object is extensive, we will only cover the basics of how we aggregated the original object and the functionality we created here. The entire source for this object can be found on the associated CD-ROM.

```
import com.ibm.xml.parser.*;

public class XMLResultSet implements java.sql.ResultSet
```

■ *Since* `XMLResultSet` *implements* `java.sql.ResultSet` *it can support all the functions of the base class, but adds additional capabilities for handling XML as a data type.*

```
{
    ResultSet inner = null;
```

■ *Because we're aggregating an existing* `ResultSet` *object, we need to hold on to the original so we can pass methods calls to it.*

```
    public XMLResultSet(java.sql.ResultSet r)
    {
```

■ *The only legal constructor for an* `XMLResultSet` *object is one that takes* `java.sql.ResultSet` *as a parameter.*

```
        inner = r;
    }
    public boolean getBoolean(int columnIndex) throws
        SQLException {
```

```
    try {
       return inner.getBoolean(columnIndex) ;
    } catch (SQLException e) {
       throw(e);
    }
  }

public  boolean getBoolean(String columnName) throws
  SQLException {
     try {
       return inner.getBoolean(columnName) ;
     } catch (SQLException e) {
       throw(e);
     }
   }
```

■   *The above functions implement the two types of retrieval operations that can be performed on the* ResultSet *object. Notice how both simply make calls to the correct method on the original* ResultSet *object.*

```
public void updateBoolean(int columnIndex, boolean x) throws
  SQLException {
     try {
       inner.updateBoolean(columnIndex, x) ;
     } catch (SQLException e) {
       throw(e);
     }
   }

public void updateBoolean(String columnName, boolean x)
   throws SQLException {
     try {
       inner.updateBoolean(columnName, x) ;
     } catch (SQLException e) {
       throw(e);
     }
   }
```

■   *The above two functions implement the two types of update operations that can be found on the* ResultSet *object. Again, we're delegating to the aggregated original.*

```
  public Document toDOM(String rawXML) {
```

■ toDOM *takes an XML document in the form of a string and returns a W3C DOM representation.*

```
Parser p = new Parser("test");
```

■ *How you create an instance of the parser is specific to each XML parser implementation. This is how it is done using the IBM XML parser.*

```
Source column = new Source(new java.io.StringReader
  (rawXML));
```

■ Source *is an object type that is used by the XML parser for reading a stream of characters that represents the XML document. We can create a* Source *object by creating a* java.io.StringReader *object that wraps the string that contains the XML document.*

```
Document doc = (Document) p.readStream(column);
```

■ *The parser* readStream *method parses the XML and builds a DOM representation in memory. It then returns that representation as a DOM* Document *object.*

```
  return (doc);
}

public String serialize(Document doc) throws SQLException {
```

■ *The serialize method takes a W3C DOM and creates a* String *object that represents the corresponding XML document. This function uses capabilities of the IBM parser that may not be found in other implementations. If this is the case, the developer may have to write code to walk the tree manually and write the corresponding XML.*

```
StringWriter sw = new java.io.StringWriter();

try {
  Visitor visitor = new ToXMLStringVisitor(sw, "UTF-16");
  Node root = doc.getDocumentElement();
```

```
new NonRecursivePreorderTreeTraversal(visitor).
  traverse(root);
return "<?xml version=\"1.0\"?>\r\n" + sw.toString();
```

■ *We need to add the XML prolog since this traversal function does not. This is optional in a well-formed XML document, but it is recommended.*

```
    } catch (Exception e) {
      throw (new SQLException(e.getMessage()));
    }
  }
  public Document getXML(int index) throws SQLException {
    try {
      return toDOM(inner.getString(index));
    } catch (SQLException e) {
      throw(e);
    }
  }

  public Document getXML(String columnName) throws
    SQLException {
    try {
      return toDOM(inner.getString(columnName));
    } catch (SQLException e) {
      throw(e);
    }
  }
```

■ *The above two functions implement the* get *operation for the XML data type. They assume that the column type is text-based and call* getString *on the original* ResultSet *object. The returned string is then passed to the* toDOM *method, where it is turned into a DOM representation. If the string does not represent well-formed XML, the returned value will be null.*

```
  public void updateXML(int index, Document doc) throws
    SQLException {
    try {
      inner.updateString(index, serialize(doc));
    } catch (SQLException e) {
      throw(e);
    }
  }
```

```
public void updateXML(String columnName, Document doc)
  throws SQLException {
  try {
    inner.updateString(columnName, serialize(doc));
  } catch (SQLException e) {
    throw(e);
  }
}
}
```

■ *The above functions implement the update operations for the XML type. These are only useful if the JDBC drivers support update functionality. Notice that it calls the original* ResultSet *object's* updateString *method after it serializes the DOM representation.*

The following code illustrates how to use the XMLResultSet object to read and write XML data to a relational database. This code operates on a database that has the following schema:

```
CREATE TABLE booktest(
   doctype char(50) primary key,
   xml blob
);
```

This database implements a simple XML document system, whereby the XML document can be retrieved by document name. The following code will take an XML file located on the local filesystem, store it in the database under the name "book.xml", and then retrieve that XML file as a DOM object, which will be serialized to the output device.

Note   This discussion assumes that book.xml is small enough to fit in the BLOB data type.

Note   This code uses the MYSQL database and MQSQL JDBC drivers, however, the project was tested against Microsoft Access using JDBC/ODBC and was found to work equally well.

```
import java.io.*;
import java.sql.*;
import org.w3c.dom.*;
```

```
import com.ibm.xml.parser.*;
import com.ncfocus.sql.XMLResultSet;
class TestXMLColumn {

    public static void main (String args[]) {

        Connection con = null;
        InputStream is = null;

        TestXMLColumn txc = new TestXMLColumn();

        try {

            Class.forName("gwe.sql.gweMysqlDriver");
```

■ *First we need to load the JDBC driver for the database.*

```
        try {
            is = new FileInputStream("test.xml");
```

■ *This line opens the file* `"test.xml"` *for reading.*

```
        } catch (FileNotFoundException notFound) {
        System.out.println("File Error: " + notFound.
            getMessage());
        }

    Document doc = (Document) new Parser("test.xml").
        readStream(is);
```

■ *Parses* `test.xml` *and create a DOM representation.*

```
    con = DriverManager.getConnection("jdbc:mysql://" +
        "localhost:3306/mysql", "root", "");
```

■ *Opens a connection to the database.*

```
        Statement stmt = con.createStatement();
```

■ *Creates a statement that will be used to execute SQL operations.*

```
XMLResultSet xr = new XMLResultSet(null);
```

■ *Creates an empty* XMLResultSet *object. This will be used to serialize the current XML document for storage into the database.*

```
String theXML = xr.serialize(doc);
```

■ *Serializes the XML document into a string.*

```
theXML = txc.FixForXML(theXML, false);
```

■ *Because this particular JDBC driver does not support update functionality properly, we need to perform an SQL INSERT operation. This means that certain characters, such as the backslash (\) need to be marked as special characters by adding another backslash before them. The method* FixForXML *handles search and replace within the string to account for this requirement.*

```
String sqlQuery = "INSERT INTO booktest VALUES" +
  "(\"book.xml\",\"";
sqlQuery += theXML + "\")";
```

■ *Here we build the SQL INSERT command.*

```
stmt.execute(sqlQuery);
```

■ *This executes the SQL INSERT operation on our database. If an error occurs an* SQLException *will be thrown.*

```
sqlQuery = "SELECT * FROM booktest WHERE booktest." +
  "doctype='book.xml'";
```

■ *Now that the XML document is written to the database, we can extract it using this SQL query.*

```
stmt.execute(sqlQuery);

xr = new XMLResultSet(stmt.getResultSet());
```

■ *We create an instance of the* XMLResultSet *that is initialized with the results of our previous SQL operation.*

```
if (xr.next()) {
```

■ *Remember, we need to position our result set before we can access a row.*

```
Document doc = xr.getXML("xml");
```

■ *Here we use the* getXML *method to retrieve the data from the column named* "xml". *This data is returned as a W3C DOM* Document *object.*

```
System.out.println(xr.serialize(doc));
```

■ *We can use the serialize method on our* XMLResultSet *object to flatten the DOM into an XML document. In this case, we will print it out to the screen. Figure 6–1 is a screen shot that illustrates the results of running this process.*

```
}

xr.close();
```

■ *When we are done with* ResultSet *objects we should invoke their close method to release resources no longer needed.*

```
} catch (Exception e) {
  System.out.println("Failure: "+e+" "+e.getMessage());
}
}

String FixForXML(String in, boolean ignorefnl) {
```

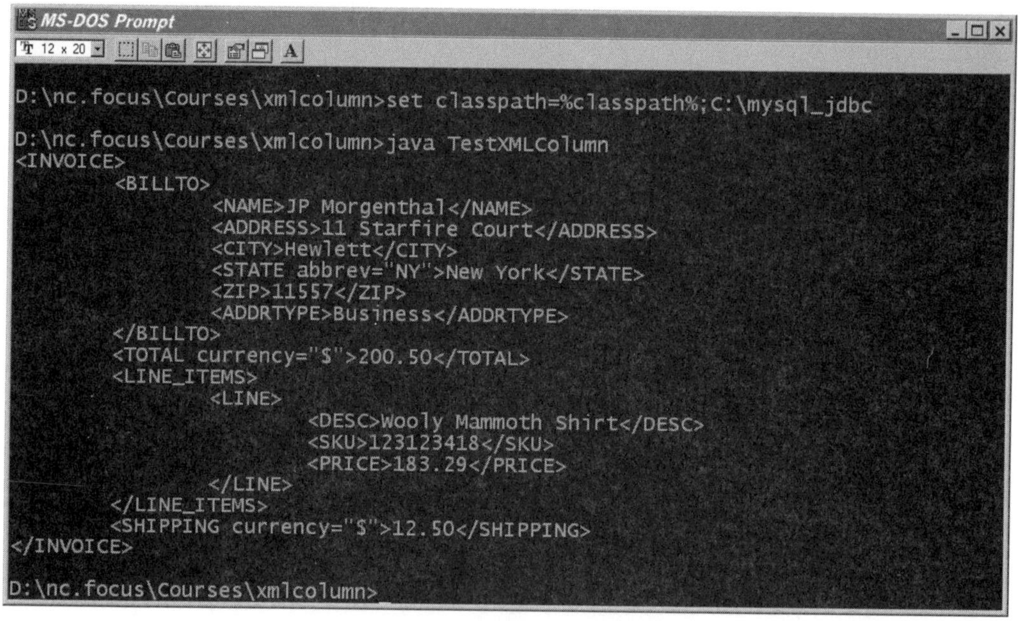

```
MS-DOS Prompt                                                    _ □ ×
T 12 x 20 ▼  □ ▣ 🖫 ⊠ 🖻🖫 A
D:\nc.focus\Courses\xmlcolumn>set classpath=%classpath%;C:\mysql_jdbc

D:\nc.focus\Courses\xmlcolumn>java TestXMLColumn
<INVOICE>
        <BILLTO>
                <NAME>JP Morgenthal</NAME>
                <ADDRESS>11 Starfire Court</ADDRESS>
                <CITY>Hewlett</CITY>
                <STATE abbrev="NY">New York</STATE>
                <ZIP>11557</ZIP>
                <ADDRTYPE>Business</ADDRTYPE>
        </BILLTO>
        <TOTAL currency="$">200.50</TOTAL>
        <LINE_ITEMS>
                <LINE>
                        <DESC>Wooly Mammoth Shirt</DESC>
                        <SKU>123123418</SKU>
                        <PRICE>183.29</PRICE>
                </LINE>
        </LINE_ITEMS>
        <SHIPPING currency="S">12.50</SHIPPING>
</INVOICE>

D:\nc.focus\Courses\xmlcolumn>
```

Figure 6–1   Screen shot of `TestXMLColumn`.

■   The `FixForXML` method will do a search and replace on a particular character. In the case of SQL, we need to preface all double-quotes (") into backslashes-double-quotes(\ "). In SQL, backslashes indicate that the next character should be taken literally; therefore, \ " needs to be represented as \\\ ".

```
  String x = FixForXMLWork(in, '\"', "\\\"", ignorefnl);
  return x;
}
String FixForXMLWork(String in, int ch, String replace,
  boolean ignorefnl) {
```

■   `FixForXMLWork` implements the actual search and replace semantics for `FixForXML`. The parameter `ignorefnl`, which means ignore first and last, allows the developer to tell the function not to analyze the first and last characters of the string, which are often quotes and need to be left alone.

```
  int firstchar, lastchar;
  if (ignorefnl) {
```

```
      firstchar = 1;
      lastchar = in.length()-1;
  } else {
      firstchar = 0;
      lastchar = in.length();
  }

  int amp = in.indexOf(ch,firstchar);
  if (amp == -1)
      return in;

  String fixedStr = null;

  int lastIdx = firstchar;

  while (amp != -1) {
      amp = in.indexOf(ch, lastIdx);
      if (amp == -1 || amp == lastchar)
          break;
      fixedStr = in.substring(0, amp);
      fixedStr += replace;
      fixedStr += in.substring(amp+1, in.length());
      lastIdx = amp+replace.length();
      in = fixedStr;
  }
  return in;
  }
}
```

This is only one implementation of this type of functionality. You might choose to implement a SAXResultSet which allows you to specify document handlers that are executed as part of the getXML method or perhaps XSLResultSet, which would automatically apply stylesheet transformations over the database column before returning it.

Regardless of its use, once the XML is stored in the database using this method, it can then be accessed by and shared with applications written in other programming languages, which is the goal of this exercise.

In addition to storing and retrieving XML from a database, there's also the issue of extracting data from a database in XML format.

Most often we wish to do this when direct database sharing is too cumbersome for our integration needs, but our data is stored in a relational database facility. In these cases, we can use XML to encapsulate the results of a database query, thus insulating us from the database schema. Many issues surround this problem. The following contribution (sections 6.2 through 6.10) by Lee Buck, CTO of Extensibility, examines this issue in finer detail and provides one possible solution.

6.2 | Modeling Spectrum

When mapping information from traditional (e.g., relational, object-oriented) data models to XML, there is no single right answer. Instead, there is a spectrum of potential approaches. At one end of the spectrum is the custom mapping of individual pieces of information from the database into a "pre-ordained" schema (e.g., an industry standard interchange format). This approach implies significant custom code to perform the mappings between the two loosely coupled schema (that of the database and that of the pre-ordained schema).

At the other end of the spectrum is a "data-dump" of the entire contents of a database with the intention of re-constituting the database with all of its relationships and data intact. This approach tends to yield a mechanical mapping onto a generic metadata schema. XMI, promulgated by the OMG, is one such generic metadata schema. In this approach, the schema is not about the business; it's about the metadata concepts themselves.

Both ends of the spectrum are common and useful ways of modeling relational data. Both have their drawbacks: the need for substantial custom code, and the obscuring of the business concepts. This chapter sets forth an approach that lies between these two extremes and applies it to relational databases. It provides mechanical mappings of key database structure concepts while retaining the notion that the schema should be about the business information. This approach has the merit of yielding straightforward understandable schemas that are congruent with existing data structures and that leverage XML concepts such as ID/IDREF. This approach is not guaranteed to provide 100% fidelity when round-tripping data from a RDBMS to XML back to an RDBMS, but whenever possible, we identify such limitations and potential workarounds.

6.3 | The Example

Let's use a simple example to work in the concrete. The following is an employee database with three tables. EMPLOYEE stores personal information and a summary of the term of the relationship. PERF_REVIEW stores performance reviews given to the employee. COMP_CHANGE stores changes to compensation resulting (usually but not always) from a performance review.

```
TABLE EMPLOYEE
      NUM     LONGINT       PRIMARY KEY
      FNAME   STRING 32
      LNAME   STRING 32
      HIRE_DATE     DATE
      TERM_DATE     DATE   MAY BE NULL


TABLE PERF_REVIEW
      EMP_NUM       LONGINT       PRIMARY KEY   FOREIGN KEY
      REVIEW_DATE   DATE   PRIMARY KEY
      REVIEW TEXT


TABLE COMP_CHANGE
      EMP_NUM       LONGINT       FOREIGN KEY
      REVIEW_DATE   DATE   MAY BE NULL
      EFF_DATE      DATE
      SALARY INT
```

At its simplest, an XML document of information drawn from this example might look like this:

```
<EMPLOYEE
     NUM = '2361'
     FNAME = 'Wilbert'
     LNAME = 'Winston'
     HIRE_DATE = '4/4/88'>
</EMPLOYEE>
```

Notice we have an element whose type is named after the table that corresponds to a row of data with attributes containing the values for each of the columns. (We could equally have had sub-elements containing the column data.) While a good start, there are crucial improvements we can make to the model:

1. Support for datatypes information.

2. Retention of key relationships.

3. Leveraging of XML's ID/IDREF facilities.

To make these improvements, we'll need to capture additional information in the schema using techniques outlined next.

6.4 | Extending the DTD

The DTD syntax is very efficient in expressing a certain set of constraints on conforming documents. However, it knows nothing about concepts such as key relationships. We'll extend the DTD to capture such additional information for the element types and attributes that we define in our schema. We'll use fixed attributes to accomplish this because the value of fixed attributes is unchangeable in individual elements, so they can be thought of as properties of the element type itself rather than of an instance. So:

1. For element types, we associate the property by adding a fixed nmtoken attribute whose name is preceded by an

e-. The value of this attribute is the value of the property. For example, to associate 'red' as the value of the 'color' property for the element type 'quark', we would define an attribute `e-color` whose fixed value was 'red'.

2. For attributes we associate the property by adding an attribute name / property value pair to a fixed `nmtokens` attribute whose name is the property name preceded by an a-. For example, to associate 'blue' as the value of the 'color' property for a particular attribute named 'bark', we would define an attribute `a-color` whose fixed value contained 'bark blue' (as well as potentially other pairs (e.g., bite pink) for the color property).

```
<!ATTLIST quark bark    CDATA    #IMPLIED
                bite    CDATA    #IMPLIED
                e-color NMTOKEN  #FIXED   'red'
                a-color NMTOKENS #FIXED   'bark blue bite
pink'
>
```

For our purposes, we'll need four such properties:

dtype   The datatype for the element type or attribute. This is used to more fully specify the allowed values for a content of type PCDATA or an attribute value of type CDATA. For a discussion of the use and meaning of the property, see the next section, Modeling Datatypes.

dsize   The storage size and/or precision for the datatype. For a discussion of the use and meaning of the property, see the next section, Modeling Datatypes.

pkey   The name of the attribute or element type(s) which corresponds to the primary key column. In the case of aggregate keys, this is a space-delimited list. This is used only on the element type corresponding to a table. For a discussion of the use and meaning of the property, see section 6.6, Modeling Relationships.

fkey   A reference to the attribute or element type which represents the column to which this attribute or element type refers. This is used only on the attribute or element type corresponding to a column that contains a foreign key. For a discussion of the use and meaning of the property, see section 6.6, Modeling Relationships.

These metadata properties are also applicable with minor modification to other schema syntaxes such as XML Data and SOX. Essentially, they become additional attributes on the element type or attribute list declaration.

6.5 | Modeling Datatypes

Traditional data sources tend to be strongly typed. While an XML document, by definition, represents information as characters, retaining knowledge about the underlying datatype is essential. The metadata property dtype (as outlined above) will be used to capture datatype information. What set of datatype values should we use? While a comprehensive list of datatypes is an elusive (if not illusory) goal, a useful set has been compiled from the various schema submissions to the W3C. We'll adopt the convention of using these datatype names.

```
string
number
dateTime

boolean
float
date
```

```
uri
int
time
```

A related problem arises around the issue of storage size. For example, how many bytes are needed to store a value of type "int" or how many characters long may a value of type string be? And even, "what is the precision of a value of type number?" We use the metadata property `dsize` to capture this information. The following meaning is assigned to values of `dsize`:

```
dtype
dsize
Example

string
maximum number of characters
23

float
bytes (4 or 8)
4

number
x.y
where
x = digits allowed to left of decimal
y = digits allowed to right of decimal
14.4

int
bytes (1, 2, 4 or 8)*
* i1, i2, i4, i8 may be used instead of int to obviate the need for the
  dsize attribute
8
```

Note that this encoding of datatype information within a DTD does not beget validation behavior by itself. Such validation is beyond the capabilities of XML 1.0 parsers. However, using these methods, you can make such information available to your custom code for proper validation. Indeed, by using notations matched in name to your `dtype` values, you can bind a reference to actual validation modules to each datatype.

6.6 | Modeling Relationships

Much of the power and complexity of mapping data to XML comes from mapping the relationships between pieces of data. In the relational world, this equates to the modeling of primary-foreign key relationships. Let's look at each in turn.

6.6.1 *Primary Keys*

A primary key provides a unique value by which a single row of a particular table may be accessed. XML has a similar concept of an ID attribute that provides unique access to an element. Many implementations of DOM provide indexed access to such elements, so leveraging the similarities is often desirable. However, a subtlety arises: XML IDs must be unique across the whole document, but a primary key is unique only within that column.

To provide the necessary global uniqueness, we use a supplemental `pkey_id` attribute to hold a version of the primary key data that we have made globally unique. To do this, we take advantage of two facts: 1) the primary key is unique within the context of the element type that contains each row (named, as you'll see, after the table itself), and 2) the element type's name is unique within the document. So, to make the locally unique name globally unique, we prepend the element type name to the key value. For example:

```
<EMPLOYEE pkey_id = "EMPLOYEE.2361">
  <EMPLOYEE.NUM>2361</EMPLOYEE.NUM>
```

```
   <EMPLOYEE.FNAME>Wilbert</EMPLOYEE.FNAME>
   <EMPLOYEE.LNAME>Winston</EMPLOYEE.LNAME>
   <EMPLOYEE.HIRE_DATE>4/4/88</EMPLOYEE.HIRE_DATE>
</EMPLOYEE>
```

6.6.2 *Foreign Keys*

The presence of foreign keys within a table provides the actual glue that binds different tables together. Just as XML's ID concept provided a useful analog for primary keys, so too its IDREF notion provides a powerful analog to foreign keys. Of course, issues of uniqueness and scope intervene here as well. To accommodate them, we use a similar technique. We create a new IDREF attribute for the table element type whose name is derived from the column name (with an `_idref` appended). Values in a document will be constructed in a similar fashion as for `pkey_id` attributes (indeed the production must match exactly; otherwise, the whole point is lost). For example:

```
<EMPLOYEE pkey_id = "EMPLOYEE.2361">
   <EMPLOYEE.NUM>2361</EMPLOYEE.NUM>
   ...

<PERF_REVIEW PERF_REVIEW.EMP_NUM_idref = "EMPLOYEE.2361">
   <PERF_REVIEW.EMP_NUM>2361<PERF_REVIEW.EMP_NUM>
   ...
```

Another problem that arises is the need to have the schema—rather than just the document—depict the relationships involved. Note that in the example above, it is the data of the PERF_REVIEW element that associates PERF_REVIEW with EMPLOYEE. So that the schema might "know" the relationship in the absence of a document instance, we define that relationship using the metadata properties `pkey` and `fkey`. For example:

```
<!ATTLIST EMPLOYEE e-pkey NMTOKEN #FIXED 'EMPLOYEE.NUM'>
```

and

```
<!ATTLIST PERF_REVIEW.EMP_NUM e-fkey NMTOKEN #FIXED 'EM-
PLOYEE.EMPLOYEE_NUM' >
```

6.6.3   *Nesting*

There is an alternative to the mechanism described above in some cases. This technique takes advantage of the fact that an XML relationship may be inferred from context (specifically, containment) as well as through ID/IDREF relationships. So, in our example, we can associate PERF_REVIEW elements with their corresponding EMPLOYEE elements by placing them inside the latter. For example:

```
<EMPLOYEE EMPLOYEE.NUM_id = "EMPLOYEE.2361"
     NUM = '2361'
     FNAME = 'Wilbert'
     LNAME = 'Winston'
     HIRE_DATE = '4/4/88'>
   <PERF_REVIEW
     REVIEW_DATE = '1/1/98'
     REVIEW = 'lousy'/>
   <PERF_REVIEW
     REVIEW_DATE = '1/1/99'
     REVIEW = 'worse'/>
</EMPLOYEE>
```

Note that this is not always desirable and is often not even possible. The following conditions must be met for this to be appropriate:

1. The foreign key must not be nullable (i.e., optional).

2. It must be the only foreign key so modeled in the table.

3. Every desired row must refer to a row that will be included.

4. The foreign key must not point to the same table.

6.7 | The Example Step-by-Step

6.7.1 *Modeling Tables*

1. Table. The table itself becomes an element type. In the document, each occurrence of an element of this type will contain a single row of the data. If we're modeling the columns of this table as attributes, the content model is EMPTY. If we're modeling the columns as elements, then the content model is a sequence of the element type names that correspond to the columns. In the latter case, we make optional (?) any elements where column values may be null.

```
<!ELEMENT EMPLOYEE EMPTY>

or
<!ELEMENT EMPLOYEE (
    EMPLOYEE.NUM,
    EMPLOYEE.FNAME,
    EMPLOYEE.LNAME,
    EMPLOYEE.HIRE_DATE,
    EMPLOYEE.TERM_DATE?
)>
```

2. Primary Key. If the table has a primary key, we capture that information with the `pkey` metadata property introduced in Section 6.4, Extending the DTD.

```
<!ATTLIST EMPLOYEE e-pkey NMTOKEN #FIXED
  'EMPLOYEE.NUM'>
```

3. To provide ID/IDREF access to key relationships we create a special ID attribute to contain a globally unique version of this key for each element.

```
<!ATTLIST EMPLOYEE pkey_id ID #REQUIRED>
```

6.7.2 *Modeling Columns as Elements*

For each column:

1. Column Name. A new element type with the same name as the column is created. In the document, each occurrence of an element of this type will contain the value of a single column of a single row of data. Because element type names must be unique throughout the whole document, you should probably qualify the column's element type name by prefixing it with the table's name.

```
<!ELEMENT EMPLOYEE.TERM_DATE (#PCDATA) >
```

2. Column Data Type. Data types are captured using the `dtype` metadata property introduced in Section 6.4, Extending the DTD.

```
<!ATTLIST EMPLOYEE.TERM_DATE e-dtype NMTOKEN
   #FIXED 'date' >
```

3. Column Nullable. As noted in number 1, if the column may contain a null value, then its reference in the table's content model is made optional.

4. Column Foreign Key. If the column contains a foreign key, we use the `fkey` metadata property to record the column's element to which the key refers.

```
<!ATTLIST PERF.REVIEW_EMP_NUM e-fkey NMTOKEN #FIXED
   'EMPLOYEE.NUM' >
```

5. To provide ID/IDREF access to key relationships, a special attribute of the table's element type may be created

to serve as an IDREF link to the element corresponding to the other table. The attribute name is formed by appending _idref to the column element type's name.

```
<!ATTLIST PERF_REVIEW PERF_REVIEW.EMP_NUM_idref IDREF
   #REQUIRED >
```

6.7.3 *Modeling Columns as Attributes*

For each column:

1. Column Name. A new attribute with the same name is created. In the document, each occurrence of this attribute for this element type will contain the value of a single column of a single row of data.

   ```
   <!ATTLIST EMPLOYEE EMPLOYEE.TERM_DATE CDATA #IMPLIED>
   ```

2. Column Data Type. Data types are captured using the dtype metadata property introduced in Section 6.4, Extending the DTD.

   ```
   <!ATTLIST EMPLOYEE a-dtype NMTOKENS #FIXED
           'EMPLOYEE.NUM           int
           EMPLOYEE.FNAME          string
           EMPLOYEE.LNAME          string
           EMPLOYEE.HIRE_DATE      date
           EMPLOYEE.TERM_DATE      date'

                      a-dsize NMTOKENS #FIXED
           'EMPLOYEE.FNAME         32
           EMPLOYEE.LNAME          32'
   >
   ```

3. Column Nullable. If the column may contain a null value, then the attribute value is made implied, if not, it is made required.

4. Column Foreign Key. If the column contains a foreign key, we use the fkey metadata property to record the table element type and attribute to which the key refers.

```
<!ATTLIST PERF_REVIEW a-fkey NMTOKENS #FIXED
      EMP_NUM     EMPLOYEE.NUM'
>
```

5. To provide ID/IDREF access to key relationships, a special attribute of the table's element type may be created
   to serve as an IDREF link to the element corresponding
   to the other table. The attribute name is formed by appending _idref to the column element type's name.

```
<!ATTLIST PERF_REVIEW EMP_NUM_idref IDREF
   #REQUIRED >
```

6.8 | Conclusion

By adopting some simple conventions, XML schemas can successfully
model information sources such as relational databases. By capturing
datatype, key relationships and ID/IDREF information, extracted data
can retain the metadata needed to facilitate processing at both sides of
an information exchange. The process set forth above is straightforward
and well suited to automation and has been implemented for a wide variety of databases in the current XML Authority schema editor product.

6.9 | Listings

6.9.1 *DTD with Columns as Elements*

```
<!ELEMENT EMPLOYEE (
   EMPLOYEE.NUM? ,
   EMPLOYEE.FNAME ,
   EMPLOYEE.LNAME ,
   EMPLOYEE.HIRE_DATE ,
   EMPLOYEE.TERM_DATE? )>

<!ATTLIST EMPLOYEE pkey_id ID    #REQUIRED
                   e-pkey NMTOKEN #FIXED 'EMPLOYEE.NUM' >
```

```
<!ELEMENT EMPLOYEE.NUM (#PCDATA )>
<!ATTLIST EMPLOYEE.NUM e-dtype NMTOKEN #FIXED 'int' >

<!ELEMENT EMPLOYEE.FNAME (#PCDATA )>
<!ATTLIST EMPLOYEE.FNAME e-dtype NMTOKEN #FIXED 'string'
                         e-dSize NMTOKEN #FIXED '32' >

<!ELEMENT EMPLOYEE.LNAME (#PCDATA )>

<!ATTLIST EMPLOYEE.LNAME e-dtype NMTOKEN #FIXED 'string'
                         e-dSize NMTOKEN #FIXED '32' >

<!ELEMENT EMPLOYEE.HIRE_DATE (#PCDATA )>
<!ATTLIST EMPLOYEE.HIRE_DATE e-dtype NMTOKEN #FIXED 'date' >

<!ELEMENT EMPLOYEE.TERM_DATE (#PCDATA )>
<!ATTLIST EMPLOYEE.TERM_DATE e-dtype NMTOKEN #FIXED 'date' >

<!ELEMENT PERF_REVIEW (
   PERF_REVIEW.EMP_NUM ,
   PERF_REVIEW.REVIEW_DATE ,
   PERF_REVIEW.REVIEW )>

<!ATTLIST PERF_REVIEW PERF_REVIEW.EMP_NUM_idref IDREF
   #REQUIRED >

<!ELEMENT PERF_REVIEW.EMP_NUM (#PCDATA )>
<!ATTLIST PERF_REVIEW.EMP_NUM e-dtype NMTOKEN #FIXED 'int'
                              e-fkey NMTOKEN #FIXED
                                 'EMPLOYEE.NUM' >

<!ELEMENT PERF_REVIEW.REVIEW_DATE (#PCDATA )>
<!ATTLIST PERF_REVIEW.REVIEW_DATE e-dtype NMTOKEN #FIXED
   'date' >

<!ELEMENT PERF_REVIEW.REVIEW (#PCDATA )>
<!ATTLIST PERF_REVIEW.REVIEW e-dtype NMTOKEN #FIXED 'string'
                             e-dSize NMTOKEN #FIXED '50' >

<!ELEMENT COMP_CHANGE (
   COMP_CHANGE.EMP_NUM ,
   COMP_CHANGE.REVIEW_DATE? ,
   COMP_CHANGE.EFF_DATE ,
   COMP_CHANGE.SALARY )>

<!ATTLIST COMP_CHANGE COMP_CHANGE.EMP_NUM_idref IDREF
   #REQUIRED >
```

```
<!ELEMENT COMP_CHANGE.EMP_NUM (#PCDATA )>
<!ATTLIST COMP_CHANGE.EMP_NUM e-dtype NMTOKEN #FIXED 'int'
                              e-fkey NMTOKEN #FIXED
                                   'EMPLOYEE.NUM' >

<!ELEMENT COMP_CHANGE.REVIEW_DATE (#PCDATA )>
<!ATTLIST COMP_CHANGE.REVIEW_DATE e-dtype NMTOKEN #FIXED
    'date' >

<!ELEMENT COMP_CHANGE.EFF_DATE (#PCDATA )>
<!ATTLIST COMP_CHANGE.EFF_DATE e-dtype NMTOKEN #FIXED 'date' >

<!ELEMENT COMP_CHANGE.SALARY (#PCDATA )>
<!ATTLIST COMP_CHANGE.SALARY e-dtype NMTOKEN #FIXED 'int' >
```

6.9.2 *DTD with Columns as Attributes*

```
<!ELEMENT EMPLOYEE EMPTY>
<!ATTLIST EMPLOYEE  pkey_id  ID         #REQUIRED
                    NUM       CDATA      #REQUIRED
                    FNAME     CDATA      #REQUIRED
                    LNAME     CDATA      #REQUIRED
                    HIRE_DATE CDATA      #REQUIRED
                    TERM_DATE CDATA      #IMPLIED
                    e-pkey    NMTOKEN    #FIXED 'NUM'
                    a-dtype   NMTOKENS   'NUM        int
                                         FNAME      string
                                         LNAME      string
                                         HIRE_DATE date
                                         TERM_DATE date'
                    a-dSize   NMTOKENS   'FNAME 32
                                         LNAME 32' >

<!ELEMENT PERF_REVIEW EMPTY>
<!ATTLIST PERF_REVIEW  PERF_REVIEW.EMP_NUM_idref IDREF      #REQUIRED
                       EMP_NUM                   CDATA      #REQUIRED
                       REVIEW_DATE               CDATA      #REQUIRED
                       REVIEW                    CDATA      #REQUIRED
                       a-dtype                   NMTOKENS 'EMP_NUM     int
                                                          REVIEW_DATE date
                                                          REVIEW      date'
                       a-fkey                    NMTOKENS 'EMP_NUM EMPLOYEE.NUM'
                       a-dSize                   NMTOKENS 'REVIEW 50' >

<!ELEMENT COMP_CHANGE EMPTY>
<!ATTLIST COMP_CHANGE COMP_CHANGE.EMP_NUM_idref IDREF      #REQUIRED
                       EMP_NUM                   CDATA      #REQUIRED
                       REVIEW_DATE               CDATA      #IMPLIED
```

```
        EFF_DATE                CDATA    #REQUIRED
        SALARY                  CDATA    #REQUIRED
        a-dtype                 NMTOKENS 'EMP_NUM      int
                                         REVIEW_DATE date
                                         EFF_DATE     date
                                         SALARY       int'
        a-fkey                  NMTOKENS 'EMP_NUM EMPLOYEE.NUM' >
```

6.9.3 *XML Data with Columns as Elements*

```
<?xml version ="1.0"?>
<!—Generated by XML Authority. Conforms to XML Data subset
   for IE 5—>
<Schema name = ""
   xmlns = "urn:schemas-microsoft-com:xml-data"
   xmlns:dt = "urn:schemas-microsoft-com:datatypes"
   xmlns:xa = "www.extensibility.com/schemas/xdr/" +
      "metaprops.xdr">
   <ElementType name = "EMPLOYEE" xa:pkey = "EMPLOYEE.NUM"
     content = "eltOnly" order = "seq">
     <AttributeType name = "pkey_id" dt:type = "ID" required
       = "yes"/>
     <attribute type = "pkey_id"/>
     <element type = "EMPLOYEE.NUM" />
     <element type = "EMPLOYEE.FNAME" />
     <element type = "EMPLOYEE.LNAME" />
     <element type = "EMPLOYEE.HIRE_DATE />
     <element type = "EMPLOYEE.TERM_DATE" minOccurs = "0"
       maxOccurs = "1"/>
   </ElementType>
   <ElementType name = "EMPLOYEE.NUM" content = "textOnly"
     dt:type = "i4"/>
   <ElementType name = "EMPLOYEE.FNAME" content = "textOnly"
     dt:type = "string"/>
   <ElementType name = "EMPLOYEE.LNAME" content = "textOnly"
     dt:type = "string"/>
   <ElementType name = "EMPLOYEE.HIRE_DATE" content =
     "textOnly" dt:type = "date"/>
   <ElementType name = "EMPLOYEE.TERM_DATE" content =
     "textOnly" dt:type = "date"/>

   <ElementType name = "PERF_REVIEW" content = "eltOnly"
     order = "seq">
     <AttributeType name = "PERF_REVIEW.EMP_NUM_idref"
       dt:type = "IDREF" required = "yes"/>
```

```
    <attribute type = "PERF_REVIEW.EMP_NUM_idref"/>
    <element type = "PERF_REVIEW.EMP_NUM" />
    <element type = "PERF_REVIEW.REVIEW_DATE />
    <element type = "PERF_REVIEW.REVIEW" />
  </ElementType>
  <ElementType name = "PERF_REVIEW.EMP_NUM" xa:fkey =
    "EMPLOYEE.NUM" content = "textOnly" dt:type = "i4"/>
  <ElementType name = "PERF_REVIEW.REVIEW_DATE" content =
    "textOnly" dt:type = "date"/>
  <ElementType name = "PERF_REVIEW.REVIEW" content =
    "textOnly" dt:type = "string"/>
  <ElementType name = "COMP_CHANGE" content = "eltOnly"
    order = "seq">
    <AttributeType name = "COMP_CHANGE.EMP_NUM_idref"
      dt:type = "IDREF" required = "yes"/>
    <attribute type = "COMP_CHANGE.EMP_NUM_idref"/>
    <element type = "COMP_CHANGE.EMP_NUM" />
    <element type = "COMP_CHANGE.REVIEW_DATE" minOccurs =
      "0" maxOccurs = "1" />
    <element type = "COMP_CHANGE.EFF_DATE" />
    <element type = "COMP_CHANGE.SALARY" />
  </ElementType>
  <ElementType name = "COMP_CHANGE.EMP_NUM" xa:fkey =
    "EMPLOYEE.NUM" content = "textOnly" dt:type = "i4"/>
  <ElementType name = "COMP_CHANGE.REVIEW_DATE" content =
    "textOnly" dt:type = "date"/>
  <ElementType name = "COMP_CHANGE.EFF_DATE" content =
    "textOnly" dt:type = "date"/>
  <ElementType name = "COMP_CHANGE.SALARY" content =
    "textOnly" dt:type = "i2"/>
</Schema>
```

6.10 | Mapping XML into Existing Schemas

So far, we've seen how to store and retrieve XML documents using text and BLOB fields in relational databases. We've also seen one method for modeling relational data in XML that captures the relationships defined by the original schema. This leads us to a discussion on mapping XML documents into existing database schemas assuming the aforementioned modeling technique, or one like it, was not used.

For example, translating an XML invoice from another company into an existing accounting system's schema would require a mapping process. Like modeling, there is no standard method for mapping XML documents into schemas, but there are few techniques that can simplify the problem.

1. **Visual Mapping Tools.** There are not many of these tools on the market, and those that do exist are expensive and only operate with their own transformation engines. However, we believe this is simply a symptom of the early XML market and that more will emerge at a reasonable cost. Visual mapping tools allow human engineers to highlight specific elements and attributes of an XML document and identify which database tables and fields these elements and attributes should be mapped into. The result of this process may be code, executable processes, or dynamic SQL statements that will handle the mapping in an automated fashion. Additionally, these tools should store the mapping so that it is easy to update whenever there may be a change to an XML document or the existing schemas.

2. **XPointer and DOM.** For developers desiring to hard code the solution, XPointer and DOM can be extremely useful tools for extracting data from XML documents. We've already explored how the DOM interface works and how it can be used to traverse the tree to extract the data and build an SQL `INSERT` or `UPDATE` statement. XPointer is another programmatic interface for extracting data from XML documents. Its syntax allows developers to define a URL that targets a specific element in an XML document. Current XPointer implementations

work in tandem with DOM and use DOM objects as return values for XPointer functions. XPointer abstracts the tree address and eliminates the need to traverse the tree manually to get to certain elements.

Unfortunately, XML hierarchies suffer from impedance mismatches with relational technologies. This means that there is not a 1:1 mapping between a hierarchy and relational operations. Moreover, there are multiple ways a hierarchy might be stored in a database, and each has performance implications. For example, mapping child elements into their own tables requires an extensive SQL JOIN operation to retrieve the entire XML document. However, a database architect could also choose to store certain parent and child elements in the same table, which leads to unnecessary duplication of data, but removes the overhead on the retrieval.

6.11 | Summary

As you can see, XML can be a useful tool for sharing data between Java and non-Java environments using a relational database. The cases we presented show how to use XML that is stored in a column within a relational database and also how to move data in and out of the database using XML as an interim format. In the next chapter, we will explore ways to exchange XML data using asynchronous messaging.

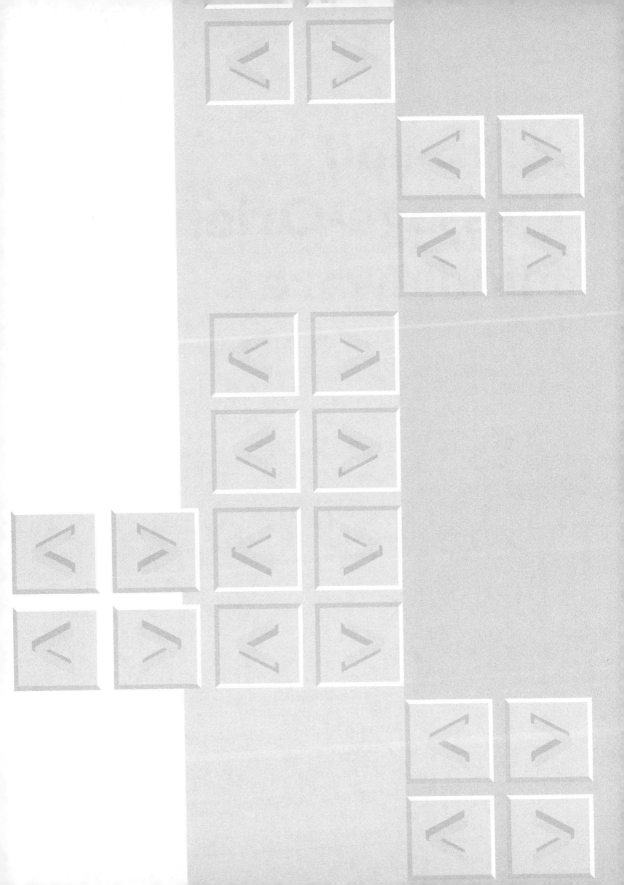

XML and
Message-Oriented
Middleware

7.1 | Introduction

Another way to exchange data between Java and non-Java environments is to use Message-Oriented Middleware (MOM). Typically, this class of software is implemented as server technology that defines message queues—holding bins for messages—or handles redistribution of messages to a group of subscribers (also known as publish/subscribe).

Asynchronous messaging allows applications to communicate over time without having to wait for the consumer to process the message. This is important when the consumer may not be available or may only be available for short time periods daily. In synchronous messaging systems, a producer will send a message to a consumer and wait for an acknowledgement. This delay is called *blocking*, and it forces the calling thread, or the entire application in a single-threaded model, to stop until the acknowledgement is sent. In the case where the consumer is not available, or only intermittently available, this could result in significant overhead for the producer application.

Of note, most asynchronous environments can operate in a synchronous mode if necessary, which is why MOM is becoming so popular as a transport medium in business today. Since business sometimes works both asynchronously and synchronously, it is useful to have a single tool that supports both models of operation. This provides for the development of simpler applications that do not need to account for different transports based upon the need of the business at a particular moment in time. For example, an accounting department may process most of its credit card authorizations off-line in a batch manner. However, in the case of a questionable customer, the department may need to authorize immediately before accepting a sales order. It is useful to have a single transport that can support both of these business requirements.

XML and MOM make a great pairing since MOM software simply manages access or distribution of data, regardless of its value. Consider the value of combining a platform- and language-neutral messaging environment with self-describing messages. This is the value of XML and MOM together and, subsequently, one of the key values of XML entirely.

Inside the Java environment, there is a standard interface to MOM software known as the Java Messaging Service (JMS). The JMS programming interface provides a way for vendors of MOM software to provide a consistent interface to Java applications, and thus make it easier to use asynchronous messaging.

Of note, JMS only partially delivers on its promise since there are too many diverse implementations of messaging software for JMS to properly embody them all. JMS has done a good job of giving developers the use of the functionality of individual messaging implementations, but use of these features reduces the ability of the code to be used with any other messaging implementations. In these cases, JMS code may be of only slightly more value than using a messaging vendor's proprietary Java interface, if one exists.

Before diving straight into the details of JMS, let's first explore the two key models of messaging that JMS supports: point-to-point and publish/subscribe.

7.1.1   *Point-to-Point Messaging*

The JMS Point-to-Point (PTP) model typically allows one producer to provide messages for one consumer in an asynchronous manner. *Consumer* is the term used to describe the application that receives the messages, and *producer* is the term used to describe the application that creates and supplies messages.

PTP connections are most often established using a mechanism called a queue. A queue is a named holding bin for messages. There are many types of queues; for example, first-in first-out, last-in first-out, random (can read messages from anywhere in the queue), and dequeues (can read and write to both ends). With PTP applications, there is an agreement that the consumer will read messages that are placed in a queue of a particular name and that the producer will write messages to this queue.

At a higher level, PTP implementations imply an agreement over the data being supplied. This agreement also embodies other information, such as the type of information that is of interest to the consumer. For example, the consumer may only be interested in stock prices, while the producer provides both stock and bond prices. Architecturally, this could be handled a couple of different ways. First, the producer could use two queues, one for stock prices and one for bond prices (see Figure 7–1). This way, the consumer only has to read from the stock price queue. Another method is for the producer to place both types of messages into the queue and for the application to

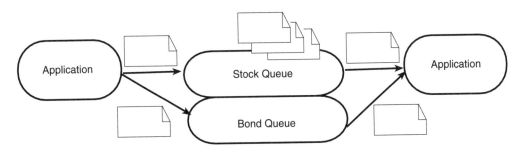

Figure 7–1   Multiple queues architecture.

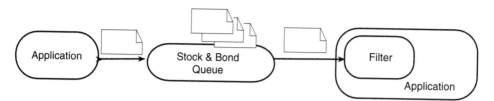

Figure 7–2   Single queue architecture.

provide automatic filtering on the consumer side as the messages are retrieved from the queue (see Figure 7–2).

Finally, PTP software also needs to provide for multiple levels in quality of service. Quality of service defines how likely it is that a message will reach its intended target. For maximum guarantee, messaging software can implement persistent queues—queues that write their values to a persistent medium in case of machine failure—as well as provide for a transacted exchange. Transactions in PTP systems can be implemented in two ways:

1. The transaction guarantees that the message was properly written to the queue.

2. The transaction guarantees that the message was received. This method requires that the consumer acknowledge receipt of the message.

In some applications, loss is acceptable; for instance, electronic mail is a PTP medium that may prove "lossy." This means that if the MOM server crashes with messages still in the queue, the consumer will not be in an indeterminate state. However, most often, PTP exchanges usually require greater levels of guaranteed delivery, and therefore usually operate in a transacted and guaranteed manner.

7.1.2 *Publish and Subscribe Messaging*

Publish/Subscribe (P/S) messaging allows a single producer to send messages to any number of consumers as a single operation. P/S software is responsible for accepting and managing subscriptions from consumers for a particular set of information known as a topic. In turn, producers publish information over a set of topics, thereby triggering a redistribution of the message to all subscribers (see Figure 7–3).

While the intention is to deliver messages asynchronously between producers and consumers, P/S differs from PTP in a few respects:

1. PTP requires that the consumer connect to a queue and pull new messages out. In contrast, P/S delivers messages directly to the subscribing consumer. This is sometimes called "push" technology, because the message is being pushed out to the consumer.

2. PTP is designed for use by one consumer and requires special handling if multiple consumers are using the same queue. P/S is designed to handle a large number of consumers.

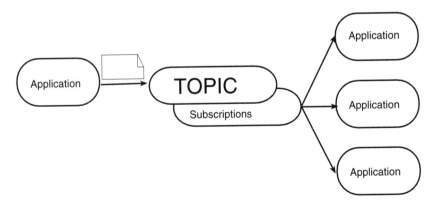

Figure 7–3   Publish/Subscribe messaging.

3. In PTP implementations, it is more likely that messages will operate in a transacted and guaranteed manner. By contrast, P/S is typically used in systems where loss of information is acceptable. However, there are some implementations of P/S messaging that provide for guaranteed messaging to a large number of consumers. This type of software is very expensive since it is a very complex problem to manage.

P/S software traditionally is implemented using one of two methods:

- **Hub-n-spoke.** In this model, there is a central redistribution point that a domain of subscribers all use. The producer sends a message to the hub, which redistributes it individually to each known subscriber. Hubs are linked together to provide scalability across a number of domains. This method is preferred when there needs to be access control over the information being published. It forces the subscriber to authenticate itself to the hub before it will receive a message. One of the downsides of the hub-n-spoke method is extreme latency of messages to remote hubs. This means that it could take a very long time to reach the last subscriber at the outermost hub. This point is usually only important when the messages being delivered have a time-based importance (see Figure 7–4).

- **Bus.** In this model, a producer broadcasts a message using a network transport capable of supporting broadcasting. This results in all machines within a certain range receiving the message. Therefore, there is an additional requirement for filtering the information locally. Also, in the case of sensitive information, there is an additional requirement to place security on reading the message vs. sending the message (see Figure 7–5).

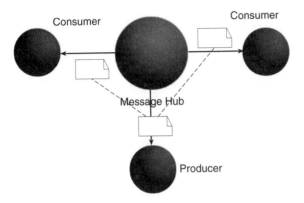

Figure 7–4   Hub-n-spoke.

JMS

The JMS API provides developers with an abstraction for accessing MOM implementations and supports both the PTP and P/S models. This abstraction works by breaking MOM systems into five core components: messages, sessions, connections, consumers, and producers. We will explore each of these components in-depth in this section.

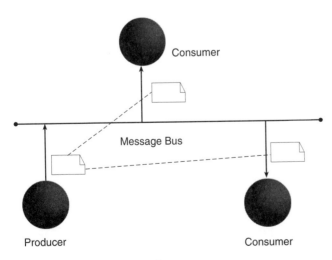

Figure 7–5   Bus topology.

The JMS message abstraction is broken into three separate sections:

- **The message header**. This part of the message is a set of properties that identifies where the message originated, the destination, the time it was sent, quality of service semantics, and other common messaging variables. This section is fixed across all implementations of JMS.

- **Message properties.** This part of the message is an extensible area that can be used to add application- or messaging-specific implementation characteristics. In addition, there are fixed properties that are prefixed with JMSX that exist across all JMS implementations, but are not required. For example, `JMSXGroupID` and `JMSX-GroupSeq` are properties that could be used to group messages together. Message properties set by the provider upon sending are available to both the producer and consumers of the message. Message properties set by the messaging system upon receipt are only available to the consumers.

- **The message body**. This is the actual data that is being delivered.

These three components make up a complete message that can be delivered to a Java or non-Java application.

Besides providing basic information to the messaging service and application, the header and properties sections can be used by a feature called the message selector, which provides filtering. The JMS message selector is an SQL-compatible facility that allows header and message properties to be used for qualification. The selector is a client-oriented function that filters messages based on selector matching.

As stated earlier, JMS supports both the PTP and P/S messaging models. Therefore, the application developer has to decide which type of messaging model to use with their application, which will lead to the selection of different JMS interfaces. This choice will identify the APIs within JMS that the developer will use for their application. We will demonstrate both the PTP and P/S interfaces in the following examples.

Regardless of which messaging model is selected, there are some fundamental interfaces that the developer must be aware of when using JMS. These interfaces are described below.

7.1.3.1 The Session Interface

A JMS `Session` is a single-threaded object that manages the exchange of messages. `Session` objects provide the following services to the JMS system:

- A `Session` is a factory for `Message` objects. A factory is a computing facility that creates new instances of other objects.

- `Sessions` act as the transaction context to allow multiple operations to be treated as a single atomic unit of work. Each transaction groups a set of message sends and a set of message receives into an atomic unit of work. Transacted messages are designed to ensure that all messages within a group are acknowledged or all are destroyed and that the session is restored to its previous state. If a transaction rollback is done, its sent messages are destroyed and the most recently consumed messages are automatically recovered.

- `Sessions` act as the context for defining message ordering.

- `Sessions` provide message persistence for messages awaiting acknowledgement.

- A `Session` acts as a container for all of its `MessageListeners`. Serialization of a `Session` preserves the `MessageListener` objects as well.

- A `Session` can create and service multiple message producers and consumers.

7.1.3.2 The Message Interface

A JMS `Message` encapsulates the header, properties, and content of a message. It allows the developer to read and write header and extended properties as typed values. Handling of the message body is done through type-specific versions of the `Message` object. By default, JMS supports the following message types:

- **BytesMessage.** Sends a message containing a stream of uninterpreted bytes.

- **MapMessage.** Sends a set of name-value pairs, where names are `String` objects and values are Java primitive types.

- **ObjectMessage.** Sends a message that contains a serializable Java object.

- **StreamMessage.** Sends a stream of Java primitives, such as `int` and `long`.

- **TextMessage.** Sends a message containing a `java.lang.StringBuffer`.

7.1.3.3 The Connection Interface

A Connection represents a link with a JMS provider. It serves the following purposes:

- Allows for one-time authentication of the user at time of creation.

- Associates client identifiers with a connection.

- Handles all client interactions through the JMS provider.

- Implements flow controls by providing start and stop mechanics.

7.1.3.4 The MessageConsumer Interface

The `MessageConsumer` is used to receive messages from a `Destination`, where a `Destination` is an abstraction of a queue or topic. `MessageConsumers` use message selectors to filter incoming messages. They have two methods of receiving messages: synchronously and asynchronously. Synchronous message delivery requires the client to call the `receive` method on the `MessageConsumer` object. To receive messages asynchronously, the client application needs to supply the `MessageConsumer` with a `MessageListener` object. When using this method of receiving, the JMS implementation will call the `MessageListener`'s `onMessage` method when a new message arrives. This allows the application to run without blocking.

7.1.3.5 The MessageProducer Interface

The `MessageProducer` is used by applications to send messages to `Destinations`. It provides an application with the ability to define quality of service and delivery mode options. `MessageProducers` are extended based upon the type of delivery service. PTP and P/S each have different methods for actually sending a message.

7.1.3.6 The MessageListener Interface

The `MessageListener` is used by the client to receive messages asynchronously. `MessageListener` has one method—`onMessage`—that is called by a `MessageConsumer` object on which it is registered.

7.1.3.7   Queues and Topics

In version 1.1 of the JMS specification, which is the one available as of this writing, implements two messaging models: PTP and P/S. These two different models produce two separate sets of interfaces for sending and receiving messages within the JMS.

PTP implementations use the message queue metaphor, and therefore operate using the Queue-based implementations of the `Session`, `MessageConsumer`, `MessageProducer`, and `Connection` objects. On the other hand, P/S uses the topics metaphor, and therefore uses the Topics-based implementations of the `Session`, `MessageConsumer`, `MessageProducer`, and `Connection` objects.

There are subtle differences in how these messaging environments work, and a developer should be familiar enough with the chosen method before using the JMS interfaces.

7.1.3.8   XML and JMS Topics

The following code examples illustrate how to send XML between applications using the P/S model. This code simply places the XML inside the body of a `TextMessage`, but you could easily develop an XML message type using the same methodology we used to create `XMLResultSet` in the JDBC section.

For these code examples, we will be using the SpiritWave JMS implementation provided by Push Technologies, Inc. These libraries can be found on the CD-ROM.

7.1.3.9   XMLProducer Class

```
public class XMLProducer
{
```

■   XMLProducer *creates* `TextMessage` *objects, puts the XML document in as the message body and then publishes it to a topic.*

```
public XMLProducer( String profileName,
           String topicName )
  throws JMSException
{
SpiritWaveBase swb = new SpiritWaveBase();
TopicConnection connection = null;
TopicPublisher publisher = null;
TopicSession session = null;
Topic topic = null;
FileInputStream is = null;

try {
  connection = swb.initTopic();
```

■ *The* `initTopic` *function creates an implementation specific* `TopicConnec-`
`tion` *Factory and then uses it to obtain a connection.*

```
session = connection.createTopicSession(swb.
  isTransacted,
  swb.acknowledgeMode);
```

■ *Here we create a* `TopicSession` *using our current connection.*

```
topic = session.createTopic(topicName);
```

■ *Notice that we create a* `TopicConnection,` `TopicSession,` *and* `Topic`
identically in the consumer and producer.

```
System.out.println("Creating TopicPublisher");
publisher = session.createPublisher( topic );
```

■ *A* `TopicPublisher` *will publish the message once to the JMS session, which*
will use its own method of redistributing the message to all of the subscribers.

```
TextMessage message = session.createTextMessage();
```

■ *Remember, the session acts as our message factory. Here we create an empty*
message with all the header properties set properly.

```
Parser parser = new Parser("test.xml");
```

■ *Here we create a new parser object to read in our* test.xml *document so we can send it as a message.*

```
try {
  is = new FileInputStream("test.xml");
    } catch (FileNotFoundException notFound) {
    System.out.println("File Error: " +
      notFound.getMessage());
    }
```

■ *Here we open the actual* test.xml *file as a* FileInputStream, *which is required by the XML4J parser in version 1.1.9.*

```
Document doc = (Document) parser.readStream(is);
```

■ *Here we parse the file to create a DOM Document.*

```
String messBody = swb.serialize(doc);
```

■ *In SpiritWaveBase, we created a function call serialize, which creates a string representation of our DOM Document object as an XML document.*

```
System.out.println(messBody);
```

■ *Here we print out the serialized document for comparison with our consumer.*

```
message.setText(messBody);
```

■ *Now we set the value of the message body to the XML document.*

```
connection.start();
```

■ *Tells the JMS implementation to start publishing messages.*

```
System.out.println("TopicConsumer Started");
publisher.publish( message );
```

■ *Here we publish the message to JMS.*

```
connection.stop();
```

■ *Tells the JMS implementation to stop publishing messages.*

```
} catch (Throwable e) {
        System.out.println(e);
} finally {
publisher.close();
session.close();
connection.close();
```

■ *Again, we clean up the used resources when the object is being destroyed.*

```
    }
 }
 ...
}
```

7.1.3.10   XMLConsumer Class

```
public class XMLConsumer
{
```

■ *The* XMLConsumer *class implements the code that subscribes to a particular topic and listens for messages being published by* XMLProducer.

```
public XMLConsumer(String profileName, String topicName)
   throws JMSException
{
  TopicConnection connection = null;
  TopicSession session = null;
  TopicSubscriber subscriber = null;
  Topic topic = null;
  SpiritWaveBase swb = new SpiritWaveBase();
```

■ *The SpiritWaveBase class implements functionality needed by* XMLConsumer *and* XMLProducer. *Some of the methods implemented on this base class pertain only to obtaining a connection from the SpiritWave JMS implementation.*

```
try
{
    connection = swb.init(profileName);
```

■ *Here we obtain a* TopicConnection *to the SpiritWave JMS implementa-tion. In this case, we're using their lightweight UDP implementation.* Topic-Connections *are only used in tandem with P/S JMS implementations.*

```
session = connection.createTopicSession(swb.
    isTransacted,
    swb.acknowledgeMode);
```

■ *From the connection, we can obtain a* TopicSession, *which will allow us to create topics and subscribers. This session is not transacted and uses DUPS_OK_ACKNOWLEDGE, which means that the client will automatically acknowledge receipt of a message once it has been processed.*

```
topic = session.createTopic(topicName);
```

■ *P/S messaging communicates over named topics.*

```
System.out.println("Creating TopicConsumer");
subscriber = session.createSubscriber( topic );
```

■ TopicSubscriber *objects listen on topics. The JMS implementation is re-sponsible for allowing multiple subscriber clients on the same topic.*

```
connection.start();
```

■ *Here we tell the connection to start receiving messages.*

```
Message message = (Message) subscriber.receive();
```

■ *Messages are retrieved through the Subscriber object. JMS implementations are required to store unacknowledged messages.*

```
if (message.getJMSType().equals("TextMessage")) {
```

■ *Here we check the type of the message to ensure that it is a* TextMessage *before we attempt to cast it.*

```
Document doc = swb.toDOM(((TextMessage)message).
   getText());
```

■ *Notice that we must cast a message to type* TextMessage *in order to call* getText *on it.*

```
System.out.println(swb.serialize(doc));
}
```

■ *Here we check to make sure that the message type is* TextMessage. *We then attempt to parse the message into a DOM Document object. If it succeeds, we can serialize the DOM to default output.*

```
connection.stop();
```

■ *Tells the JMS implementation we want to stop receiving messages.*

```
} catch (JMSException e) {
System.out.println(e.getMessage());} finally {
subscriber.close();
session.close();
connection.close();
```

■ *When the object is being destroyed, we want to make sure we release all the resources. This is critical if the JMS implementation communicates with a non-Java messaging implementation.*

```
   }
   ...
   }
}
```

Note *When running these examples from the CD-ROM, wait until all the consumer applications have posted their "Started" message before running the producer. Otherwise, messages being published might be lost.*

7.1.4 *XML and JMS Queues*

The source code for passing an XML message between two applications using the queuing method is almost identical to the source code shown above for doing this with P/S. Therefore, we will only show the differences between the corresponding components here.

7.1.4.1 XMLSender Class

```
public class XMLSender
{
   public XMLSender( String queueName )
     throws JMSException
     {
     SpiritWaveBase swb = new SpiritWaveBase();
     QueueConnection connection = null;
     QueueSession session = null;
     QueueSender sender = null;
     Queue queue = null;
     FileInputStream is = null;

     try {
       connection = swb.initQueue();
       session = connection.createQueueSession(swb.
         isTransacted,
         swb.acknowledgeMode);
       queue = session.createQueue(topicName);
       System.out.println("Creating QueueSender");
       sender = session.createSender( queue );
       sender.setDeliveryMode(DeliveryMode.NON_PERSISTENT);
       connection.start();
       sender.send( message );
                         ( ... same as XMLProducer ...)
       connection.stop();
```

```
          sender.close();
                          ( ... same as XMLProducer ...)
     }
```

7.1.4.2 XMLReceiver Class

```
public class XMLReceiver
{     public XMLReceiver( String    queueName )
        throws JMSException
     {
     QueueConnection connection = null;
     QueueSession session = null;
     QueueReceiver receiver = null;
     Queue queue = null;
     SpiritWaveBase swb = new SpiritWaveBase();

     try
     {

        connection = swb.initQueue();
        session = connection.createQueueSession(swb.
          isTransacted,
          swb.acknowledgeMode);
        queue = session.createQueue( queueName );
        System.out.println("Creating QueueReceiver");
        receiver = session.createReceiv"er( queue );
        connection.start();
        System.out.println(QueueReceive Started");

                        ( ... same as XMLConsumer ...)

        connection.stop();
        receiver.close();

                        ( ... same as XMLConsumer ...)

     }
```

The key differences between these methods can be summarized as follows:

- In the Publish/Subscribe example, we can have many instances of XMLConsumer for each XMLProducer.

■ In the queue-based example, we can only have one XML-Receiver/XMLSender pair per queue.

This example illustrates messaging between two JMS-based applications; however, either end of this asynchronous messaging pipe could be replaced with a non-Java application using a generic MOM solution.

7.2 | Summary

Message-Oriented Middleware (MOM) provides our applications with a level of abstraction that supports both synchronous and asynchronous delivery of messages. Because of this abstraction, we can deal with both highly connected and often-disconnected environments without having our applications cognizant of this point.

JMS is a Java API that provides a consistent interface to MOM implementations. It allows us to represent messages as Java objects that are natively supported by our application. When we desire to send XML messages between our applications, as is commonly being done in e-commerce applications today, then JMS allows us to create an abstract representation of the XML message that we can pass to a SAX or DOM processing facility.

In the next chapter, we will see how the metadata support that XML provides us can be used to enable directory and naming service implementations.

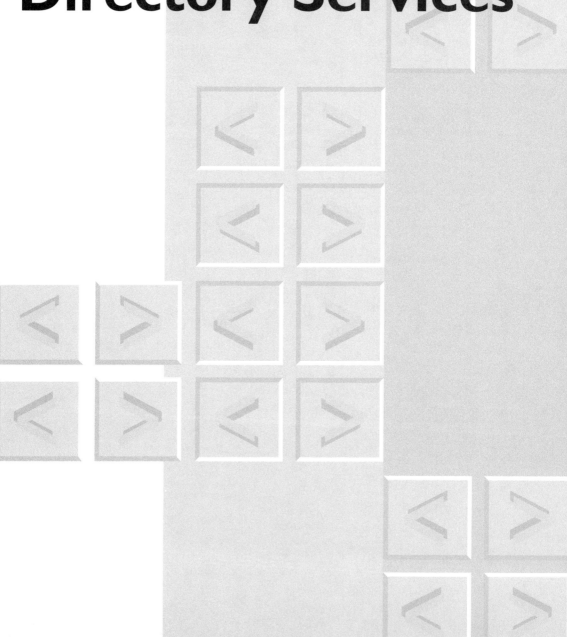

XML and
Directory Services

8.1 | Introduction

For many people, EAI implies inter- and intra-departmental integration initiatives. This belief understates the power of the solutions being designed to solve EAI requirements. A well-designed EAI solution serves extra-organizational concerns as well as inter- and intra-departmental concerns. That is, the manner in which one would integrate applications between organizations could use the same methodologies used to integrate applications across departments.

This distinction is important because inter- and intra-departmental integration and extra-organizational integration operate over different mediums. Inter- and intra-departmental integration can be handled using the enterprise's Local Area Network (LAN) and/or Wide Area Network (WAN), which provide a consistent level of connectivity and service for an organization as a whole.

However, when we cross organizational boundaries, we are faced with new hurdles, which include low bandwidth, incompatible hardware and transfer mediums, long periods of disconnect, and security constraints. Application and data transparency can minimize the impact that these hurdles have on development of our applications. Thus, we can design applications that work equally well in both internal and external integration projects. For example, long periods of disconnect can be overcome by using store-and-forward Message-Oriented Middleware (MOM). Using MOM in this fashion allows our applications to pull data from a named queue that can be fed by both inter- and extra-organizational applications. MOM shields our processing application from knowing if it is in an environment subject to extended periods of disconnect or it is in a fully-connected one. Solutions that address these needs by design offer more promise than those that assume an always-connected, large-bandwidth, homogeneous environment.

Therefore, the concept of application and data transparency is extremely pertinent to EAI. Transparency is provided by hiding the implementation of data access from a client application. To accomplish this feat, we need to have services that provide an alias for a physical resource and that use that alias to render service for a client application instead of having the application access the resource directly.

In chapters 5, 6, & 7 we covered services that allow us to move data between Java and non-Java environments, which provide a level of transparency to the application as we illustrated above with the MOM example. This chapter covers a service that provides application and data transparency across applications: Directory services. Through transparency, we free our systems to be more responsive to changes in business that are brought about by e-business initiatives.

8.2 | Directory Services

There are tens of thousands of electronic resources in most companies. These include workstations, servers, printers, network services, phones, digital certificates, documents, databases, and the list goes on ad infinitum. During the course of automating the tracking and management of these resources, the concept of a directory service was born.

Directory services are distributed, federated lists of pointers to other sources of information. The type of information one might find in a directory is metadata about other information sources within the organization. For example, a directory usually has information about people, such as their phone numbers and building locations. Other metadata that might be found in a directory could be more application-centric—for example, the physical server that houses the human resources databases. In building this distributed and highly available source of metadata, applications have a common source to query for location-specific information, thus providing a very necessary level of transparency, which is a critical component of EAI.

Directory services and XML share tremendous synergy. Directory services and XML are both hierarchical data representations that have content and attributes (see Figure 8–1). Indeed, one could view an

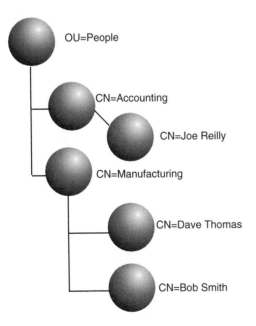

Figure 8–1   Directory service representation.

XML document as a persistent representation of a directory service, especially if that XML document pointed to other resources. Moreover, by adding an XML document as a branch of the directory service, one complements the power of replication and high availability of directory services with an extensible source of content that is reusable across multiple processes. This section will cover more of this concept in the later section titled "*XML Extends the Power and Reach of Directory Services.*"

Directory services can be extremely useful for integration projects. Integration is driven by the need for metadata, whether it is about message formats, application components, or configuration data. Directories provide an excellent mechanism for the storage and retrieval of this metadata. However, some implementations of directory services can be very rigid in their schema definition, which limits the use of the directory service for new data types.

This section will explore using XML documents to provide information for a directory service implementation. Because the metadata is stored in XML documents, it is immediately extensible and can support new data types very easily. The following contribution sidebar by Andrew Roberts, CTO of Bowstreet, examines using XML documents to extend the capabilities of directory services without necessarily having to amend the directory schema for each new object type.

As you can see, XML, in combination with a directory service, offers application developers the opportunity to have a highly available source of metadata at their disposal. In the next section, we will explore how to access these metadata repositories from within a Java application.

8.2.1 *The Java Naming and Directory Interface*

There are many implementations of directory services, each supporting a unique model of querying and management. For example, Novell offers its Novell Directory Services and Sun Microsystems uses

Extending Directory Services with XML

Traditionally, Directory Services have been used to manage the human and computing resources within an organization. For the most part these resources consist of users, printers, and network equipment, such as file servers and printers. The main value of these directories is as an "address book" that provides managed access to corporate resources.

The growth in the number and complexity of internal resources, along with open standards such as LDAP (Lightweight Directory Access Protocol), has spurred the acceptance of directories in corporations. More resources are being managed, and more applications are making use of the data stored in these "address books."

XML now allows companies to trade information and processes in a standard markup across corporate boundaries. These relationships, the information shared, and the business processes of how to share it are all new resources that need to be managed. All the business functionality that exists within an organization and across the Internet will benefit from the organized management directory services can bring. There is no better way to manage descriptions, access and location of these thousands of web services.

The combination of XML and Directory Services technologies pushes the limits on how data is stored, shared and accessed. Using the structural and hierarchical management strengths of a directory to manage the millions of XML documents is a natural fit. Using directories to store these XML documents as elements provides the ease of management across an enterprise that is needed to make effective use of the information.

In addition, XML can be used to dynamically extend the schema of objects stored in a directory. Directories traditionally have captured metadata about the structure of information. XML changes things, because XML associates content with structural definition. By introducing XML content to a directory, we blur the line between structure and content. XML and directories allow for a continuous transition between the directory's structural metadata, and the XML document's content. Using XML to extend the directory's schema allows more meta-information about the documents to be accessed. Directories begin to contain a hierarchical view of XML schemas defining the contents of XML documents within.

Directory tools can be used to search the attributes of all managed elements. Soon, they will be able to reach into XML documents stored within the directories. Within an organization, this becomes extraordinarily powerful. Having the ability to at once search metadata and content throughout all of the business resources within an organization is one of the key components of knowledge management.

Given the open and flexible nature of XML, new types of objects can now be stored in directories, such as services, functionality, data and all business resources. Companies are

(continued)

Extending Directory Services with XML (continued)

expanding their vision of corporate resources to include information and functionality that exists in their partners' enterprises and across the Internet. They need the ability to store, search, replicate, share and manage information about all the resources. Directories are the only solution that scales to the millions of elements across multiple locations needed for this. Using XML to describe the elements provides the next dimension of scalability on what can be stored.

The next major step is for companies to begin publishing information about services and functionality within the directories for use by partners. It will become increasingly important for these Internet trading relationships to be able to share resource information in a directory-independent fashion. XML provides yet another mechanism for allowing directories to scale.

Using industry-standard XML schemas such as Directory Services Markup Language (DSML), directory resources can be queried and replicated between disparate systems. DSML allows companies to create XML documents to send to other directories to perform schema updates, query resources, etc. Directories are the right tool for managing metadata about resources. XML is the answer for describing all application/resource data. DSML is the missing piece that allows these two to work together and which provides a common ground for all XML-based applications to make better use of directories.

This cross-corporate communication allows the Internet and XML to begin to treat heterogeneous repositories as a massive federated directory of business resources. Multiple directories, working together allow businesses to make the most effective use of all of their resources.

NIS+. In an attempt to provide a consistent-access mechanism for Java applications, Sun Microsystems, with its partners, has developed the Java Naming and Directory Services Interface (JNDI).

JNDI is a framework that consists of two programming interfaces glued together by a generic naming services layer (see Figure 8–2). This architecture allows multiple service providers to plug in their own implementation of naming or directory services for use within an application. In turn, applications can use multiple directory services simultaneously to create a federated namespace for an application.

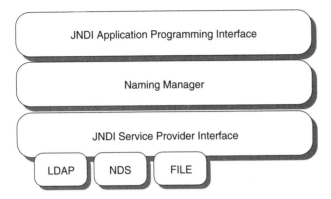

Figure 8–2 The JNDI architecture.

Federated naming is a term used to describe multiple naming service instances all linked together as one consistent view. This view then propagates a consistent namespace that can resolve a composite name. Example 8.1 illustrates a namespace that is supported by the X.500 and LDAP directory services. The elements of this composite name might actually span X.500, LDAP, and NDS implementations, but it is the role of the federated naming service to resolve this name correctly.

Resolution of the composite name in Example 8.1 results in either a directory service context from which attributes and other contexts can be retrieved, or a node object that contains the information we are looking for. If comparing the directory service to the DOM, a context is equivalent to an element node.

Example 8.1: A composite name.

```
C="NC.Focus", OU=people, CN="Morgenthal, JP"
```

This is accomplished by making the node of one directory service tree a context of another directory service tree (see Figure 8–3). To build a federated namespace, the directory service implementation that the application is communicating with must be able to communicate directly with other instances of directory services.

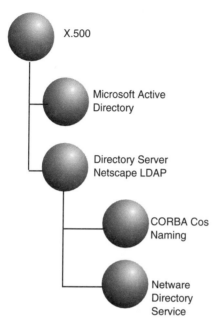

X.500

Microsoft Active
Directory

Directory Server
Netscape LDAP

CORBA Cos
Naming

Netware
Directory
Service

Figure 8–3 Federated naming.

For example, a company using X.500 as its primary directory may desire to link digital certificates, stored in LDAP, to people objects in NDS. To retrieve a certificate based on a person's name, it could manually read the context from X.500 and then manually access the LDAP service using that information. Or, if the X.500 implementation speaks LDAP natively, it can resolve the entire composite name correctly and access the digital certificate object directly.

The JNDI is a Java Standard Extension. Java Standard Extensions are not part of the core libraries that ship with the Java Virtual Machine and therefore must be installed separately. Applications use the javax.naming class library to access JNDI functionality. They configure this library using predefined environment variables stored in the system properties file or using library functions. We will explore these configuration parameters as part of the coverage of the application that tests the XML-based directory service provider.

As previously mentioned, JNDI is divided up into two programming interfaces: the Application Programming Interface (API) and the Service Provider Interface (SPI). We will explore both of these interfaces as we design a service provider that allows applications to treat XML documents like directory services and then build an application that uses that service provider class. For purposes of simplicity, our version of the XML SPI will not support composite names. Therefore, it will only support one element per lookup. This means that to find the element FIRST_NAME inside the element PERSON, the developer must perform two lookups.

8.2.1.1 XML Document Service Provider

The following Java classes provide an implementation of the JNDI SPI. They are intended to allow XML documents to act effectively as a directory or naming service. Because XML documents are hierarchical and for the most part object-oriented, they make excellent resources for supporting a federated naming service.

SPIs require two specific interfaces to be implemented: the `InitialContextFactory` implementation and the `Context` implementation. The `InitialContextFactory` implements a large number of methods that we do not provide functionality for; therefore we will not present those methods here. Instead, these may be found in the full source listings on the associated CD-ROM.

`XMLInitCtxFactory` is our implementation of the `InitialContextFactory`. The role of this interface is to provide to the `javax.naming` classes a `Context` object based upon the environment that it provides. This will be the application's starting point from which it can traverse the directory service hierarchy.

8.2.1.2 XMLInitCtxFactory

```
public class XMLInitCtxFactory implements
  InitialContextFactory {
```

- XMLInitCtxFactory *is an implementation of the* InitialContextFactory *interface. It has only one method,* getInitialContext.

```
public Context getInitialContext(Hashtable env) {
```

- *The context factory returns a Context object and takes one parameter, which is a Hashtable that contains key/value pairs representing the configuration data for each JNDI implementation.*

```
Context xr = null;
try {
  xr = new XMLCtx(env);
```

- *Here we create an instance of the Context object for our implementation. This means using our Context object implementation—XMLCtx.*

```
} catch (Exception e) {
  System.out.println(e);
}
return xr;
```

- *And we return the Context object to the calling client.*

```
  }
}
```

XMLCtx is our implementation of a Context object. Context objects keep our place in the hierarchy as we traverse the directory service content. They also allow us to search and modify information in the directory service based upon the Context's current location. To an application that is using a directory service, Context objects look identical even though they may be operating over very different datatypes. For example, one Context implementation might be using an XML document, such as our implementation below, while another might be operating over a relational database. This consistent view is important if we wish to create a federated hierarchy.

8.2.1.3 XMLCtx

```
class XMLCtx implements Context {

    String xmlFile = null;
    Hashtable myEnv = null;
    Document myDoc = null;
    Element currentNode = null;

    XMLCtx(Hashtable env) throws NamingException {
```

■ *This is the constructor for our Context object.*

```
    try {
```

■ *The environment passed into our implementation of the Context requires a key called* java.naming.provider.url. *This is the pointer to the XML document that provides the content for our directory service.*

```
        xmlFile = (String) env.get("java.naming.provider." +
            "url");
        myEnv = env;
```

■ *Because the context can spawn other contexts, we are responsible for preserving this information as part of our context.*

```
        NonValidatingDOMParser nvp = new NonValidating
            DOMParser();
        nvp.parse(xmlFile);
```

■ *Here we are calling the parser to parse our XML document and create a DOM representation for us to use.*

```
        myDoc = nvp.getDocument();
        if (myDoc == null)
            throw new NamingException(xmlFile+" is not a" +
                "valid XML document");
```

■ *We attempt to get the document root from the parser. If it is null, then there was an error parsing the file.*

```
currentNode = myDoc.getDocumentElement();
```

■ *We set the initial context to point to the root element in the DOM.*

```
    } catch (Exception e) {
      System.out.println(e);
    }
}

public Object lookup(String name) throws NamingException {
```

■ *This function looks for the first element of a particular type, whose name is provided as the parameter to the lookup function.*

```
    if (name.equals("")) {
      return (new XMLCtx(myEnv));
    }
```

■ *Ensures that the element type name provided is valid.*

```
    NodeList nodes = currentNode.getElementsByTagName(name);
    if (nodes.getLength() == 0)
      return null;
```

■ *Uses the DOM function* getElementsByTagName *to look for an element of type name. Notice that we start our search from* currentNode. *This is because* currentNode *will be updated (below) to point to the first occurrence of this name. Therefore, searches are conducted within the scope of* currentNode.

```
    currentNode = (Element) nodes.item(0);
```

■ *Here we set* currentNode *to point to the first element found by our search.*

```
    return currentNode;
  }
  . . .
}
```

Now that we have our `InitialContextFactory` and `Context` objects, we can build an application that will use the `javax.naming` library to perform a lookup over any XML document we prescribe. The `Lookup` class implementation, below, uses these classes to locate either a single element within an XML document, or it can find a single sub-element of a parent element in the XML document.

8.2.1.4 Directory Service Lookup

```
class Lookup {
    public static void main(String[] args) {
        if (args.length < 1) {
        System.err.println("usage: java Lookup" +
          "<name_of_object_1>
             [<name_of_object_2>]");
```

■ *This is a stand-alone application that takes up two command-line arguments. These arguments are type names of elements that we are looking for in our naming service. If a second name is provided, it is looked for within the scope of the first name.*

```
      System.exit(-1);
    }

    Properties env = System.getProperties();
```

■ *We define two important system properties at application startup. The first is* `java.naming.factory.initial=com.ncfocus.xml.jndi.XMLInitCtx` Factory, *which is the name of the class we want JNDI to use for locating the initial context. This is not the only way to tell JNDI how to find the initial context; the JNDI specification details the methods that can be used to accomplish this task. This is just the simplest method for our example. The other property is the* `java.naming.` `provider.url`, *which will point to our XML file.*

```
String currentNodeName = null;
try {
    Context ctx = new InitialContext(env);
```

■ *Here we ask JNDI to create* InitialContext *using our system properties. Because we set the* java.naming.factory.initial *to point to our SPI, JNDI will create an instance of* XMLInitCtxFactory, *which in turn will create an instance of* XMLCtx.

```
    Node n = (Node) ctx.lookup(args[0]);
```

■ *Here we perform a lookup on our Context object using the first name we provided on the command line. We cast the returned object to a DOM Node object.*

```
    if (args.length == 2) {
```

■ *If a child of the first element is also provided on the command line, this block of code will locate that element based on the current* Context.

```
    n = (Node) ctx.lookup(args[1]);
```

■ *Since our context object* ctx *now points to our first element, the next search will be conducted only on that element's children.*

```
    if (n != null)
        System.out.println(n.getNodeName()+" found inside as a" +
"child of"
            +currentNodeName);
```

■ *If we successfully find the second element within the first, then we print out this line.*

```
    else
        System.out.println(args[1]+" is not a child of "
            +currentNodeName);
```

■ *Otherwise, we print out this line.*

```
System.out.println(n.getFirstChild().getNodeValue());
```

■ *Here we print out the value of the second node found to prove that it is the node we are looking for.*

```
    }
  } catch (Exception e) {
    System.out.println(e);
      e.printStackTrace();
  }
    }
}
```

Below is the output of executing the `Lookup` class against the following XML document:

```xml
<?xml version="1.0"?>
<INVOICE>
  <SHIPTO>
     <NAME>JP Morgenthal</NAME>
     <ADDRESS>50 Charles Lindbergh Blvd, Ste. 400</ADDRESS>
     <CITY>Uniondale</CITY>
     <STATE abbrev="NY">New York</STATE>
     <ZIP>11553</ZIP>
     <ADDRTYPE>Business</ADDRTYPE>
   </SHIPTO>
   <BILLTO>
     <NAME>JP Morgenthal</NAME>
     <ADDRESS>11 Grosso Road </ADDRESS>
     <CITY>Hewlett </CITY>
     <STATE abbrev="NY">New York</STATE>
     <ZIP>11557</ZIP>
     <ADDRTYPE>Business</ADDRTYPE>
   </BILLTO>
   <TOTAL currency="$">200.50</TOTAL>
   <LINE_ITEMS>
     <LINE>
          <DESC>Wooly Mammoth Shirt</DESC>
          <SKU>123123418</SKU>
          <PRICE>183.29</PRICE>
     </LINE>
   </LINE_ITEMS>
   <SHIPPING currency="$">12.50</SHIPPING>
 </INVOICE>
```

```
D:\nc.focus\Javaxmlbook\src\jndi>run Lookup BILLTO
   ADDRESS

BILLTO has 13 children
ADDRESS found inside as a child of BILLTO
11 Grosso Road

D:\nc.focus\Javaxmlbook\src\jndi>
```

Figure 8–4   Find ADDRESS in BILLTO.

In Figure 8–4 and Figure 8–5, we can see how the Context object provides us with different views of the data based upon its location within the directory service hierarchy. In Figure 8–4 when we ask for ADDRESS when our context is pointing to BILLTO, we see that the value returned is different from when we ask for ADDRESS when our context is pointing to SHIPTO (Figure 8–5).

This example merely provides us with the basis for building a powerful naming system using XML documents. Some of the enhancements that could be added include: composite name parsing (to evaluate multiple elements at once, e.g., accounting/person/tom), XPointer support for federating over multiple XML documents and, of course, binding/unbinding (adding and removing elements on the tree).

```
D:\nc.focus\Javaxmlbook\src\jndi>run Lookup SHIPTO
   ADDRESS

SHIPTO has 13 children
ADDRESS found inside as a child of SHIPTO
50 Charles Lindbergh Blvd, Ste. 400

D:\nc.focus\Javaxmlbook\src\jndi>
```

Figure 8–5   Find ADDRESS in SHIPTO.

With directory services, we have a way to abstract the physicality of resources within an enterprise. In the next section, we will explore a programming model that facilitates development of flexible applications that can respond rapidly to changes in business: a critical component of systems that support e-business.

8.3 | Summary

Metadata is a key ingredient for implementing the application and data transparency that is necessary for a successful EAI project. Directory services provide a procedural interface for applications to store and retrieve metadata, and share that metadata globally. JNDI is a Java API that allows our applications to treat multiple directory service implementations identically, and thereby, facilitate the development of federated directory services.

Also in this chapter you saw that there's tremendous synergy between XML as a way to represent and store metadata, and directory and naming services use of metadata. This relationship is so synergistic, that we were able to demonstrate in this chapter how to build a naming and directory services implementation that uses XML documents.

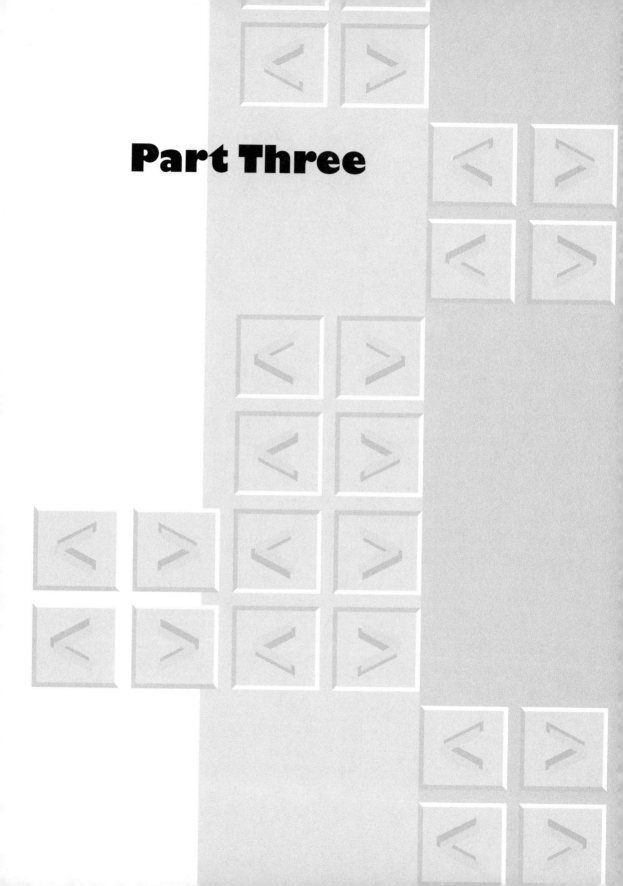

Part Three

Programming Models for EAI

The Declarative Programming Model

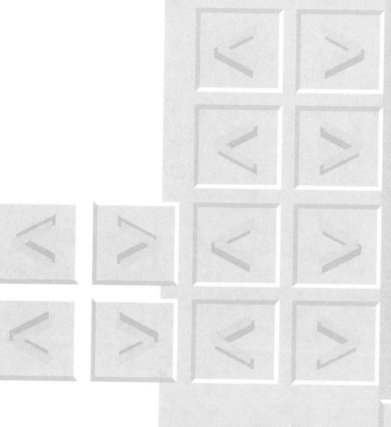

9.1 | Introduction

In Chapters 4 through 8 we explored using Enterprise Java APIs as a solution for EAI problems. Five methods we explored are:

- **Serializing the state of Java object graphs into XML.** This allows us to move a Java object's state to non-Java applications in a readily usable form.

- **Data sharing using relational databases.** Sometimes using a shared database can be a bit limiting when maintaining non-relational or semi-relational data. XML stored in text and BLOB database fields can simplify this task. In this chapter, we built a JDBC `ResultSet` object that treated text and BLOB columns like a real XML data type, returning and storing DOM `Document` objects.

- **Encapsulating database query results.** To isolate applications from needing to know where data is physically

191

stored, we can allow our applications to obtain the results of a database query as an XML document. In this scenario, we can provide a proxy application that knows how to communicate with the database and generates XML documents on behalf of other applications from SQL queries. If the schema or database changes in the future, we simply can update the proxy application. This also allows us to provide higher availability of our database server since processing can be offloaded to other machines.

- **Using Message-Oriented Middleware (MOM).** This is one of the most popular methods of application integration today. The Java Messaging Service (JMS) provides a consistent interface to these environments and allows us to exchange XML documents synchronously and asynchronously. We extended this facility to include support for XML as a real datatype in a manner similar to that of JDBC.

- **Using XML for a persistent representation of data that can be used for naming and directory service implementations.** There will eventually be specific methods for querying an XML document, but XML is an excellent format for storing metadata information that may be needed to provide transparency of application and data.

This part focused on technologies that facilitate sharing and exchanging data between applications. In the next part, we will begin to look at programming models for EAI.

So far in the book, I have tried to provide a good understanding of how XML and Java can be used to solve application integration problems. You can use these two technologies together to allow applications to directly exchange or share information, or to build a new application that aggregates many other applications' data. This part expands upon that knowledge by providing new models for architecting EAI solutions.

I will show how declarative environments make solutions more flexible and maintainable in the face of rapid changes in business processing. We will explore further ways to provide declarative environments without removing the procedural interfaces needed by programmers and architects. Moreover, I will show how to bind behavior to constantly changing documents.

This chapter will also show you how to use XML and Java to build dynamic applications. These applications dynamically bind Java components together at runtime based on processing a given XML document type. The result of this dynamic late-binding is the creation of a unique application specialized to the needs of its input.

In Chapter 2 we defined the terms declarative and procedural. We described the declarative environment as one that does not dictate the steps to completing a goal, while a procedural environment has rigid control over both the steps and the goal. These modes play a significant role in the overall effectiveness of an EAI solution, especially whether or not it will work extra-organizationally, as well as intra-organizationally. Indeed, it is because of developers' reliance upon procedural models that the EAI problem has been created.

The need for EAI was spawned by lack of adherence to a simple theorem of computing:

> *"Usage defines meaning and must be consistent, otherwise the meaning is broken."*

For example, if we assume that the algebraic equation $a + b = c$ will perform an arithmetic function for us, then we are also assuming that a and b are numbers. That is, the addition (+) operator has certain meaning when operating in the realm of numbers. If the addition (+) operator operates in the realm of strings, then c cannot be a number, but instead will be a concatenation of strings a and b. But, in the case where a is a number, and b is a string, the meaning of the addition operator is broken, and thus will not work.

In this instance, we can create a new meaning for the addition operator by forcing the number to be turned into a string, or the string into a number, and once again conforming to one of our known realms. However, accomplishing this feat requires the system to make this decision on its own, at runtime, based upon the inputs it has been provided. This changes the operator from a procedural one into a declarative one.

The difference is subtle, but important. Developers have a desire to have tight control over what is happening in an application (procedural), but this results in a rigid, hard-to-maintain application. Declarative environments provide us with the flexibility and maintainability we desire, but require the programmer to give up too much. To eliminate this rift, we compromise. We provide the developer with a procedural interface that delivers the façade that the programmer is in control, while in effect they are feeding information to a declarative environment that is enacting behavior as it sees fit.

An excellent example of this need for both a declarative environment with a procedural interface is the Object-Oriented Programming (OOP) paradigm. Pure OOP has been rejected in recent years in favor of a more pragmatic approach, such as that provided by C++. The original intent of OOP was to send an object a message and have the object respond in kind with a behavior based upon that message. *Polymorphism* is a term in OOP that describes multiple objects that accept the same message, but provide different behaviors.

By this pure definition of OOP, we see a well-defined interface for sending the object a message, but cannot control the outcome or the goal. The interface provides the programmer with a structure and a method of communications necessary to write application logic. However, the object is an encapsulated unit that will decide how it will react to the message, hence the declarative environment we need for development of flexible and easily maintainable applications.

Procedural models are very important to programmers and architects. This is because programmers and architects need to have conceptual entities, such as structures and objects that can manipulate inside their code. It's very difficult to develop software that is 100% declarative in nature, as we will see shortly. The trick for software developers is to use objects to define a framework or meta-object model that can house many different types of information without permanently tying an application to a specific structure or type.

Declarative environments are extremely powerful and highly flexible, but do not necessarily offer the productivity needed for associating behavior with specific datatypes. That is, declarative environments are mostly rule based and possibly recursive—they call upon themselves to complete a task—in nature. This means that the engineer who changes one rule needs to have a big-picture understanding of the implications that the change will have to the rest of the system. In a large-scale development effort, this is almost an impossibility as the developer usually has a narrow scope of responsibility for the project.

The rest of this chapter will explore one solution that provides developers a procedural interface, while still providing the power of a declarative environment. We've termed this solution the Declarative Programming Model (DPM). While the declarative programming model is not a new concept, it is finding new life thanks to the formation of a widely accepted, self-describing data format—XML.

Our DPM creates a memory space of XML containers that store structured and unstructured data and allow developers to dynamically add or remove information from the model through a programmatic interface, which in turn generates an event that a user can associate with a declarative behavior. Applications communicate with the space using an XML-based Remote Procedure Call (RPC) facility that accepts messages over HTTP. This type of system can be implemented very easily using the likes of any application server that implements an XML interface.

This example is also very useful because it shows how to integrate XML into a solution. That is, it illustrates the development of an XML vocabulary that will be used for this solution and how that vocabulary is declared and implemented using code.

9.2 | The Declarative Programming Model

The Declarative Programming Model is a very simple abstraction of a shared memory space that facilitates the adding, deleting, and changing of XML documents for a group of client applications. XML provides us with a high degree of extensibility that does not require fixed schema declarations. This means that users can add new data objects and add data to existing data objects at will.

In addition to simply providing an environment for living and growing data objects, we can also associate behavior with changes over existing data objects. As we issue changes on a particular element within an already declared data object, it will fire an event that results in a corresponding process. For example, if we place a CAR data object in the memory space and associate a CAR process with that data object, then changing the element <RUNNING_STATE> from OFF to ON would indicate that we wish the car's state to be running (see Figure 9–1). However, because this is a declarative environment, the process associated with change events for CAR objects will determine the outcome of this change.

The purpose of this example is to provide a basis for understanding the power of declarative processing environments. The example we will develop here allows us to simply associate behavioral logic with any document, continually add new elements to this document while it is in memory, and act on those changes as they occur. There are a

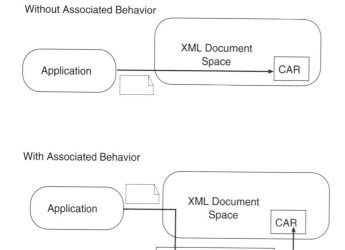

Figure 9–1 Associating behavior with documents.

number of initiatives under way by vendors to provide similar, but more powerful, functionality over XML-based data objects. However, this example will provide you with an understanding of how declarative processing environments, when coupled with XML, can solve many data sharing and processing problems.

The power provided by this type of environment can be a double-edged sword. On one hand, we can add or change PASSENGER in our CAR object at any time. But, if we attempt to add a PASSENGER using the element type name PASENGER, which is incorrectly spelled, then the behavior we expect to occur will not happen. In addition, we will most likely end up storing a new piece of information that will have no bearing on any of our operations and take up space in memory.

One way around the problem of adding incorrect elements is to provide some document validation for updates. This can be done by using a document type declaration and a validating XML parser. By validating updates and not the in-memory data object, we do not limit our document by having a fixed schema, but we do limit the types of elements that can be added. For example, we can have a DTD that states that PASSENGER is a valid element type that is allowed inside of updates, but we do not state where a PASSENGER element can be added inside of the data object. This way we can validate update messages before they are applied to our existing data object, but maintain the flexibility we desire for our programming model.

9.3 | The Declarative Programming Model XML Document Type

The most important part of our DPM is defining the DTD we will use for operating on our shared memory space. The operations we will support include: add document, remove document, and add element to document. The vocabulary for these operations is defined below:

The root element for each operation is called OPERATION. It has no attributes and possibly two children.

Within OPERATION we can have two legal child element types: DOCUMENT and ASSOCIATION. DOCUMENT defines the documents to be added to the shared memory space, as well as the elements to be added to a document. The ASSOCIATION element allows us to associate a particular document with a Java class file located within our memory space. For this example, there can be only one ASSOCIATION per DOCUMENT, therefore if one already exists, it will be overwritten. Also, if an ASSOCIATION is declared for a non-existent DOCUMENT, it is simply ignored.

DOCUMENT has two attributes: type and name. The type attribute defines the type of operation we will be performing and assumes that the value will be one of the following: add, remove, or set. The name attribute defines the document type name that will be associated with this document in the shared memory space. If a document of a certain type already exists, subsequent add operations with this name will be ignored.

To pass parser validation, we are required to hide the document we wish to add inside a CDATA section. If we do not, we will be told that the document we are adding has children not defined in the DTD. The first CDATA section of DOCUMENT will act as the root element for the document to be added in memory.

Alternatively, we could have declared DOCUMENT to have an "open" content model; that is, one with a content spec of "ANY". We could then have used the internal subset of the DOCTYPE declaration to declare the element types that occur as children of DOCUMENT in this particular instance, without modifying the shared DTD for OPERATION.

Note *For the sake of simplicity, this example will assume that all* set *operations are to occur on the root element. Additionally, this example does not provide facilities for removing or changing sub-elements since this would require sophisticated matching capabilities.*

ASSOCIATION has no content and two attributes: classname and documentname. The classname attribute specifies the fully-qualified Java class name that will be executed whenever an operation is applied to the document specified by the documentname attribute.

The DTD is provided in Example 9.1 below:

Example 9.1: DPG DTD.

```
<!ELEMENT OPERATION (DOCUMENT? , ASSOCIATION? )>
<!ELEMENT DOCUMENT (#PCDATA)>
<!ATTLIST DOCUMENT type (add | remove | set ) #REQUIRED>
<!ATTLIST DOCUMENT name CDATA #REQUIRED>
<!ELEMENT ASSOCIATION EMPTY>
<!ATTLIST ASSOCIATION documentname CDATA #REQUIRED>
<!ATTLIST ASSOCIATION classname CDATA #REQUIRED>
```

9.3.1 *Associating Behavior with Objects*

To simplify the process of associating behavior with objects in this example, we have devised a very simple interface for declaring associations between entire documents and Java classes. The association itself is described in XML using the ASSOCIATION element. There is also a Java interface definition for document handlers that defines entry points for initializing, shutting down, and distributing operation events. In the example we are going to develop, we will not handle the problems of incorrect elements being added.

The interface for DPM document handlers is defined below:

```
import org.w3c.dom.*;

public interface    {
   public void init(Node doc);
```

- *Issued whenever an* ASSOCIATION *is processed.*

```
   public void shutdown(Node doc);
```

- *Issued on a remove operation.*

```
   public boolean event(Node doc, Node request);
```

■ *Issued before an operation is performed. Returning false will stop the set operation from being applied.*

```
}
```

The `DPGMemory` class will implement the logic to handle storing, updating, and removing documents from our memory space.

9.3.2 *The Shared Memory Space Application*

```
import java.util.Hashtable;
import java.io.*;
import org.w3c.dom.*;
import org.xml.sax.*;
import com.ibm.xml.parser.*;
import DPMDocHandler;

public class DPGMemory {
```

■ *The `DPGMemory` class implements a memory space that stores DOM Node objects that are referenced by a document name.*

```
  Hashtable docList = null;
  Hashtable associations = null;
```

■ *These two hashtables will store the document and its associations as referenced by a document name.*

```
  DPGMemory() throws Exception {
    docList = new Hashtable(10);
    associations = new Hashtable(10);
  }

  Node getFirstChildElement(Node newDoc) {
```

■ `getFirstChildElement` *is a utility function that strips the document we want to add out of the* CDATA *section in which we have embedded it.*

```
  try {
    NodeList nl = newDoc.getChildNodes();
    if (nl != null){
      for (int i=0; i<nl.getLength(); i++)
        if (nl.item(i).getNodeType() == Node.
          CDATA_SECTION_NODE) {
          Document tmp = toDOM(nl.item(i).getNodeValue());
          Node toReturn = tmp.getDocumentElement();
          return toReturn;
        }
    }
  } catch (Exception e) {
    System.out.println(e.getMessage());
  }
  return null;
}

Document toDOM(String rawXML) throws Exception {
  ... Same as Chapter 6 ...
}


public String serialize(String docName){
```

■ *Our serialize routine takes a DOM Node object. This overloaded version looks up the Node object to be serialized in our memory space and then calls the routine to serialize that Node object.*

```
  Node toSerialize = null;

  try {
    toSerialize = (Node) docList.get(docName);
    return "<?xml version='1.0'?>\r\n"+serialize(to
      Serialize);
  } catch (Exception e) {
    return null;
  }
}

public String serialize(Node doc) throws Exception {
  ... Same as Chapter 6 ...
}

public boolean evaluateOperation(String XML) throws
  Exception {
```

■ *evaluateOperation will examine OPERATION XML documents and apply the DOCUMENT element and ASSOCIATION element behaviors.*

```
Document newDoc = toDOM(XML);
if (newDoc == null)
  throw new Exception("Operation message is not valid" +
    "XML");

Element root = newDoc.getDocumentElement();
if (root.hasChildNodes() == false)
  return false;
```

■ *Sees if DOCUMENT or ASSOCIATION exists.*

```
NodeList nl = root.getElementsByTagName("DOCUMENT");
if (nl.getLength() > 0){
```

■ *Evaluates DOCUMENT, if one exists.*

```
Element op = (Element) nl.item(0);

String name = op.getAttribute("name");
if (name == null)
  throw new Exception("Improperly formed DOCUMENT" +
    "message:" +
      "missing attribute 'name'");
```

■ *Retrieves the name attribute from the DOCUMENT element.*

```
String opType = op.getAttribute("type");
if (opType == null)
  throw new Exception("Improperly formed DOCUMENT :" +
      "missing attribute 'type'");
```

■ *Retrieves the attribute type from the DOCUMENT element.*

NOTE   *We could use a validating parser and the DTD to ensure that this document matches our requirements before processing. If so, we would not have needed to do such rigorous checking in the code.*

```
if (opType.equals("add")) {
  if (add(name, op) == false)
      throw new Exception ("Error adding document to" +
          "memory space");
} else if (opType.equals("remove")) {
  if (remove(name) == false)
      throw new Exception ("Error removing document" +
          "+name+" from" +
          "memory space");
} else if (opType.equals("set")) {
  if (set(name, op) == false)
        throw new Exception ("Error performing set" +
          "operation on"
          +name);
} else
    throw new Exception("Improperly formed DOCUMENT" +
        "message:"
        Attribute type may only be add, remove, or set");
}
```

■   *Based upon the value of the attribute type, we're going to perform an* add, re-move, *or* set *operation.*

```
nl = root.getElementsByTagName("ASSOCIATION");
```

■   *Check for* ASSOCIATION. *We do this second in case the* OPERATION *document includes the* DOCUMENT *element against which the* ASSOCIATION *is going to be made.*

```
if (nl.getLength() > 0){
  Element op = (Element) nl.item(0);
  String classname = op.getAttribute("classname");
  String documentname = op.getAttribute("documentname");
```

■   *Retrieves the* classname *and* documentname *attributes from the* ASSOCIA-TION *element.*

203

```
if (classname == null || documentname == null)
  throw new Exception ("Improperly formed ASSOCIATION" +
    message:" +
    "classname or documentname attribute is missing");
```

■ *If* classname *or* documentname *does not exist, it is an error since our DTD states these are required attributes.*

```
Node node = (Node) docList.get(documentname);
if (node == null)
  return false;
```

■ *If the document does not exist, just ignore the* ASSOCIATION.

```
associations.put(documentname, classname);
```

■ *Stores the association for future processing.*

```
Class toRun = Class.forName(classname);
DPMDocHandler xa = (DPMDocHandler) toRun.new
  Instance();
```

■ *Creates an instance of the document handler object.*

```
if (xa != null)
  xa.init(node);
```

■ *If the instance creation succeeded, calls the* init *function. Consequently, the instance creation can fail if the classname cannot be found in the local classpath.*

```
  }
  return true;
}
public boolean add(String name, Node newDoc){
```

■ *The* add *function will place the document contained within the* DOCUMENT *element into the memory space associated with the name provided by the* name *parameter.*

```
Node clone = getFirstChildElement(newDoc).
   cloneNode(true);
```

■ *This function finds the first element of the* DOCUMENT *element. Since we're using* DOCUMENT *as a container, no text can come before the contained document's root element. If it does, it's ignored. We need to clone that node since we cannot have the same node in two different document per the DOM specification.*

```
if (clone != null) {
   docList.put(name, clone);
```

■ *Here we put the document into the memory space. If there's already a document of this name, it is overwritten.*

```
      return true;
   }
   return false;
}

public boolean remove(String docName) {
```

■ *The* remove *function deletes the document from the memory space.*

```
   try {
      String classname = (String) associations.get(docName);
      if (classname != null) {
         Class toRun = Class.forName(classname);
         DPMDocHandler xa = (DPMDocHandler) toRun.new
            Instance();
         Node node = (Node) docList.get(docName);
         xa.shutdown(node);
```

■ *If the document has an associated document handler, we need to call that document handler's* shutdown *function before removing the document.*

```
      }
    } catch (Exception e) {
    }
    if (docList.remove(docName) == null)
      return false;
```

■ *Here we actually remove the document from the memory space.*

```
    return true;
  }

  public boolean set(String name, Node newDoc){
```

■ *The* set *operation appends a new element to an existing document in the memory space.*

```
    Node toUpdate = (Node) docList.get(name);
    if (toUpdate == null)
      return false;
```

■ *First we need to retrieve the document to be updated.*

```
    Node clone = getFirstChildElement(newDoc).cloneNode
      (true);
    if (clone == null)
      return false;
```

■ *Next we need to extract the element to be appended out of the* DOCUMENT *element container. Again, since this is already part of an existing XML document, we need to clone the node to get a copy that we can append to our existing document.*

```
    try {
      String classname = (String) associations.get(name);
      if (classname != null) {
        Class toRun = Class.forName(classname);
        DPMDocHandler xa = (DPMDocHandler) toRun.new
          Instance();
```

```
        if (xa.event(toUpdate, clone) == false)
          return false;
```

■ *If there is an associated document handler, we need to first call that document handler's* event *function. If this function returns false, we will not perform the* append *operation.*

```
        }
      } catch (Exception e) {
      }

      if (toUpdate.appendChild(clone) != null)
```

■ *If all is fine, we append the child to the existing document.*

```
        return true;

      return false;
    }
}
```

Now that we have our memory space operational, we need to build our test case. Below we have defined a number of documents that contain operations, which define a car and passengers that will be added to the car (see Example 9.2 through Example 9.5). These operations will then be applied against our memory space to create a new aggregate CAR document that contains our PASSENGERs.

9.3.3 *The CAR Data Object Operations*

Example 9.2: Document to add a CAR to the memory space.

```
<?xml version="1.0"?>
<!DOCTYPE OPERATION SYSTEM "DPG.DTD">

<OPERATION>
    <DOCUMENT name="mycar" type="add"><![CDATA[
```

```
      <CAR make="Jeep" model="Laredo" color="red">
      </CAR>]]>
    </DOCUMENT>
    <ASSOCIATION classname="MyDocHandler" documentname="mycar"/>
</OPERATION>
```

Example 9.3: Document to add a PASSENGER to the CAR.

```
<?xml version="1.0"?>
<!DOCTYPE OPERATION SYSTEM "DPG.DTD">


<OPERATION>
        <DOCUMENT name="mycar" type="set"><![CDATA[
    <PASSENGER>
      <SEAT>Front Passenger</SEAT>
      <NAME>Fred Willoughby</NAME>
      <AGE>26</AGE>
      <HEIGHT measurment="inches">72</HEIGHT>
    </PASSENGER>]]>
   </DOCUMENT>
</OPERATION>
```

Example 9.4: Document to add second PASSENGER to the CAR.

```
<?xml version="1.0"?>
<!DOCTYPE OPERATION SYSTEM "DPG.DTD">


<OPERATION>
        <DOCUMENT name="mycar" type="set"><![CDATA[
    <PASSENGER>
      <SEAT>Driver's Side Rear</SEAT>
      <NAME>Tanya Westerly</NAME>
      <AGE>30</AGE>
      <HEIGHT measurment="inches">65</HEIGHT>
    </PASSENGER>]]>
   </DOCUMENT>
</OPERATION>
```

Example 9.5: Document to remove CAR document from memory space.

```
<?xml version="1.0"?>
<!DOCTYPE OPERATION SYSTEM "DPG.DTD">
```

```
<OPERATION>
  <DOCUMENT name="mycar" type="remove"/>
</OPERATION>
```

In addition to simply adding PASSENGERs to our CAR document, we're going to implement a document handler that allows us to evaluate the name of the PASSENGER being added and adds its own element to show that it has been called.

9.3.4 *The CAR Document Handler*

```
import java.io.StringWriter;
import com.ibm.xml.parser.*;
import org.w3c.dom.*;
import DPMDocHandler;
public class MyDocHandler implements DPMDocHandler {
      public void init(Node doc) {
```

■ *The* init *function will be called when the document handler is installed. It will only be installed if the document for which it is being installed already exists.*

```
    try {
      System.out.println("Initializing MyDocHandler");
      System.out.println("Document:");
      System.out.println(serialize(doc));
    } catch (Exception e) {
      System.out.println("MyDocHandler: "+e);
    }
  }

  public void shutdown(Node doc){
```

■ *The* shutdown *function is called when a* remove *operation is processed. In this sample document handler, we simply print out the document in its current state in memory.*

```
    System.out.println("MyDoc Handler Notified Of Document" +
      Removal:");
```

```
try {
  System.out.println(serialize(doc));
} catch (Exception e) {
  System.out.println("MyDocHandler: "+e);
}
}

public boolean event(Node doc, Node request){
```

■ *The* event *function is called when* set *operations are processed.*

```
try {
  NodeList nl =
    ((Element)request).getElementsByTagName
      ("PASSENGER");
  for (int i=0; i<nl.getLength(); i++) {
    Node n = nl.item(i);
    NodeList passengers = ((Element)n).getElementsBy
      TagName("NAME");
    for (int j=0; j<passengers.getLength(); j++) {
      Node name = passengers.item(j);
      NodeList children = name.getChildNodes();
      for (int k=0; k<children.getLength(); k++) {
        Node text = children.item(k);
        if (text.getNodeType() == Node.TEXT_NODE)
            System.out.println("Adding Passenger:"+
                "text.getNodeValue());
      }
    }
  }
```

■ *This set of logic looks to see if a* PASSENGER *element is being added to the document. If it is, this logic will pull out the name of the* PASSENGER *and print it to the standard output device. This logic is also a good example of how cumbersome the DOM can be for locating information within an XML document.*

```
Document theXML = toDOM(serialize(doc));
Element e = theXML.createElement("DOCHANDLER_ADDED_
  ELEMENT");
Text t = theXML.createTextNode("I was created by a"+
  "document handler");
```

```
   e.appendChild(t);
   doc.appendChild(e);
```

■ *Here we add a new element called* DOCHANDLER_ADDED_ELEMENT *to illustrate that we can also affect the current document and the updating document before the set operation occurs.* **NOTE:** *We use the function* toDOM *to create a* DOCUMENT *object for us since we need one to act as our factory and the IBM XML4J parser does not allow direct instancing of* DOCUMENT *objects.*

```
   } catch (Exception e) {
      System.out.println("MyDocHandler: "+e);
   }
   return true;
}

Document toDOM(String rawXML) throws Exception {
   ... same as in Chapter 6 ...
}
public String serialize(Node doc) throws Exception {
   ... same as in Chapter 6 ...
}
}
```

The following application allows us to submit multiple OPERATION XML documents on the same instance of the memory space. We will use it to add PASSENGERs to an empty CAR. The remove operation will print out the resulting XML document after all of our add operations.

9.3.5   *DPM Test Application and Results*

```
import java.io.*;
import org.w3c.dom.*;
import com.ibm.xml.parser.*;
import DPGMemory;

class TestMemorySpace {
   public static void main (String args[]) {
      try {
         DPGMemory space = new DPGMemory();
```

■ *Creates an instance of the document memory space. In this case, the memory space will operate locally to a single application. But, this could be built into a server process that allows multiple clients to submit* OPERATION *documents.*

```
for (int i=0; i<args.length; i++) {
```

■ *Loops over the arguments to the applications, which should be a list of* OPERA-TION *XML documents.*

```
NonValidatingTXDOMParser parser = new
NonValidatingTXDOMParser();
```

■ *This is an IBM XML4J parser-specific class that is needed to make this example work.*

```
parser.parse(args[i]);
Document doc = parser.getDocument();
String theXML = space.serialize(doc);
```

■ *Prints the document read to the standard output device to show that this is the file we will be submitting to the memory space.*

```
System.out.println(theXML);
System.out.println(args[i]+":"+space.evaluate
    Operation(theXML));
```

■ *Evaluates the* OPERATION *document and prints the results of submitting it to the memory space.*

```
      }
    } catch (Exception e) {
      System.out.println("Failure: "+e);
      e.printStackTrace(System.out);
    }
  }
}
```

The result of running this application using the OPERATION documents we defined above is illustrated in Table 9–1 below:

Table 9–1   Results of running test application.

```
<OPERATION>
   <DOCUMENT name="mycar" type="add"><![CDATA[
     <CAR make="Jeep" model="Laredo" color="red">
     </CAR>]]>
   </DOCUMENT>
   <ASSOCIATION classname="MyDocHandler" documentname="mycar"/>
</OPERATION>

Initializing MyDocHandler

Document:

<CAR make="Jeep" model="Laredo" color="red">
</CAR>

adda.xml: true

<OPERATION>
        <DOCUMENT name="mycar" type="set"><![CDATA[
     <PASSENGER>
       <SEAT>Front Passenger</SEAT>
       <NAME>Fred Willoughby</NAME>
       <AGE>26</AGE>
       <HEIGHT measurment="inches">72</HEIGHT>
     </PASSENGER>]]>
    </DOCUMENT>
</OPERATION>

Adding Passenger: Fred Willoughby

set1.xml: true

<OPERATION>
         <DOCUMENT name="mycar" type="set"><![CDATA[
     <PASSENGER>
       <SEAT>Driver's Side Rear</SEAT>
       <NAME>Tanya Westerly</NAME>
       <AGE>30</AGE>
       <HEIGHT measurment="inches">65</HEIGHT>
     </PASSENGER>]]>
```

(continued)

```
</DOCUMENT>
```

Table 9–1   Results of running test application. (*continued*)

```
</OPERATION>

Adding Passenger: Tanya Westerly

set2.xml: true

<OPERATION>
   <DOCUMENT name="mycar" type="remove"/>
</OPERATION>

MyDoc Handler Notified Of Document Removal:

<CAR make="Jeep" model="Laredo" color="red">
    <DOCHANDLER_ADDED_ELEMENT>I was created by a document
      handler</DOCHANDLER_ADDED_ELEMENT><PASSENGER>
      <SEAT>Front Passenger</SEAT>
      <NAME>Fred Willoughby</NAME>
      <AGE>26</AGE>
      <HEIGHT measurment="inches">72</HEIGHT>
    </PASSENGER><DOCHANDLER_ADDED_ELEMENT>I was created by a
      document handler</DOCHANDLER_ADDED_ELEMENT><PASSENGER>
      <SEAT>Driver's Side Rear</SEAT>
      <NAME>Tanya Westerly</NAME>
      <AGE>30</AGE>
      <HEIGHT measurment="inches">65</HEIGHT>
   </PASSENGER></CAR>

remove.xml: true
```

9.4 | Summary

This chapter illustrated one method of building a declarative processing environment. The declarative programming environment provides us with a mechanism for dynamically handling new data object types without significant re-coding and testing. By manipulating shared XML documents, we are able to change the behavior for operating over XML documents and can thereby create dynamic applications that have a very low maintenance requirement. This concept can be extended to enhance any type of processing requirement, not just XML. For example, we could use the XML OPERATION documents to initiate a database transaction or create a new user interface. We also illustrated in this chapter the creation of a new XML vocabulary, using DTD syntax, and showed how that vocabulary gets integrated into the overall solution.

In the next chapter, we will explore Bill la Forge's MDSAX environment. MDSAX is an extension of the SAX processing we saw in Chapter 3. It allows for dynamically introducing filtering of the XML document at the time of parsing. By processing documents in this way, we create applications that have the ability to dynamically change the semantics of an original XML document, as well as validate in a more robust manner than just using DTDs. Processing documents with MDSAX is very similar to the declarative programming environment that we have described here, but operates at a much lower level and requires less memory overhead.

Dynamic Applications

10

10.1 | Introduction

Up until this point we have examined how the EAI problem can be solved by connecting two applications together directly or through a declarative processing environment. Both of these solutions move toward relieving the problem by making the solution more flexible and maintainable, but still requiring maintenance when changes occur. This chapter introduces the concept of using dynamic applications to provide us with the seamless integration we desire from EAI.

We are not attempting to introduce the concept of a system with artificial intelligence or any like capability. Dynamic applications are simply modules or components that are linked together at runtime based upon some input and a repository of information that describes how to interpret that input.

The beauty of dynamic applications is that they require the least maintenance of all the systems architectures we have discussed so far. Indeed, a single value changed in a repository can produce a radically different outcome based upon the same input. And, the technology that we will use to allow these diverse components to be sewn together mechanically is XML. XML plays a significant role in the design of the dynamic application runtime environment, as well as the communications between components.

At the conclusion of this chapter we will explore, in-depth, Bill la Forge's MDSAX, which is one example of a dynamic application runtime environment. Using MDSAX we can extend the SAX processing philosophy so that we can dynamically string together serial XML document handlers to provide us with dynamic application semantics.

10.2 | MDSAX

MDSAX is a filter framework for processing SAX events.

Table 10–1 illustrates the three alternatives for processing XML documents.

MDSAX represents the ideal solution to document processing. The application receives only what it needs and in a form that it can

Table 10–1   Parsing alternatives.

Alternative	Description
Traditional Parsers	Transform a document into an internal representation (or model) that is passed to the invoking application.
Event Parsers	Create a series of events that are passed (via callbacks) to the invoking application while a document is being parsed.
MDSAX	Configurable system for transforming a document into an application-specific representation, which is passed to the invoking application.

process directly. Moreover, the application works with neither document object models nor parse events.

In this section, we will begin by introducing filters, a new kind of programming component, which can be plugged into applications to simplify the processing of XML documents. We will consider briefly the kinds of operations a filter might perform and then examine how a particular filter, the inheritance filter by John Cowan, transforms documents for easier processing.

We will then turn our attention to MDSAX, a framework for building structures of filters, and consider some additional operations a filter might perform within that context. We will see how these additional capabilities give MDSAX the ability to transform documents into application-specific structures.

We will look closely at the structures supported by MDSAX, the use of a document to control how other documents are processed, and the capabilities provided by the many filters that work with MDSAX. Finally, we will look at using MDSAX to create entire applications, a re-implementation of the Java Developer's Kit's (JDK) simple Swing example using this technology, and some of the security implications of moving documents rather than JavaBeans across the Web.

10.3 | SAX Filters

Applications that use a SAX parser must process the events that the parser produces. Often this task is simplified by using a filter to pre-process these events. A filter sits between the SAX parser and an application, processing the events from the parser before passing them on to the application (see Figure 10–1). Therefore, a filter must implement the SAX `Parser` interface and interact with the application as if it were the parser. A filter must also implement various event handler interfaces, including `org.xml.sax.DocumentHandler`,

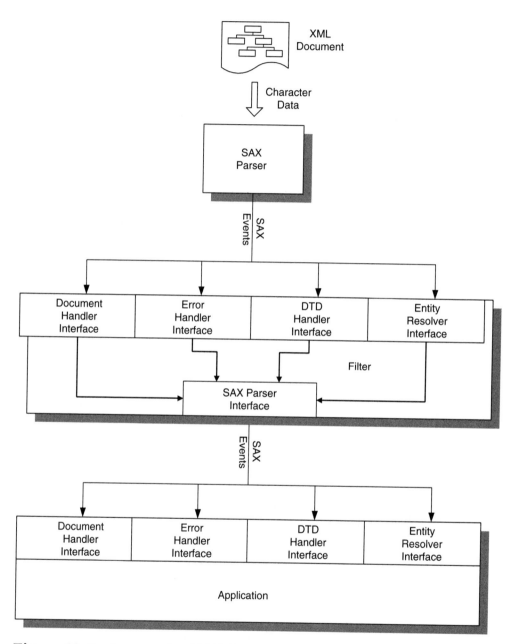

Figure 10–1   An example of SAX filtering.

and interact with the parser as if it were the application. Inserting a filter between a SAX parser and an application can often be done with very few changes to the application.

There are three different ways a filter can have an effect:

1. A filter can alter the event stream that passes through it by modifying or dropping various events. By this we mean that filters can be used to enhance a parser, providing support for new features like namespaces. Filters can also be used to simplify the tasks performed by an application, discarding events not needed by the application, and transforming the remainder into a form expected by the application.

2. A filter can reject the events passed to it by throwing an exception. Throwing exceptions is how a filter can participate in the validation of a document. And, while a parser may be the best tool for validating a document against a DTD or other schema, a filter may be the best place to validate a document against the requirements of a particular application.

3. Filters can be used to extract information from a document and pass it to the application, although this would require an additional interface between the filter and the application. For example, a filter might build a table of all the links found in a document.

10.3.1 *Filters as Components*

A filter is a component that implements the `org.xml.sax.parser` interface. It receives events from another component that also implements the `org.xml.sax.parser` interface. Starting with a parser, a series of filters can be strung together at runtime, with the application receiving events from the last filter in the series.

Many filters contain internal state data. A stack of elements can be used to track the active element. A well-written filter will be serially reusable, reinitializing its internal state data when a `startDocument` event is received.

Filters, like other types of components, are often configurable. For example, when using an inheritance filter (defined below), the filter must be configured for the inheritable attributes specific to the application.

10.3.2 *The Inheritance Filter*

Attributes generally only affect the processing of the element to which they are assigned. Inheritable attributes are an exception to this rule, as they affect the subordinate elements to which they are assigned. This can add to the complexity of an application, as it must now track the scope of these attributes to determine which inheritable attributes should be applied to the elements being processed.

The inheritance filter, written by John Cowan, makes it easier for an application to deal with inheritable attributes. This filter tracks the nesting structure of a document and, when it encounters an inheritable attribute, it adds that attribute to all the subordinate elements. Thus, inherited attributes act as default attributes unless specifically overridden. The application can now simply process the document element by element, without regard to which attributes are inheritable and without regard to the scope of those attributes. By default, only the attributes `xml:space` and `xml:lang` are inheritable.

Let's look at a simple example (see Example 10.1) :

Example 10.1: xml:lang.

```
<a xml:lang="en">
    <b>Hello.</b>
    <b xml:lang="de">Gutten tag.</b>
    <b>Hi!</b>
</a>
```

The inheritance filter transforms this document, propagating the xml:lang attribute down to all the elements contained by the element to which it was assigned, except where it is overridden by a new value. Example 10.2 illustrates this.

Example 10.2: Overridden attributes.

```
<a xml:lang="en">
    <b xml:lang="en">Hello.</b>
    <b xml:lang="de">Gutten tag.</b>
    <b xml:lang="en">Hi!</b>
</a>
```

The inheritance filter is configurable, letting you specify additional inheritable attributes unique to your application. This filter also allows you to manage namespace processing by making the xmlns attribute inheritable, as well as any attribute that begins with "xmlns:".

Components like the inheritance filter can be plugged into a wide range of applications. The utility of a component is often increased by making it configurable. This characteristic also makes it less likely that the component will need to be changed for use in any particular application.

Filters working in the framework of MDSAX can still perform the same operations as standalone filters, transforming the stream of events passing through them, throwing exceptions when errors are detected in the document being processed and extracting information. However, the MDSAX framework expands on that set of operations in several ways by enabling the following:

1. Stack filters, which contain a series of filters through which all events are passed. This organizational role allows several filters to be handled together as a single filter.

2. Event routers, which are filters that route the events they receive through a selected filter that is subordinate to the

router. Often the criterion used when selecting a filter to process a particular event depends on the name of the current element type.

3. Context filters, which within the MDSAX framework are always the top-level filters. The context filter is a kind of stack filter, but it also holds an element stack (see Figure 10–2), which is used to track the nesting of XML elements in the document being parsed. Each entry in this stack holds the element type name and attribute list, so

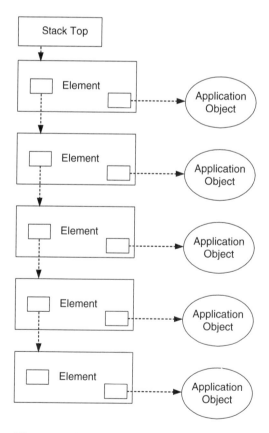

Figure 10–2   An Element stack.

that the information about a parent element (or any ancestor) is available when processing an element.

4. x filters can be used to transform elements into components. With x filters, the stack entry holds a reference to the application-specific component that was created by the filter. These filters are also responsible for linking the created application-specific objects to their parent elements. Again, the element stack is useful for accessing an object created from a parent element.

Additionally, filters can be used to set the properties of an object created from an element based on information held by a child element.

Before an application can use MDSAX, the structure of filters used to process an application's documents must be assembled and configured. The composition of this filter structure is the key to the transformation of XML documents into application-specific structures. Filters can be used to transform or prune parse events. In addition, event routers can be used to select events based on document type or element type. Together, filters and routers can be configured to construct a wide range of structures.

MDSAX is an open framework. It includes a basic toolkit of filters and routers, but custom components can also be developed, as these components are little more than SAX filters. Configuration of these components into the filter structure used by MDSAX can be done programmatically using the MDSAX API, or with a document written using the Context Markup Language (ContextML), which we will review shortly.

MDSAX includes initialization logic to construct a rather simple filter structure that can then be used by MDSAX to transform ContextML documents into additional filter structures. These structures, in turn, can then be used by MDSAX to transform other documents into application-specific structures. This results in MDSAX configuring its own filter structures, thus creating a simple bootstrap process.

10.3.3   *Basic Components*

Two classes of filters that are used to build filter structures are stack filters and routers. A stack filter is a filter that can be configured to hold several other filters arranged in a stack, as show in Figure 10–3. A stack filter gives us the capability of treating a group of filters as a single filter. SAX events that are passed to a stack filter will be passed to each of the filters held by the stack filter.

Routers are the second class of filters from which filter structures are built. Like a stack filter, a router is a filter that can be configured to hold several other filters as depicted in Figure 10–4. In contrast to a stack filter, a router will pass the SAX events that it receives to only one filter.

The filters held by a router each have a key attribute. The value of the key attribute is used to determine which filter receives any given SAX event. In the case of an element router, the key is matched to the name of the current element.

There are a number of routers included in the MDSAX download. But while they all work by comparing the key attributes of the filters they hold, they differ in which information the keys are matched against and how they handle the default case when there is no match.

The context filter is a type of stack filter that is the top-level filter used by MDSAX. The context filter holds a single chain of filters stacked serially to process SAX events one after the other. The context filter maintains a context for the filters it holds. This shared context includes an element stack that is used to assemble and configure application-specific structures into which the XML documents are being transformed.

The context filter also extends the `org.xml.sax.Parser` interface, adding a `build` method, which works just like the `Parser.parse` method, except that it returns the application-specific structure created by the transformation process (see Figure 10–5). When using MDSAX, the application calls this `build` method to transform a document into the internal form needed by the application.

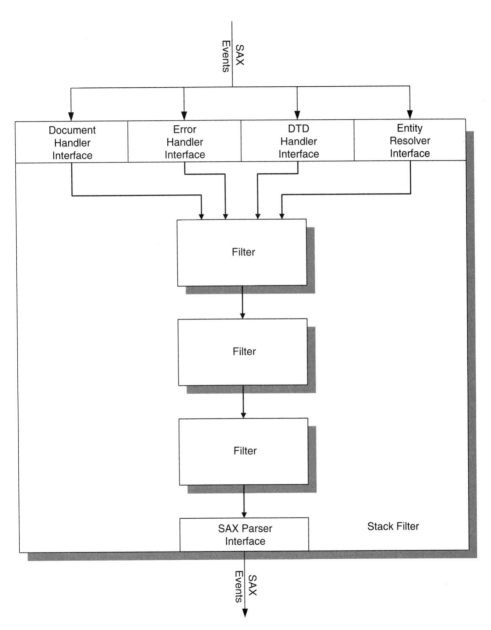

Figure 10–3   Stack filter.

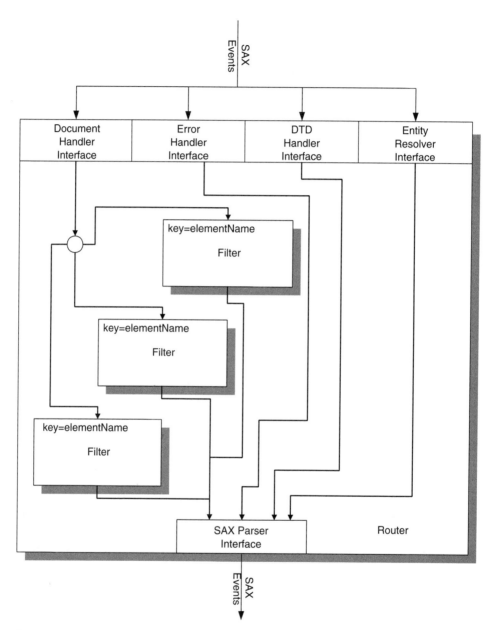

Figure 10–4 A router filter.

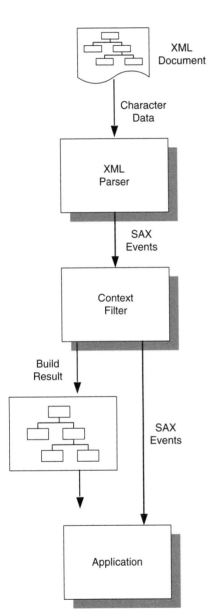

Figure 10–5   Context filter.

We have already briefly examined the element stack, which is part of the shared context maintained by the context filter (see Figure 10–2). The element filter (see Figure 10–6) pushes an element on the stack when it receives a `startElement` event and it removes the ele-

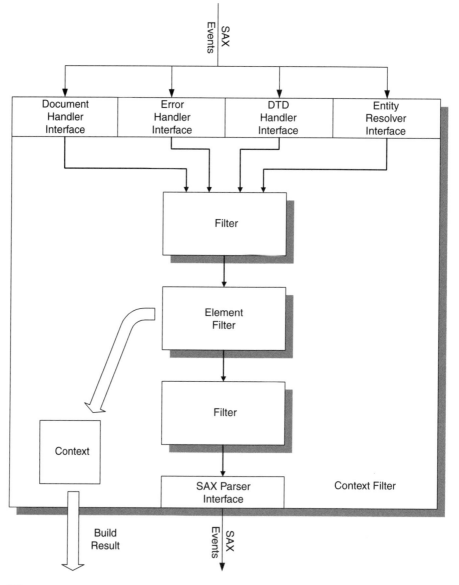

Figure 10–6   Element filter.

ment from the stack when it receives an `endElement` event. But, it does this while maintaining references to both the current and parent elements. The parent element reference is actually the stack top. When a `startElement` is encountered, the current element is pushed onto the stack and the current element is set to null. When an `endElement` is encountered, the parent element is saved in the current element reference before popping the stack.

10.3.4 *Filter Factories*

The only filter structure used by MDSAX is a tree of filter objects whose root node is an instance of the context filter. When a node in the tree has children, the implementation of the parent/child links depends on the class used to implement the node. For example, if the node is an instance of the stack filter class, or is an instance of a class that extends the stack filter class, then references to the children are held by an instance of `java.util.Vector`. Alternatively, the children of an element router are held by a hashtable. And, configuration of the filters within a filter structure is nothing more than assigning appropriate values to the properties of a filter.

In MDSAX, filters often participate in the processing of a document and have state information that changes while a document is being processed. If a filter is well-defined, it can be used to process any number of documents; so, filter structures built entirely from well-defined filters are serially reusable. But, this means that filter structures are not thread-safe; therefore, two threads cannot use the same filter structure at the same time.

MDSAX does not support the direct configuration of filters. Instead, MDSAX works with filter factories. When a ContextML document is processed, it is transformed into a structure of filter factories. Unlike filters, which participate directly in document processing, filter factories have no associated state except for their configuration. In other words, a filter factory structure is thread-safe.

Filter factories create filter components whose behavior depends on how the filter factory was configured. Filter factories for stack filters and routers hold other filter factories. And, when a stack filter or router is created by a filter factory, the factories held by the filter factory are each directed to create a filter, which is then held by the newly created stack filter or router.

When using several threads to process multiple documents, the filter factory structures can be shared by all threads. This is accomplished by having each thread create its own filter structures from the common filter factory structures. These filter factory structures are held in a cache, eliminating the need to reprocess the original ContextML documents that were used to produce them.

10.3.5 *Bootstrap*

MDSAX initialization builds a boot filter structure (see Figure 10–7) that can process only a simplified version of ContextML. This initial structure is used to process the bootstrap document (see Example 10.4), constructing in turn a more elaborate filter structure. When the initial structure processes the bootstrap document, SAX events are first passed through an element filter. This element filter creates the element objects in our context stack. An element router is then used to direct the events to different filters, depending on the type of element being processed.

Subordinate to the element router in the boot filter structure are several x filters, one for each type of element used in the bootstrap document. Each x filter creates a different kind of filter factory, attaches it to the top element object in the element stack, and then, when appropriate, adds that filter factory to the stack filter factory or router factory associated with the parent element object.

Once the parse of the bootstrap document completes, the filter factory attached to the base element object in the element stack is returned. This factory is then used to spawn a filter structure that is used to process other documents.

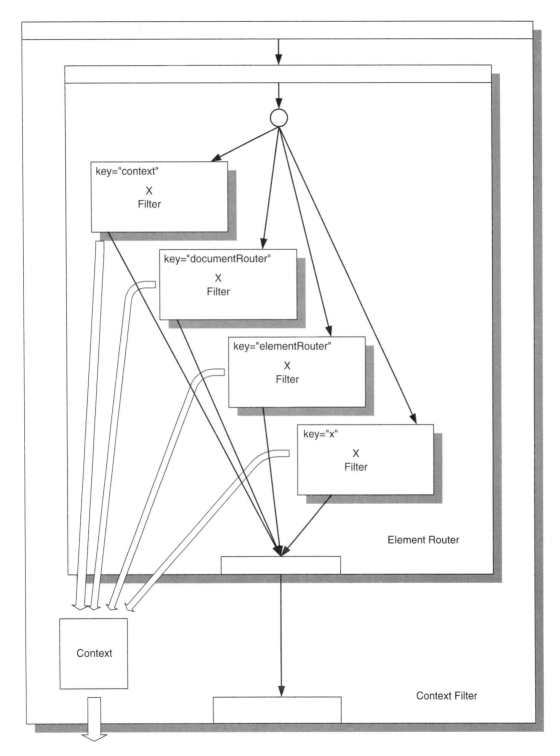

Figure 10–7   The boot filter structure.

Table 10–2   Filter Factory Classes

Element	Class
Att	com.jxml.mdsax.schema.MDAtt
AttList	com.jxml.mdsax.schema.MDAttlistFactory
Context	com.jxml.mdsax.MDContextFactoryImpl
DocumentRouter	com.jxml.mdsax.MDDocumentRouterFactory
Element	com.jxml.mdsax.MDElementFactoryImpl
ElementRouter	com.jxml.mdsax.MDElementRouterFactory
Stack	com.jxml.mdsax.MDFilterStackFactoryImpl
Trace	com.jxml.mdsax.MDTraceFilterFactory
X	com.jxml.mdsax.MDXFactoryImpl

The initial filter structure of MDSAX handles only the minimum number of elements needed to implement a simplified version of ContextML, mapping them to the filter factory classes given in Table 10–2.

We will be looking at the various elements listed above in more detail in the section on ContextML, but at this point, an example of a ContextML document should be helpful. The following ContextML document (Example 10.3), when processed by MDSAX, results in a filter structure that is identical to the boot filter structure created by the MDSAX initialization logic:

Example 10.3: Boot filter structure expressed as a ContextML document.

```
<context>
  <element/>
  <elementRouter>
    <x key="att"
       resultClass="com.jxml.mdsax.schema.MDAtt"/>
    <x key="attList"
       resultClass="com.jxml.mdsax.schema.MDAttlistFactory"/>
    <x key="context"
       resultClass="com.jxml.mdsax.MDContextFactoryImpl"/>
    <x key="documentRouter"
       resultClass="com.jxml.mdsax.MDDocumentRouterFactory"/>
    <x key="element"
       resultClass="com.jxml.mdsax.MDElementFactoryImpl"/>
```

```
      <x key="elementRouter"
        resultClass="com.jxml.mdsax.MDElementRouterFactory"/>
      <x key="stack"
        resultClass="com.jxml.mdsax.MDFilterStackFactoryImpl"/>
      <x key="trace"
        resultClass="com.jxml.mdsax.MDTraceFilterFactory"/>
      <x key="x"
        resultClass="com.jxml.mdsax.MDXFactoryImpl"/>
    </elementRouter>
</context>
```

In the above document, the root element (the outermost element) is named `context`. Documents are often typed based on their root element, and documents of type ContextML are classified by their root element, which must have the name `context`.

Note that the `context` element in this document has two child elements, `element` and `elementRouter`. The `element` element is mapped into an element factory when the filter factory structure is created. A filter factory structure is then used to create a filter structure, which has a corresponding element filter. Then, when the filter structure is used to process a document, the element filter creates the entries in the element stack and initializes the element tag name and attribute list each time it is passed a `startElement` event.

The `elementRouter` element is mapped into an element router factory. This factory creates the element router filter that directs parse events based on the current element being parsed. Every element under `elementRouter` has a `key` attribute. The element router filter ultimately uses these `key`s when choosing a subordinate filter to process the parser events for each element in the document being parsed.

There are nine elements subordinate to `elementRouter`, one for each type of element that is supported in the simplified version of ContextML. These are all `x` elements, which map to the x factory. This factory creates an `x` filter that, in turn, creates a factory object for every matching element whose parse events are routed to it by the event router filter. As a result, the document being parsed is transformed into a structure of factory objects for creating filter structures.

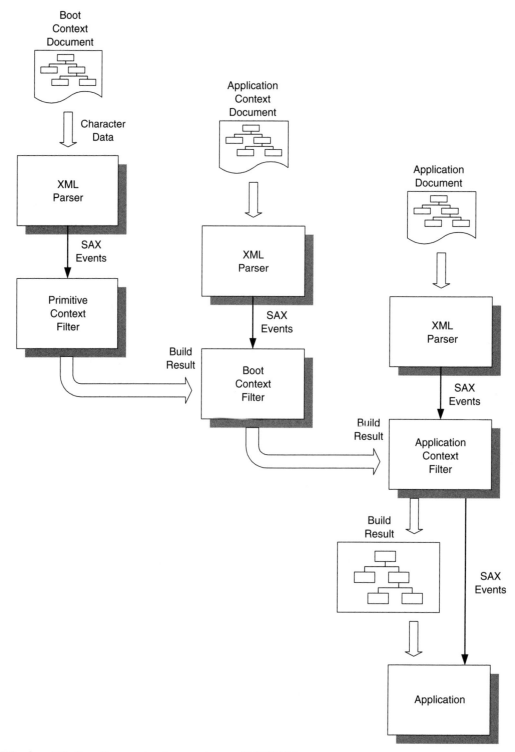

Figure 10–8   Successive invocations of MDSAX.

In a typical application, MDSAX is invoked three times in succession (see Figure 10–8):

1. As part of the bootstrap process, the built-in filter structure is used to process the bootstrap document. The result is a more comprehensive filter structure capable of processing the full ContextML, not just a simplified subset.

2. The filter structure from the bootstrap process is next used to process a ContextML document that defines how an application document is to be processed. The result is a filter structure for processing an application-specific document type.

3. Finally, a document of a type specific to the application is processed, transforming it into the form expected by the application.

The specification of how to process a ContextML document is not hard-coded in MDSAX, but is given in the bootstrap document. It is then a simple matter of updating the bootstrap document when adding new filter and filter factory components—the code for MDSAX does not need to be updated. Example 10.4 is the bootstrap document included with the MDSAX download.

Example 10.4: Bootstrap document.

```
<context>
   <element/>
   <documentRouter>

      <elementRouter key="context">
        <stack key="context">
          <x resultClass="com.jxml.mdsax.MDContextFactoryImpl"/>
        </stack>

        <stack key="element">
          <attList>
            <att name="key" type="CDATA" status="#IMPLIED"/>
```

```
    </attList>
    <x resultClass="com.jxml.mdsax.MDElementFactoryImpl"/>
  </stack>

  <stack key="documentRouter">
    <attList>
      <att name="key" type="CDATA" status="#IMPLIED"/>
    </attList>
    <x resultClass="com.jxml.mdsax.MDDocumentRouterFactory"/>
  </stack>

  <stack key="stack">
    <attList>
      <att name="key" type="CDATA" status="#IMPLIED"/>
    </attList>
    <x resultClass="com.jxml.mdsax.MDFilterStackFactoryImpl"/>
  </stack>

  <stack key="elementRouter">
    <attList>
      <att name="key" type="CDATA" status="#IMPLIED"/>
    </attList>
    <x resultClass="com.jxml.mdsax.MDElementRouterFactory"/>
  </stack>

  <stack key="passAll">
    <attList>
      <att name="key" type="CDATA" status="#IMPLIED"/>
</attList>
    <x resultClass="com.jxml.mdsax.MDPassAllFactory"/>
  </stack>

  <stack key="trace">
    <attList>
      <att name="key" type="CDATA" status="#IMPLIED"/>
      <att name="prefix" type="CDATA" status="#IMPLIED"/>
    </attList>
    <x resultClass="com.jxml.mdsax.MDTraceFilterFactory"/>
  </stack>

  <stack key="display">
    <attList>
      <att name="key" type="CDATA" status="#IMPLIED"/>
      <att name="heading" type="CDATA" status="#IMPLIED"/>
      <att name="displayReference" type="idref" status=
        "#IMPLIED"/>
    </attList>
```

```
  <x resultClass="com.jxml.mdsax.MDDisplayFilterFactory"/>
</stack>

<stack key="devNull">
  <attList>
    <att name="key" type="CDATA" status="#IMPLIED"/>
  </attList>
  <x resultClass=
    "com.jxml.mdsax.restructure.MDDevnullFactory"/>
</stack>

<stack key="flatten">
  <attList>
    <att name="key" type="CDATA" status="#IMPLIED"/>
  </attList>
  <x resultClass=
    "com.jxml.mdsax.restructure.MDFlattenFactory"/>
</stack>

<stack key="flattenable">
  <attList>
    <att name="name" type="CDATA" status="#REQUIRED"/>
  </attList>
  <x resultClass="com.jxml.mdsax.restructure.MDFlattenable"/>
</stack>

<stack key="redirectRouter">
  <attList>
    <att name="key" type="CDATA" status="#IMPLIED"/>
  </attList>
  <x resultClass=
    "com.jxml.mdsax.restructure.MDRedirectRouterFactory"/>
</stack>

<stack key="att">
  <attList>
    <att name="name" type="CDATA" status="#REQUIRED"/>
    <att name="type" type="CDATA" value="CDATA"/>
    <att name="status" type="CDATA" status="#IMPLIED"/>
    <att name="value" type="CDATA" status="#IMPLIED"/>
  </attList>
  <x resultClass="com.jxml.mdsax.schema.MDAtt"/>
</stack>

<stack key="attList">
  <attList>
    <att name="key" type="CDATA" status="#IMPLIED"/>
```

```
   </attList>
   <x resultClass="com.jxml.mdsax.schema.MDAttlistFactory"/>
 </stack>

 <stack key="namespace">
   <attList>
     <att name="key" type="CDATA" status="#IMPLIED"/>
   </attList>
   <x resultClass=
     "com.jxml.mdsax.transform.MDNamespaceFactory"/>
 </stack>

 <stack key="unnamespace">
   <attList>
     <att name="key" type="CDATA" status="#IMPLIED"/>
   </attList>
   <x resultClass=
     "com.jxml.mdsax.transform.MDUnnamespaceFactory"/>
 </stack>

 <stack key="inheritance">
   <attList>
     <att name="key" type="CDATA" status="#IMPLIED"/>
     <att name="namespace" type="CDATA" status="#IMPLIED"/>
   </attList>
   <x resultClass=
     "com.jxml.mdsax.transform.MDInheritanceFactory"/>
 </stack>

 <stack key="inheritable">
   <attList>
     <att name="attribute" type="CDATA" status="#REQUIRED"/>
   </attList>
   <x resultClass="com.jxml.mdsax.transform.MDInheritable"/>
 </stack>

 <stack key="xaf">
   <attList>
     <att name="key" type="CDATA" status="#IMPLIED"/>
     <att name="architecture" type="CDATA" status="#REQUIRED"/>
   </attList>
   <x resultClass="com.jxml.mdsax.transform.MDXAFFactory"/>
 </stack>

 <stack key="x">
   <attList>
     <att name="key" type="CDATA" status="#IMPLIED"/>
```

```
      <att name="resultClass" type="CDATA" status="#REQUIRED"/>
  </attList>
  <x resultClass="com.jxml.mdsax.MDXFactory"/>
</stack>

<stack key="xb">
  <attList>
    <att name="key" type="CDATA" status="#IMPLIED"/>
    <att name="resultClass" type="CDATA" status="#REQUIRED"/>
  </attList>
  <x resultClass="com.jxml.mdsax.MDResultFactory"/>
</stack>

<stack key="xs">
  <attList>
    <att name="key" type="CDATA" status="#IMPLIED"/>
    <att name="resultClass" type="CDATA" status="#REQUIRED"/>
  </attList>
  <x resultClass="com.jxml.mdsax.beans.MDXSFactory"/>
</stack>

<stack key="xel">
  <attList>
    <att name="key" type="CDATA" status="#IMPLIED"/>
    <att name="listenerClass" type="CDATA" status="#REQUIRED"/>
    <att name="eventSourceClass" type="CDATA" status=
      "#REQUIRED"/>
  </attList>
  <x resultClass="com.jxml.mdsax.beans.MDXELFactory"/>
</stack>

<stack key="xpl">
  <attList>
    <att name="key" type="CDATA" status="#IMPLIED"/>
    <att name="property" type="CDATA" status="#REQUIRED"/>
  </attList>
  <x resultClass="com.jxml.mdsax.beans.MDPropertyLink"/>
</stack>

<stack key="parentRouter">
  <attList>
    <att name="key" type="CDATA" status="#IMPLIED"/>
  </attList>
  <x resultClass="com.jxml.mdsax.MDParentRouterFactory"/>
</stack>

<stack key="apRouter">
```

```
          <attList>
            <att name="key" type="CDATA" status="#IMPLIED"/>
            <att name="redirect" type="CDATA" status="#IMPLIED"/>
            <att name="nsAtt" type="CDATA" status="#IMPLIED"/>
          </attList>
          <x resultClass="com.jxml.mdsax.MDAPRouterFactory"/>
        </stack>

        <stack key="document">
          <x resultClass=
            "com.jxml.coins.dvdom.DVDocumentFilterFactory"/>
        </stack>

        <stack key="cElement">
          <attList>
            <att name="key" type="CDATA" status="#IMPLIED"/>
          </attList>
          <x resultClass="com.jxml.coins.CElementFactory"/>
        </stack>

      </elementRouter>
    </documentRouter>
</context>
```

Example 10.4 is similar to Example 10.3, except for the use of stack elements subordinate to elementRouter. A stack element is mapped to the stack factory, which in turn is used to create a stack filter. A stack filter, while serving as a single filter, is a wrapper for a series of filters through which all the parse events given to the stack filter are passed. This means we can now route the parse events for a given type of element to multiple filters.

In the bootstrap document, the parse events for each type of element are processed first by an attribute list filter and then by an x filter. The attList element is mapped to an attribute list factory that then creates the attribute list filter. The att elements subordinate to attList are mapped to an att object, which configures the attribute factory, giving rise to the same functionality that is normally implemented in a DTD. The advantage here is that it is under the control of the application and could be easily extended to be much more particular than any generic schema might be.

10.3.6 *ContextML*

There are 28 elements defined in ContextML. But, as the bootstrap document illustrates, you can do a lot using only a few of them. The large number of elements supported by MDSAX and ContextML are there to broaden the scope of problems you can address. Each element in ContextML is mapped into the filter factory defined in the bootstrap document.

Let's start with the basic elements: context, document, element, and cElement. The context element is the root element of ContextML. Its corresponding filter implements the MDContextFilter interface that includes the build method used by an application to transform a document into the desired internal representation.

The document element is optional, but must occur before element or cElement. Use of the document element turns on DOM construction.

The element or cElement should then precede any other element. These elements construct the element objects on the element stack. cElement is only used after the document element, as it creates DOM Element objects (see Table 10–3).

The stack element and various router elements provide the structure to a ContextML document. The stack element lets us group together several filters and treat them as a single filter. This is important when working with routers, as events passed to a router are only processed by one of the filters that are subordinate to the router. However, by targeting a stack instead of a single filter, we essentially can target a chain of filters.

The documentRouter element is useful when designing a filter structure that can process different types of documents. It routes all events based on the root element type. Of note, processing instructions that occur before the root element are queued and then forwarded to the subordinate filter structure, once the root element of the document being processed is encountered.

The elementRouter and apRouter are probably the most useful routers, as they provide a means to differentiate how events are

Table 10–3   Basic ContextML elements.

Element	Use	Attributes	Child Elements
context	The root element for a ContextML document.	None.	ContextML elements identifying how this MDSAX processor should handle documents.
element	Must appear somewhere in all ContextML document processing. Used by MDSAX to establish the context of the current element being processed in the overall document tree. Location can vary, but determines the current context.	key – used for routing when element is a child of a router element.	None.
cElement	Used in place of element when constructing a DOM. It is the cElement filter that turns the element stack into the DOM tree.	key – used for routing when cElement is a child of a router.	None.
document	Used to select a DOM implementation.	None.	None.

processed based on the current element type. The apRouter provides additional flexibility by letting the application make selections based on root element type name, parent elements, and even namespaces, in combination with the current element type. The parentRouter will likely be used in combination with the elementRouter for special cases where the apRouter is simply not fast enough.

The redirectRouter works a little like the documentRouter, except that it routes events based on the current element, but when there is no match for the current element, it routes the events the same way it routed the events for the parent element.

Table 10–4 describes the filter structure elements.

Table 10–4 Filter structure elements.

Element	Use	Attributes	Child Elements
stack	Identifies a group of filters managed together as a single stack of filters. While its internal structure may contain multiple layers of filters, to MDSAX it looks like a single filter.	key – used for routing when the stack is a child of a router element.	ContextML elements representing the filters "contained" in the stack.
documentRouter	Sends events to different filters (or sets of filters), depending on the root element of the document currently being processed.	key – used for routing when the documentRouter itself is a child of a router element.	ContextML elements whose key attribute matches the root elements for documents that should follow that path.
elementRouter	Sends events to different filters (or sets of filters), depending on the name of the element type currently being processed.	key – used for routing when the elementRouter itself is a child of a router element.	ContextML elements whose key attributes match the ancestor element type names for document information that should follow that path.
parentRouter	Event routing based on the parent element.	key – used for routing when parentRouter is a child of a router.	ContextML elements whose key attributes match the ancestor element type names for document information that should follow that path.

(continued)

Table 10–4   Filter structure elements. *(continued)*

Element	Use	Attributes	Child Elements
redirectRouter	A sub-tree router. Similar to element-Router, except that when there is no match, the default is to route the events for an unknown element the same way its parent's events were routed.	key – used for routing when redirect-Router is a child of a router element.	ContextML elements whose key attributes match the ancestor element type names for document information that should follow that path.
apRouter	A sub-tree router that routes based on the name of the current element type and its location in the document tree. Similar to redirectRouter, except that when there is no match, may route to the default pattern (where key=""), or the routing that the parent element followed, depending on whether the redirect attribute is false, missing, or true, respectively.	key – used for routing when apRouter is a child of a router element. Redirect – takes true or false. (Treated as false if missing.) If true, routing for elements that don't match a pattern will follow their parent element's routing. If false, routing for elements that don't match a pattern will be handled by the default pattern. nsAtt – takes true or false. (Treated as false if missing.) If true, looks for namespace information in the xmlns attributes generated by the inheritance filter. If false, assumes namespaces have been processed to URI^local_name by the namespace filter.	ContextML elements whose key attributes match the ancestor element names for document information that should follow that path.

Filters can be used to change the structure of a document, especially when used in combination with a router. For example, when devNull is subordinate to elementRouter, it drops all occurrences of an element, but when placed subordinate to redirectRouter, it drops the elements and all subordinate elements.

The passAll filter is helpful when working with a router—it is the same as a stack filter with no contents—because it does nothing. Often when working with a router there may be cases where no processing is needed. For those cases, the passAll filter can be used.

A flatten filter, like devNull, can be used to restructure a document. A flatten filter operates by retaining all of an element's contents and only drops the startElement and endElement events.

The xaf filter supports documents that employ architectural forms. A document using architectural forms can define various subsets of information that can be selected by the document processor. MDSAX supports this by letting you specify the desired architectural form as an attribute on the xaf element when using ContextML.

Table 10–5 describes the transformation filter structure elements.

ContextML gives you a means of specifying how to transform an XML document into a structure of application-specific objects. But things don't always go the way you expect. When that happens, you can use trace and display filters to look at either the events or how the document is being transformed at various points in your filter structure. A trace element can even be put in the bootstrap document. Trace and display filters illustrate the power of this architecture, as debugging can easily be added without affecting the processing code.

Table 10–6 describes the debugging filter structure elements.

DTDs are very handy when composing a document—they ensure that the document conforms to the author's understanding of how the document should be structured. When processing documents, there is no assurance that even valid documents will have exactly the structure expected—that is often left to the application to determine.

The attList filter is intended to support unique application validation requirements. The configuration of the attList filter is han-

Table 10–5   Transformation filter structures.

Element	Use	Attributes	Child Elements
passAll	Passes all elements through without any change.	key – Used for routing when passAll is a child of a router element.	None.
devNull	Drops all events.	key – Used for routing when devNull is a child of a router element.	None.
flatten	Indicates that some elements are to be discarded and their content promoted to be content in the parent element. (Effectively, strips tags out based on the keys of child flattenable elements.)	key – Used for routing when devNull is a child of a router element.	Flattenable elements whose keys indicate the elements to be flattened.
flattenable	Used to identify elements that can be stripped out of a document and replaced by their content. Must appear within a flatten element.	name – Contains the name of an element type whose contents can be flattened into the parent element.	None.
xaf	Turns on architectural forms processing, which provides sophisticated transformations of documents from one DTD to another.	key – Used for routing when xaf is a child of a router element. architecture – The name of the architecture that is the destination for the transformation.	None.

Table 10–6 Debugging filter structures.

Element	Use	Attributes	Child Elements
trace	Displays information about the events it receives on the system console. (The -v option to MDMain uses trace to display the final SAX events that MDSAX returns to the application.)	key – Used for routing when trace is a child of a router element. Prefix – Allows prefixing of the displayed information, simplifying the task of sorting out the display when multiple traces are in use.	None.
display	Sets up child elements that may display the contents of the XML document.	Key – Used for routing when display is a child of a router element. heading – Allows prefixing of the displayed information, simplifying the task of sorting out the display when multiple traces are in use. displayReference – An optional refid attribute to an element that processes the output.	display doesn't know anything about any child elements, but xpl can be used to identify element types that set a parent refid to reference an element in another document. displayOutput, for example, must have display as its parent, so that it can set the refid property.

dled by the att elements that are subordinate to the attList element in ContextML and is not subject to the control of the document author. Validation and defaulting of attribute values that are critical to correct document processing are no longer dependent on the DTD, allowing the use of faster, non-validating parsers.

Table 10–7 describes the validation filter structure elements.

The namespace element provides one of the two ways of handling namespaces provided with MDSAX. Unfortunately, the mangled ele-

Table 10–7   Validation filter structures.

Element	Use	Attributes	Child Elements
att	Specifies an attribute value that should be added to an element, and has the same capabilities for the filter as a DTD has for a ponser. The value parameter is optional and only specifies a default or required value.	name – The name of the attribute to be added. type – The type of the attribute to be added. Acceptable values are the same as for a DTD: ID, IDREF, etc. Defaults to CDATA. status – The status of the attribute to be added. Acceptable values are the same as for a DTD: #REQUIRED, #IMPLIED, #FIXED. value – The default or required value of the attribute to be added.	None.
attList	Contains att elements used to add attributes to elements.	key – Used for routing when attList is a child of a router element.	att elements.

ment type name that results may not be useable to build a DOM. One possibility is to use the namespace filter, do some processing that depends on it, and then use the unnamespace filter to undo the effects of the namespace filter.

Table 10–8 describes the namespace filter structure elements.

The inheritance filter is useful for processing inheritable attributes. When an inheritance element is specified in ContextML, only inheritable elements can be subordinate to it. These inheritable elements are used to specify the attributes that the inheritance filter is to treat as inheritable—any inheritable attribute that occurs on a startElement event is passed to the inheritance fil-

Table 10–8 Namespace filter structure.

Element	Use	Attributes	Child Elements
namespace	Resolves namespace prefixes to URIs and attaches them to the element type name (separated by a ^).	Key – Used for routing when namespace is a child of a router element.	None.
unnamespace	Removes namespaces, rebuilding the document in a format as close to the original as possible. (When multiple prefixes have been declared for a namespace, this uses the most recent.)	key – Used for routing when unnamespace is a child of a router element.	None.

ter and is subsequently added to all subordinate startElement events.

The inheritance filter can also be used to simplify namespace processing, especially when used together with apRouter. By treating all xmlns attributes as inheritable, subsequent namespace processing does not need to deal with the location of an element in a document—because all namespace information has been duplicated in the element's attribute list. This is particularly handy if a DOM is being built and subsequently restructured.

Table 10–9 describes inheritance filter structures.

The xb filter is the central player in MDSAX—it is responsible for all object composition. Each xb filter is configured, via the resultClass attribute in ContextML, to construct a particular type of object. Then, when the xb filter receives a startElement event, it creates an object and sets the reference in the current element object to point to it.

The xb filter is also responsible for processing ID attributes. In addition to an element stack, the shared context also holds a map that associates IDs with the application objects created by the xb filter.

Table 10–9   Inheritance filter structures.

Element	Use	Attributes	Child Elements
inheritance	Turns on the inheritance of attributes specified by the name attributes of inheritable child elements. Typically used to ease processing of XML's xml:space and xml:lang attributes.	key - Used for routing when inheritance is a child of a router element. namespace - True or false. If true, makes all xmlns attributes inheritable.	Inheritable elements.
inheritable	Identifies attributes that are treated as inheritable. All child elements will have the same value as the parent element, unless they specifically override that value. (And their child attributes will then inherit the new value from them.)	attribute - The name of the attribute to be made inheritable.	None.

After creating an application object, if the startElement contains any attributes of type ID, the xb filter is responsible for associating the attribute ID value with the application object it created.

The xb filter makes use of the java.reflection and java.beans packages for creating and configuring components. The java.reflection package provides the capability for discovering methods and invoking them.

The java.beans package provides information about properties, which are defined by declaring a get or set method that fits a particular format. In addition to this default approach to determining properties, a programmer can also explicitly declare the properties of a class by defining a BeanInfo class with the same name, but extended by "BeanInfo".

The `java.beans` package also includes a `PropertyEditor` interface for updating a property. Each property editor works with a particular type of property. The JDK includes a number of undocumented property editors that are used by MDSAX. The `java.beans` package also includes a means for defining new kinds of property editors. When this is done in an application program, those new property editors can be used by MDSAX.

The final responsibility of the `xb` filter is to update any properties that have the same name as the attributes found in the `startElement` event. This could be a very slow process, except that the necessary `BeanInfo` is retrieved when the `xb` filter is specified, rather than when a `startElement` event is processed. How the property is updated also depends on the type of attribute. If the attribute is an `IDREF`, then the value of the attribute is used as a key to the `ID` map held in the shared context. The value associated with the `id` is then used to update the application object's bean property. Otherwise, a property editor is used to convert the attribute value to the appropriate type and set the property.

Note   The logic given here for `ID`/`IDREF` processing has been somewhat simplified. The actual implementation is such that an `IDREF` can be used before the `ID` is defined. When this happens, the bean property of the previously constructed application object will be updated when the `startElement` event defining the ID is finally processed.

The `x` and `xs` filters are extensions of the `xb` filter. These filters build parent/child relationships between selected types of application objects. The `x` filter is used to configure structures of filter factories. When the application objects of the parent element implement the stack or router interface, the `x` filter will call the appropriate method on that application object to add the subordinate filter factory.

The `xs` filter creates Swing objects. It recognizes various `Swing` classes and, when it can, creates the appropriate parent/child relationships.

The `xel` filter is used to register event sources with event listeners. The `xel` filter is configured to work with a particular listener interface, which means that the necessary Java reflection can be done when the filter is created and not when it is processing parse events. When the xel filter receives a startElement event, the attribute list for that event must include an eventDestination IDREF attribute. The parent application object is assumed to be the event source, which is then registered with the application object associated with the IDREF.

The xpl filter is used to set a bean property of an application object in one document to reference an application object generated by processing another document. The filter is configured with the property attribute, which is used to identify the bean property to be configured. When the filter receives a startElement event, it updates that property on the application object of the parent element. The startElement event must contain an href attribute, which is used to identify a second document to be processed. The href attribute may contain a #. If it does, the text following the # is the id value of the application object that is to be referenced. Otherwise, the application object associated with the root element of the document is used.

Table 10–10 describes application filter elements.

10.3.7   *MDMain*

Included in the download for MDSAX is a driver program, com.jxml.mdsax.MDMain. This program is useful for standalone processing of documents and as a starting point for applications that use MDSAX. Additionally, the MDMain program includes some debugging aids.

This program accepts up to six arguments: three optional switches, an optional URL, and two required URLs (see Table 10–11). The switches can be entered in any order. Two of the switches, -v and -s, are strictly to help with debugging.

Table 10–10 Application filter structures.

Element	Use	Attributes	Child Elements
x	Defines filter element mappings with support for routers, stacks, and other parent/child relationships unique to filters.	key - Used for routing when x is a child of a router. resultClass - Defines the class of the result attached to the x element.	None.
xb	Defines generic element mappings with no parent/child relationships.	key - Used for routing when xb is a child of a router. resultClass - Defines the class of the result attached to the xb element.	None.
xs	Defines Swing element mappings with parent/child Swing.	key - Used for routing when xs is a child of a router element. resultClass - Defines the class of the result attached to the xs element.	None.
xel	Defines element mappings for establishing event source/listener connections.	key - Used for routing when xel is a child of a router element. listenerClass - Name of the listener interface class. eventSourceClass - Name of the class or interface of the event source.	None.
xpl	Defines element mappings for connecting parent result object properties (typically defined as refid attributes) to elements in other documents.	key - Used for routing when xpl is a child of a router element. property - Name of the bean property of the result associated with the parent element.	None.

Table 10–11   MDMain command-line switches.

Switch	Result
-v	Displays (visualizes) final output of all SAX events, reflecting all MDSAX processing.
-s	Displays (shows) final `resultMap` contents (useful if filters created objects during the parse).
-r	Executes (runs) the result object that is built by MDSAX (useful for testing and running program composition).

You will recall from Figure 10–8 that MDSAX works with three documents: the bootstrap document, the ContextML document, and the application document. The URLs for these documents must be passed to MDMain as command-line arguments after any switches are specified. The first is optional, and when not present, the bootstrap document is taken from the Java CLASSPATH. These arguments are described in Table 10–12 below.

Table 10–12   MDMain command-line parameters.

URL Argument	Importance
bootURL	Overrides the default boot file at `classpath:///com/jxml/context.xml`. Defines the structure that should be used to process the `contextURL` document, if different from the default (optional, but comes first if it appears).
contextURL	ContextML document describing the structure of the filters that should be built to process the `appURL` document. It provides "marching orders" for filter factories (required).
appURL	Application document to be processed (required).

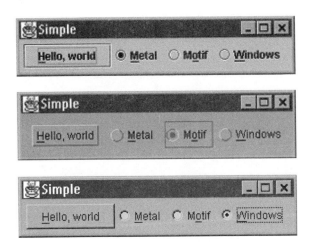

Figure 10–9 Output from Simple.

10.3.8   *A Swing Example*

JDK 1.2 from JavaSoft includes the `Simple` example. As shown in Figure 10–9, `Simple` consists of a `Frame`, a `Panel`, a `Button` that does not do anything, and three radio buttons, where the radio buttons change the look and feel of the display.

As is typical of most GUI programs, the `Simple` program from Sun Microsystems includes a high ratio of glue code to application code. Making matters worse, the glue code is application-specific and difficult to read and/or maintain. MDSAX lets you replace the glue code with an XML document, which is naturally tree-structured, making it a good way to describe how the `Swing` components are to be configured. We are left with 81 lines of Java code to describe the application logic.

The following code is the `Swing Simple` example from the JDK, but without all the glue code.

```
import java.awt.*;
import java.awt.event.*;
import javax.swing.*;

public class SFrame extends JFrame
    implements Runnable, ActionListener
```

■ SFrame *is now the only class we need to define.*

```
{
```

■ *We begin by defining three properties:* metalButton, motifButton, *and* windowsButton.

```
    protected JRadioButton metalButton, motifButton,
      windowsButton;

      public void
    setMetalButton(JRadioButton metalButton)
    {
      this.metalButton=metalButton;
    }
      public void
    setMotifButton(JRadioButton motifButton)
    {
      this.motifButton=motifButton;
    }

      public void
    setWindowsButton(JRadioButton windowsButton)
    {
      this.windowsButton=windowsButton;
    }

      public void
    run()
```

■ *The run method is called by the* MDMain *program when the root element of the document being processed is transformed into an* SFrame *object.*

```
    {
      addWindowListener(
        new WindowAdapter()
          {
            public void windowClosing(WindowEvent e)
            {
              System.exit(0);
            }
```

```
      });
    pack();
    setVisible(true);
    updateState();
  }

    public void
  actionPerformed(ActionEvent e)
```

■ *The* `actionPerformed` *method is called when a radio button is selected to change the look and feel.*

```
    {
      String lnfName = e.getActionCommand();

      try
      {
        UIManager.setLookAndFeel(lnfName);
        SwingUtilities.updateComponentTreeUI(this);
        pack();
      } catch (Exception exc)
      {
        JRadioButton button = (JRadioButton)e.getSource();
        button.setEnabled(false);
        updateState();
        System.err.println(
          "Could not load LookAndFeel: " + lnfName);
      }
    }
    public void
  updateState()
```

■ *The* `updateState` *method is used to select the radio button that reflects the current look and feel.*

```
  {
    String lnfName = UIManager.getLookAndFeel()
      .getClass().getName();
    if (lnfName.indexOf("Metal") >= 0)
      metalButton.setSelected(true);
    else if (lnfName.indexOf("Windows") >= 0)
      windowsButton.setSelected(true);
```

```
        else if (lnfName.indexOf("Motif") >= 0)
          motifButton.setSelected(true);
        else
          System.err.println(
            "SimpleExample is using an unknown L&F: "
            + lnfName);
      }
    }
```

We should observe a few things from the code above:

1. The class SFrame extends the Swing class JFrame. Among other things, this gives SFrame a title property.

2. The class SFrame is runnable. The run method included in this class is the start of the application.

3. The class SFrame is an ActionListener.

4. The class SFrame includes three properties: MetalButton, MotifButton, and WindowsButton. These properties are of type JRadioButton.

The MDSAX Simple example is executed by the following command line:

```
java com.jxml.mdsax.MDMain -r file:appContext.xml file:a.xml
```

This command uses the MDMain class to convert file a.xml into a structure of objects, as specified by file appContext.xml. The -r switch on this command tells MDMain to call the run method on the root object in the structure that was created.

The a.xml file is the document that describes how various objects are to be initialized and assembled. (See Example 10.5, below.)

Example 10.5: Simple application document a.xml.

```
<sFrame
 title="Simple"
 ID="frame1"
 metalButton="MetalButton"
 motifButton="MotifButton"
 windowsButton="WindowsButton">
```

```
<panel constraints="Center">
 <button text="Hello, world">
  <buttonProperties mnemonic="h"/>
 </button>
 <buttonGroup ID="bg1"/>
 <radioButton
  text="Metal"
  ID="MetalButton"
  actionCommand=
     "javax.swing.plaf.metal.MetalLookAndFeel">

  <buttonProperties buttonGroup="bg1" mnemonic="m"/>
  <action eventDestination="frame1"/>
 </radioButton>
 <radioButton
  text="Motif"
  ID="MotifButton"
  actionCommand=
     "com.sun.java.swing.plaf.motif.MotifLookAndFeel">

  <buttonProperties buttonGroup="bg1" mnemonic="o"/>
  <action eventDestination="frame1"/>
 </radioButton>
 <radioButton
  text="Windows"
  ID="WindowsButton"
  actionCommand=
     "com.sun.java.swing.plaf.windows.WindowsLookAndFeel">

  <buttonProperties buttonGroup="bg1" mnemonic="w"/>
  <action eventDestination="frame1"/>
 </radioButton>
 </panel>
</sFrame>
```

Just as in the Declarative Programming Model example, notice how easily we can associate behavior with elements. However, in contrast to the DPG Memory example, this document defines the association at the element level instead of at the document level.

The elements in this document have two different uses. Some of the elements are transformed into objects, as shown in Table 10–13. The other two elements, `buttonProperties` and `action`, are used to configure the object associated with the element's parent. The `buttonProperties` element sets the mnemonic of the parent button and ties that parent button to a button group. The `action` ele-

Table 10–13 XML Swing elements.

XML Element Type	Java Class
sFrame	com.jxml.mdsax.beans.examples.simple.Sframe
panel	javax.swing.Jpanel
button	javax.swing.JButton
buttonGroup	javax.swing.ButtonGroup
radioButton	javax.swing.JRadioButton

ment is used to register the object associated with its parent element. The parent object must be a source of action events and is registered with an action listener.

To transform a.xml into a set of Swing objects, we use appContext.xml, which is an instance of ContextML.

```
<context>
```

■ *For ContextML,* context *must be the root element. It is transformed into a context filter, which provides a common operating environment for the filters that it holds.*

```
<element/>
```

■ *An* element *(or* cElement*) is always required to create entries in the element stack.*

```
<attList>
```

■ *This* attList *will be applied to all the elements of the document to be processed (i.e.* a.xml *in Example 10.5). This* attList *declares an* ID *attribute for all types of elements.*

```
    <att name="ID" type="id" status="#IMPLIED"/>
  </attList>

  <elementRouter>
```

■ *The remainder of this document deals with individual element types. And since no default has been defined for* elementRouter *(via a key attribute with a value of ""), any element type found in the document being processed which does not match one of the keys provided will cause an exception to be thrown.*

```
  <stack key="buttonGroup">
```

■ *Maps* buttonGroup *elements onto the class* javax.swing.ButtonGroup.

```
    <xs resultClass="javax.swing.ButtonGroup"/>
  </stack>

  <stack key="button">
```

■ *Maps* button *elements into the class* javax.swing.Jbutton. *Then adds the button to the component created by the* parent *element.*

```
    <xs resultClass="javax.swing.JButton"/>
  </stack>

  <stack key="radioButton">
```

■ *Maps* radioButton *elements into the class* javax.swing.JradioButton. *Then adds the button to the component created by the* parent *element.*

```
    <xs resultClass="javax.swing.JRadioButton"/>
  </stack>

  <stack key="panel">
```

■ *Maps* panel *elements into the class* javax.swing.JPanel. *Then adds the panel to the component created by the* parent *element.*

```
<xs resultClass="javax.swing.JPanel"/>
</stack>

<stack key="sFrame">
```

■ *Maps* sFrame *elements into the class* com.jxml.mdsax.beans.examples.
simple.SFrame. *Also, declares attributes* metalButton, motifButton, *and*
windowsButton *as required* IDREFS.

```
<attList>
  <att
    name="metalButton"
    type="idref"
    status="#REQUIRED"/>
  <att
    name="motifButton"
    type="idref"
    status="#REQUIRED"/>
  <att
    name="windowsButton"
    type="idref"
    status="#REQUIRED"/>
</attList>
<xs resultClass=
  "com.jxml.mdsax.beans.examples.simple.SFrame"/>
</stack>
<stack key="buttonProperties">
```

■ *Maps* buttonProperties *elements into the class* com.jxml.mdsax.beans.
MDButtonProperties. *Also, declares the attribute* buttonGroup *as an* IDREF
and declares attribute mnemonic as well.

```
<attList>
  <att
    name="buttonGroup"
    type="idref"
    status="#IMPLIED"/>
  <att name="mnemonic" status="#IMPLIED"/>
</attList>
<xs resultClass=
  "com.jxml.mdsax.beans.MDButtonProperties"/>
```

```
</stack>
<stack key="action">
```

■ *Declares element* action *as a connector for registering an* ActionListener *with an* AbstractButton.

```
  <xel listenerClass=
    "java.awt.event.ActionListener"
    eventSourceClass="javax.swing.AbstractButton"/>
  </stack>
 </elementRouter>
</context>
```

Note In this example, ContextML was used to define a transformation, but a.xml, was written using application-specific markup. This can be done rather simply as long as the structure of the application objects being produced roughly corresponds to the structure of the document being processed.

10.3.9 *Security Benefits*

Using MDSAX to transform an XML document into a composition of objects is extremely safe—much safer than the instantiation of a serialized JavaBean, as well as being faster. This is because an XML document can be validated and because the mapping from XML element types to Java classes is controlled entirely by a separate ContextML document.

The inherent security of this kind of processing holds enormous potential for the movement of object compositions across the Internet as it gives the receiver complete control. Greater flexibility can be achieved using serialized JavaBeans, but only at the cost of "sandboxing"—a notoriously slow process that is not suitable for Web servers.

10.4 | Summary

We started with a look at filters, which sit between a SAX parser and an application, and the three kinds of things a filter can do: document transformation, document validation, and information extraction. We then looked at how the *inheritance* filter, written by John Cowan, can be used to transform XML documents to support inheritable attributes.

Following that, we turned our attention to MDSAX—a framework for building structures of filters with a shared context. We saw that there were five more things a filter in MDSAX could do: manage a sequence of filters, route events between filters, maintain a common context, instantiate objects, and configure objects built by other filters. These additional capabilities give MDSAX the ability to transform documents into application-specific structures.

Additionally, we looked at some of the basic filters used by MDSAX, its bootstrap process, and ContextML, which together allow us to write an XML document that governs the transformation of application documents into application-specific structures.

Finally, we saw how to run MDSAX as an application in an example that re-implements the `Swing Simple` example from the JDK. We also saw some of the security benefits of passing documents instead of program logic.

The result of using MDSAX for application processing is a lightweight mechanism for dynamically binding functional behavior together using MDSAX. It allows us to link filters together serially at runtime to produce a variety of results using the same processing logic. Additionally, it provides a framework for routing and processing events produced by an XML parser. And, it allows us to extend existing application functionality in a simple and easily configurable manner.

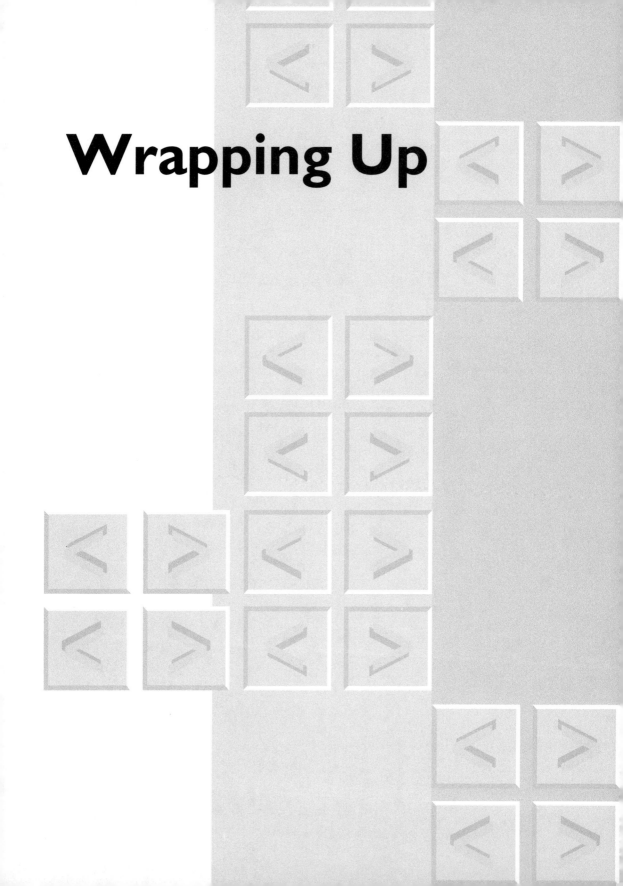

Wrapping Up

I n this part, we introduced two programming models for EAI. The DPM presented a shared declarative environment for the aggregation of data using XML. Using this model, you can develop a set of runtime engines that do not need to change whenever there is a change in a business process. This enables you to build solutions faster that require less testing. This model also allows you to modify the behavior for processing a particular document without affecting other documents that will be processed by the same engine.

MDSAX extends the SAX programming model by using an XML document to configure the runtime processing environment, and thereby creates a dynamic runtime engine. Additionally, MDSAX allows you to manipulate the document at an element level, where DPM only operates over complete documents.

Both of these models are helpful in building more maintainable and flexible EAI solutions. The DPM focuses on the needs of dynamic data aggregation for the purposes of sharing with multiple applications, while MDSAX focuses on transformation of XML data into application-specific structures. Of course, these models can be combined to facilitate the transformation of the dynamically aggregated data for native use by applications.

Now that you have reached the end of this book, I hope you have a better understanding of the Enterprise Application Integration problem and how XML and Java can assist you in building solutions for it. This chapter will provide a brief synopsis of the key points made throughout the book.

- EAI is about creating a seamless interaction between business systems. In order for this to occur, we need to have consistent definitions of business and system entities.

- The EAI problem has been created by people and systems not adhering to a single definition of business and system entities throughout their organization. Through their lack of adherence, they have broken the definition, thus causing a breach that needs to be bridged. EAI solutions provide this bridge.

- For integration across organizations, it is highly unlikely that there will be a consistent definition of business and system entities and, therefore, the EAI solutions will be needed to bridge this gap.

- Declarative environments provide the best solutions for EAI, since they allow local definitions of business and system entities to change, while leaving their global meanings unchanged.

- Most EAI solutions are designed to allow two disparate systems to share or exchange data.

- XML and Java are a powerful combination for building EAI solutions. Java offers late-binding, object-oriented programming, and a homogeneous platform. XML provides us with a consistent data format that allows us to store structured and unstructured data.

- To use XML documents, we must first parse them to identify if they are well-formed and possibly valid.

- We can use the Simple API for XML (SAX) to build applications to process XML that require low memory footprints and only allow one part of the XML document to be seen at a time. SAX also allows our applications to use XML parsers as software components.

- The W3C Document Object Model (DOM) supports another method of processing XML documents. This one has high memory requirements, but allows the application to examine the entire document at once.

- Using XML with Enterprise Java APIs allows us to use rigid, procedural interfaces to exchange and share structured and unstructured data.

- The Java Reflection API is very useful for allowing us to transform internal Java application structures into XML documents for use in sharing with non-Java applications.

- The Java Database Connectivity (JDBC) API allows us access relational databases in a generic manner from Java applications. It also allows us to treat common database BLOB data as rich XML documents.

- The Java Messaging Service (JMS) allows us to exchange XML documents with Java and non-Java applications. It also allows us to treat XML as a native Java object.

- The Java Naming and Directory Interface (JNDI) is very important for providing access to our applications and data in a transparent manner. This transparency is very important for long-term maintenance of EAI solutions. We can also use XML documents to provide information to JNDI, thus allowing us to use XML as a source of directory and naming metadata.

Appendix A
REC-xml-19980210

Extensible Markup Language (XML) 1.0

W3C Recommendation 10-February-1998

This version:

> http://www.w3.org/TR/1998/REC-xml-19980210
> http://www.w3.org/TR/1998/REC-xml-19980210.xml
> http://www.w3.org/TR/1998/REC-xml-19980210.html
> http://www.w3.org/TR/1998/REC-xml-19980210.pdf
> http://www.w3.org/TR/1998/REC-xml-19980210.ps

Latest version:

> http://www.w3.org/TR/REC-xml

Previous version:

> http://www.w3.org/TR/PR-xml-971208

Editors:

Tim Bray (Textuality and Netscape)
Jean Paoli (Microsoft) <jeanpa@microsoft.com>
C. M. Sperberg-McQueen (University of Illinois at Chicago)

Abstract

The Extensible Markup Language (XML) is a subset of SGML that is completely described in this document. Its goal is to enable generic SGML to be served, received, and processed on the Web in the way that is now possible with HTML. XML has been designed for ease of implementation and for interoperability with both SGML and HTML.

Status of this document

This document has been reviewed by W3C Members and other interested parties and has been endorsed by the Director as a W3C Recommendation. It is a stable document and may be used as reference material or cited as a normative reference from another document. W3C's role in making the Recommendation is to draw attention to the specification and to promote its widespread deployment. This enhances the functionality and interoperability of the Web.

This document specifies a syntax created by subsetting an existing, widely used international text processing standard (Standard Generalized Markup Language, ISO 8879:1986(E) as amended and corrected) for use on the World Wide Web. It is a product of the W3C XML Activity, details of which can be found at http://www.w3.org/XML. A list of current W3C Recommendations and other technical documents can be found at http://www.w3.org/TR.

This specification uses the term URI, which is defined by [Berners-Lee et al.], a work in progress expected to update [IETF RFC1738] and [IETF RFC1808].

The list of known errors in this specification is available at http://www.w3.org/XML/xml-19980210-errata.

Please report errors in this document to xml-editor@w3.org.

Extensible Markup Language (XML) 1.0

Table of Contents

Appendices

1. *Introduction*

Extensible Markup Language, abbreviated XML, describes a class of data objects called XML documents and partially describes the behavior of computer programs which process them. XML is an application profile or restricted form of SGML, the Standard Generalized Markup Language [ISO 8879]. By construction, XML documents are conforming SGML documents.

XML documents are made up of storage units called entities, which contain either parsed or unparsed data. Parsed data is made up of characters, some of which form character data, and some of which form markup. Markup encodes a description of the document's storage layout and logical structure. XML provides a mechanism to impose constraints on the storage layout and logical structure.

A software module called an **XML processor** is used to read XML documents and provide access to their content and structure. It is assumed that an XML processor is doing its work on behalf of another module, called the **application**. This specification describes the required behavior of an XML processor in terms of how it must read XML data and the information it must provide to the application.

1.1 Origin and Goals

XML was developed by an XML Working Group (originally known as the SGML Editorial Review Board) formed under the auspices of the World Wide Web Consortium (W3C) in 1996. It was chaired by Jon Bosak of Sun Microsystems with the active participation of an XML Special Interest Group (previously known as the SGML Working Group) also organized by the W3C. The membership of the XML Working Group is given in an appendix. Dan Connolly served as the WG's contact with the W3C.

The design goals for XML are:

1. XML shall be straightforwardly usable over the Internet.

2. XML shall support a wide variety of applications.

3. XML shall be compatible with SGML.

4. It shall be easy to write programs which process XML documents.

5. The number of optional features in XML is to be kept to the absolute minimum, ideally zero.

6. XML documents should be human-legible and reasonably clear.

7. The XML design should be prepared quickly.

8. The design of XML shall be formal and concise.

9. XML documents shall be easy to create.

10. Terseness in XML markup is of minimal importance.

This specification, together with associated standards (Unicode and ISO/IEC 10646 for characters, Internet RFC 1766 for language identification tags, ISO 639 for language name codes, and ISO 3166 for country name codes), provides all the information necessary to understand XML Version 1.0 and construct computer programs to process it.

This version of the XML specification may be distributed freely, as long as all text and legal notices remain intact.

1.2   Terminology

The terminology used to describe XML documents is defined in the body of this specification. The terms defined in the following list are used in building those definitions and in describing the actions of an XML processor:

may

Conforming documents and XML processors are permitted to but need not behave as described.

must

> Conforming documents and XML processors are required to behave as described; otherwise they are in error.

error

> A violation of the rules of this specification; results are undefined. Conforming software may detect and report an error and may recover from it.

fatal error

> An error which a conforming XML processor must detect and report to the application. After encountering a fatal error, the processor may continue processing the data to search for further errors and may report such errors to the application. In order to support correction of errors, the processor may make unprocessed data from the document (with intermingled character data and markup) available to the application. Once a fatal error is detected, however, the processor must not continue normal processing (i.e., it must not continue to pass character data and information about the document's logical structure to the application in the normal way).

at user option

> Conforming software may or must (depending on the modal verb in the sentence) behave as described; if it does, it must provide users a means to enable or disable the behavior described.

validity constraint

> A rule which applies to all valid XML documents. Violations of validity constraints are errors; they must, at user option, be reported by validating XML processors.

well-formedness constraint

> A rule which applies to all well-formed XML documents. Violations of well-formedness constraints are fatal errors.

match

> (Of strings or names:) Two strings or names being compared must be identical. Characters with multiple possible representations in ISO/IEC 10646 (e.g. characters with both precomposed and base+diacritic forms) match only if they have the same representation in both strings. At user option, processors may normalize such characters to some canonical form. No case folding is performed. (Of strings and rules in the grammar:) A string matches a grammatical production if it belongs to the language generated by that production. (Of content and content models:) An element matches its declaration when it conforms in the fashion described in the constraint "Element Valid".

for compatibility

> A feature of XML included solely to ensure that XML remains compatible with SGML.

for interoperability

> A non-binding recommendation included to increase the chances that XML documents can be processed by the existing installed base of SGML processors which predate the WebSGML Adaptations Annex to ISO 8879.

2. *Documents*

A data object is an **XML document** if it is well-formed, as defined in this specification. A well-formed XML document may in addition be valid if it meets certain further constraints.

Each XML document has both a logical and a physical structure. Physically, the document is composed of units called entities. An entity may refer to other entities to cause their inclusion in the document. A document begins in a "root" or document entity. Logically, the document is composed of declarations, elements, comments, character references, and processing instructions, all of which are indicated in the document by explicit markup. The logical and physical structures must nest properly, as described in "4.3.2 Well-Formed Parsed Entities".

2.1 Well-Formed XML Documents

A textual object is a well-formed XML document if:
Taken as a whole, it matches the production labeled document.
It meets all the well-formedness constraints given in this specification.

Each of the parsed entities which is referenced directly or indirectly within the document is well-formed.

Document

```
[1]  document  ::=  prolog element Misc*
```

Matching the document production implies that:

1. It contains one or more elements.

2. There is exactly one element, called the **root**, or document element, no part of which appears in the content of any other element. For all other elements, if the start-tag is in the content of another element, the end-tag is in the content of the same element. More simply stated, the elements, delimited by start- and end-tags, nest properly within each other.

As a consequence of this, for each non-root element C in the document, there is one other element P in the document such that C is in the content of P, but is not in the content of any other element that is in the content of P. P is referred to as the **parent** of C, and C as a **child** of P.

2.2   Characters

A parsed entity contains **text**, a sequence of characters, which may represent markup or character data. A **character** is an atomic unit of text as specified by ISO/IEC 10646 [ISO/IEC 10646]. Legal characters are tab, carriage return, line feed, and the legal graphic characters of Unicode and ISO/IEC 10646. The use of "compatibility characters", as defined in section 6.8 of [Unicode], is discouraged.

Character Range

```
[2]   Char   ::=    #x9 | #xA | #xD | [#x20-   /*  any Unicode char-
                    #xD7FF] | [#xE000-#xFFFD]      acter, excluding
                    | [#x10000-#x10FFFF]           the surrogate
                                                   blocks, FFFE, and
                                                   FFFF. */
```

The mechanism for encoding character code points into bit patterns may vary from entity to entity. All XML processors must accept the UTF-8 and UTF-16 encodings of 10646; the mechanisms for signaling which of the two is in use, or for bringing other encodings into play, are discussed later, in "4.3.3 Character Encoding in Entities".

2.3   Common Syntactic Constructs

This section defines some symbols used widely in the grammar.

S (white space) consists of one or more space (#x20) characters, carriage returns, line feeds, or tabs.

White Space

```
[3]   S   ::=   (#x20 | #x9 | #xD | #xA)+
```

Characters are classified for convenience as letters, digits, or other characters. Letters consist of an alphabetic or syllabic base character possibly followed by one or more combining characters, or of an ideographic character. Full definitions of the specific characters in each class are given in "B. Character Classes".

A **Name** is a token beginning with a letter or one of a few punctuation characters, and continuing with letters, digits, hyphens, underscores, colons, or full stops, together known as name characters. Names beginning with the string "xml", or any string which would match ((('X'|'x') ('M'|'m') ('L'|'l'))), are reserved for standardization in this or future versions of this specification.

Note: The colon character within XML names is reserved for experimentation with name spaces. Its meaning is expected to be standardized at some future point, at which point those documents using the colon for experimental purposes may need to be updated. (There is no guarantee that any name-space mechanism adopted for XML will in fact use the colon as a name-space delimiter.) In practice, this means that authors should not use the colon in XML names except as part of name-space experiments, but that XML processors should accept the colon as a name character.

An Nmtoken (name token) is any mixture of name characters.

Names and Tokens

```
[4]  NameChar  ::=  Letter | Digit | '.' | '-' | '_' | ':' |
                    CombiningChar | Extender

[5]  Name      ::=  (Letter | '_' | ':') (NameChar)*

[6]  Names     ::=  Name (S Name)*

[7]  Nmtoken   ::=  (NameChar)+

[8]  Nmtokens  ::=  Nmtoken (S Nmtoken)*
```

Literal data is any quoted string not containing the quotation mark used as a delimiter for that string. Literals are used for specifying the content of internal entities (EntityValue), the values of attributes (AttValue), and external identifiers (SystemLiteral). Note that a SystemLiteral can be parsed without scanning for markup.

Literals

```
[9]   EntityValue    ::=  '"' ([^%&"] | PEReference |
                          Reference)* '"'

                     |   "'" ([^%&'] | PEReference |
                          Reference)* "'"

[10]  AttValue       ::=  '"' ([^<&"] | Reference)* '"'

                     |   "'" ([^<&'] | Reference)* "'"

[11]  SystemLiteral  ::=  ('"' [^"]* '"') | ("'" [^']* "'")

[12]  PubidLiteral   ::=  '"' PubidChar* '"' | "'" (PubidChar -
                          "'")* "'"

[13]  PubidChar      ::=  #x20 | #xD | #xA | [a-zA-Z0-9] |
                          [-'()+,./:=?;!*#@$_%]
```

2.4   Character Data and Markup

Text consists of intermingled character data and markup. **Markup** takes the form of start-tags, end-tags, empty-element tags, entity references, character references, comments, CDATA section delimiters, document type declarations, and processing instructions.

All text that is not markup constitutes the **character data** of the document.

The ampersand character (&) and the left angle bracket (<) may appear in their literal form *only* when used as markup delimiters, or within a comment, a processing instruction, or a CDATA section. They are also legal within the literal entity value of an internal entity declaration; see "4.3.2 Well-Formed Parsed Entities". If they are needed elsewhere, they must be escaped using either numeric character references or the strings "&" and "<" respectively. The right angle bracket (>) may be represented using the string ">", and must, for compatibility, be escaped using ">" or a character reference when it appears in the string "]]>" in content, when that string is not marking the end of a CDATA section.

In the content of elements, character data is any string of characters which does not contain the start-delimiter of any markup. In a CDATA section, character data is any string of characters not including the CDATA-section-close delimiter, "]]>".

To allow attribute values to contain both single and double quotes, the apostrophe or single-quote character (') may be represented as "'", and the double-quote character (") as """.

Character Data

[14] `CharData  ::=  [^<&]* - ([^<&]* ']]>' [^<&]*)`

2.5   Comments

Comments may appear anywhere in a document outside other markup; in addition, they may appear within the document type declaration at places allowed by the grammar. They are not part of the document's character data; an XML processor may, but need not, make it possible for an application to retrieve the text of comments. For compatibility, the string "--" (double-hyphen) must not occur within comments.

Comments

[15] `Comment  ::=  '<!--' ((Char - '-') | ('-' (Char - '-')))*`
                    `'-->'`

An example of a comment:

```
<!-- declarations for <head> & <body> -->
```

2.6   Processing Instructions

Processing instructions (PIs) allow documents to contain instructions for applications.

Processing Instructions

```
[16]  PI         ::=  '<?' PITarget (S (Char* - (Char* '?>'
                      Char*)))? '?>'
[17]  PITarget   ::=  Name - (('X' | 'x') ('M' | 'm') ('L' | 'l'))
```

PIs are not part of the document's character data, but must be passed through to the application. The PI begins with a target (`PITarget`) used to identify the application to which the instruction is directed. The target names "`XML`", "`xml`", and so on are reserved for standardization in this or future versions of this specification. The XML Notation mechanism may be used for formal declaration of PI targets.

2.7 CDATA Sections

CDATA sections may occur anywhere character data may occur; they are used to escape blocks of text containing characters which would otherwise be recognized as markup. CDATA sections begin with the string "`<![CDATA[`" and end with the string "`]]>`":

CDATA Sections

```
[18]  CDSect   ::=  CDStart CData CDEnd
[19]  CDStart  ::=  '<![CDATA['
[20]  CData    ::=  (Char* - (Char* ']]>' Char*))
[21]  CDEnd    ::=  ']]>'
```

Within a CDATA section, only the `CDEnd` string is recognized as markup, so that left angle brackets and ampersands may occur in their literal form; they need not (and cannot) be escaped using "`&lt;`" and "`&amp;`". CDATA sections cannot nest.

An example of a CDATA section, in which "`<greeting>`" and "`</greeting>`" are recognized as character data, not markup:

```
<![CDATA[<greeting>Hello, world!</greeting>]]>
```

2.8 Prolog and Document Type Declaration

XML documents may, and should, begin with an **XML declaration** which specifies the version of XML being used. For example, the following is a complete XML document, well-formed but not valid:

```
<?xml version="1.0"?>
<greeting>Hello, world!</greeting>
```

and so is this:

```
<greeting>Hello, world!</greeting>
```

The version number "1.0" should be used to indicate conformance to this version of this specification; it is an error for a document to use the value "1.0" if it does not conform to this version of this specification. It is the intent of the XML working group to give later versions of this specification numbers other than "1.0", but this intent does not indicate a commitment to produce any future versions of XML, nor if any are produced, to use any particular numbering scheme. Since future versions are not ruled out, this construct is provided as a means to allow the possibility of automatic version recognition, should it become necessary. Processors may signal an error if they receive documents labeled with versions they do not support.

The function of the markup in an XML document is to describe its storage and logical structure and to associate attribute-value pairs with its logical structures. XML provides a mechanism, the document type declaration, to define constraints on the logical structure and to support the use of predefined storage units. An XML document is **valid** if it has an associated document type declaration and if the document complies with the constraints expressed in it.

The document type declaration must appear before the first element in the document.

Prolog

[22]	prolog	::=	XMLDecl? Misc* (doctypedecl Misc*)?
[23]	XMLDecl	::=	'<?xml' VersionInfo EncodingDecl? SDDecl? S? '?>'
[24]	VersionInfo	::=	S 'version' Eq (' VersionNum ' | " VersionNum ")
[25]	Eq	::=	S? '=' S?
[26]	VersionNum	::=	([a-zA-Z0-9_.:] | '-')+
[27]	Misc	::=	Comment | PI | S

The XML **document type declaration** contains or points to markup declarations that provide a grammar for a class of documents. This grammar is known as a document type definition, or **DTD**. The document type declaration can point to an external subset (a special kind of external entity) containing markup declarations, or can contain the markup declarations directly in an internal subset, or can do both. The DTD for a document consists of both subsets taken together.

A **markup declaration** is an element type declaration, an attribute-list declaration, an entity declaration, or a notation declaration. These declarations may be contained in whole or in part within parameter entities, as described in the well-formedness and validity constraints below. For fuller information, see "4. Physical Structures".

Document Type Definition

[28]	doctypedecl	::=	'<!DOCTYPE' S Name (S ExternalID)? S? ('[(markupdecl | PEReference | S)* ']' S?)? '>'	[VC: Root Element Type]
[29]	markupdecl	::=	elementdecl | AttlistDecl | EntityDecl | NotationDecl | PI | Comment [	VC: Proper Declaration/ PE Nesting]
				WFC: PEs in Internal Subset]

The markup declarations may be made up in whole or in part of the replacement text of parameter entities. The productions later in this specification for individual nonterminals (`elementdecl`, `AttlistDecl`, and so on) describe the declarations *after* all the parameter entities have been included.

Validity Constraint: Root Element Type

The `Name` in the document type declaration must match the element type of the root element.

Validity Constraint: Proper Declaration/PE Nesting

Parameter-entity replacement text must be properly nested with markup declarations. That is to say, if either the first character or the last character of a markup declaration (`markupdecl` above) is contained in the replacement text for a parameter-entity reference, both must be contained in the same replacement text.

Well-Formedness Constraint: PEs in Internal Subset

In the internal DTD subset, parameter-entity references can occur only where markup declarations can occur, not within markup declarations. (This does not apply to references that occur in external parameter entities or to the external subset.)

Like the internal subset, the external subset and any external parameter entities referred to in the DTD must consist of a series of complete markup declarations of the types allowed by the non-terminal symbol `markupdecl`, interspersed with white space or parameter-entity references. However, portions of the contents of the external subset or of external parameter entities may conditionally be ignored by using the conditional section construct; this is not allowed in the internal subset.

External Subset

```
[30]  extSubset      ::=  TextDecl? extSubsetDecl
[31]  extSubsetDecl  ::=  ( markupdecl | conditionalSect |
                           PEReference | S )*
```

The external subset and external parameter entities also differ from the internal subset in that in them, parameter-entity references are permitted *within* markup declarations, not only *between* markup declarations.

An example of an XML document with a document type declaration:

```
<?xml version="1.0"?>
<!DOCTYPE greeting SYSTEM "hello.dtd">
<greeting>Hello, world!</greeting>
```

The system identifier "hello.dtd" gives the URI of a DTD for the document.

The declarations can also be given locally, as in this example:

```
<?xml version="1.0" encoding="UTF-8" ?>
<!DOCTYPE greeting [
  <!ELEMENT greeting (#PCDATA)>
]>
<greeting>Hello, world!</greeting>
```

If both the external and internal subsets are used, the internal subset is considered to occur before the external subset. This has the effect that entity and attribute-list declarations in the internal subset take precedence over those in the external subset.

2.9   Standalone Document Declaration

Markup declarations can affect the content of the document, as passed from an XML processor to an application; examples are attribute defaults and entity declarations. The standalone document declaration, which may appear as a component of the XML declaration, signals whether or not there are such declarations which appear external to the document entity.

Standalone Document Declaration

```
[32]  SDDecl  ::=  S 'standalone' Eq (("'"       [ VC: Standalone
                   ('yes' | 'no') "'") | ('"'     Document
                   ('yes' | 'no') '"'))           Declaration ]
```

In a standalone document declaration, the value "yes" indicates that there are no markup declarations external to the document entity (either in the DTD external subset, or in an external parameter entity referenced from the internal subset) which affect the information passed from the XML processor to the application. The value "no" indicates that there are or may be such external markup declarations. Note that the standalone document declaration only denotes the presence of external *declarations*; the presence, in a document, of references to external *entities*, when those entities are internally declared, does not change its standalone status.

If there are no external markup declarations, the standalone document declaration has no meaning. If there are external markup declarations but there is no standalone document declaration, the value "no" is assumed.

Any XML document for which standalone="no" holds can be converted algorithmically to a standalone document, which may be desirable for some network delivery applications.

Validity Constraint: Standalone Document Declaration

The standalone document declaration must have the value "no" if any external markup declarations contain declarations of:

- attributes with default values, if elements to which these attributes apply appear in the document without specifications of values for these attributes, or

- entities (other than amp, lt, gt, apos, quot), if references to those entities appear in the document, or

- attributes with values subject to normalization, where the attribute appears in the document with a value which will change as a result of normalization, or

- element types with element content, if white space occurs directly within any instance of those types.

An example XML declaration with a standalone document declaration:

```
<?xml version="1.0" standalone='yes'?>
```

2.10   White Space Handling

In editing XML documents, it is often convenient to use "white space" (spaces, tabs, and blank lines, denoted by the nonterminal S in this specification) to set apart the markup for greater readability. Such white space is typically not intended for inclusion in the delivered version of the document. On the other hand, "significant" white space that should be preserved in the delivered version is common, for example in poetry and source code.

An XML processor must always pass all characters in a document that are not markup through to the application. A validating XML processor must also inform the application which of these characters constitute white space appearing in element content.

A special attribute named xml:space may be attached to an element to signal an intention that in that element, white space should be preserved by applications. In valid documents, this attribute, like any other, must be declared if it is used. When declared, it must be given as an enumerated type whose only possible values are "default" and "preserve". For example:

```
<!ATTLIST  poem xml:space (default|preserve)
'preserve'>
```

The value "default" signals that applications' default white-space processing modes are acceptable for this element; the value "preserve" indicates the intent that applications preserve all the white space. This declared intent is considered to apply to all elements within the content of the element where it is specified, unless overriden with another instance of the xml:space attribute.

The root element of any document is considered to have signaled no intentions as regards application space handling, unless it provides a value for this attribute or the attribute is declared with a default value.

2.11 End-of-Line Handling

XML parsed entities are often stored in computer files which, for editing convenience, are organized into lines. These lines are typically separated by some combination of the characters carriage-return (#xD) and line-feed (#xA).

To simplify the tasks of applications, wherever an external parsed entity or the literal entity value of an internal parsed entity contains either the literal two-character sequence "#xD#xA" or a standalone literal #xD, an XML processor must pass to the application the single character #xA. (This behavior can conveniently be produced by normalizing all line breaks to #xA on input, before parsing.)

2.12 Language Identification

In document processing, it is often useful to identify the natural or formal language in which the content is written. A special attribute named xml:lang may be inserted in documents to specify the language used in the contents and attribute values of any element in an XML document. In valid documents, this attribute, like any other, must be declared if it is used. The values of the attribute are language identifiers as defined by [IETF RFC 1766], "Tags for the Identification of Languages":

Language Identification

```
[33]  LanguageID   ::=   Langcode ('-' Subcode)*
[34]  Langcode     ::=   ISO639Code | IanaCode | UserCode
[35]  ISO639Code   ::=   ([a-z] | [A-Z]) ([a-z] | [A-Z])
[36]  IanaCode     ::=   ('i' | 'I') '-' ([a-z] | [A-Z])+
[37]  UserCode     ::=   ('x' | 'X') '-' ([a-z] | [A-Z])+
[38]  Subcode      ::=   ([a-z] | [A-Z])+
```

The Langcode may be any of the following:

- a two-letter language code as defined by [ISO 639], "Codes for the representation of names of languages"

- a language identifier registered with the Internet Assigned Numbers Authority [IANA]; these begin with the prefix "i-" (or "I-")

- a language identifier assigned by the user, or agreed on between parties in private use; these must begin with the prefix "x-" or "X-" in order to ensure that they do not conflict with names later standardized or registered with IANA

There may be any number of Subcode segments; if the first subcode segment exists and the Subcode consists of two letters, then it must be a country code from [ISO 3166], "Codes for the representation of names of countries." If the first subcode consists of more than two letters, it must be a subcode for the language in question registered with IANA, unless the Langcode begins with the prefix "x-" or "X-".

It is customary to give the language code in lower case, and the country code (if any) in upper case. Note that these values, unlike other names in XML documents, are case insensitive.

For example:

```
<p xml:lang="en">The quick brown fox jumps over
the lazy dog.</p>
<p xml:lang="en-GB">What colour is it?</p>
<p xml:lang="en-US">What color is it?</p>
<sp who="Faust" desc='leise' xml:lang="de">
  <l>Habe nun, ach! Philosophie,</l>
  <l>Juristerei, und Medizin</l>
  <l>und leider auch Theologie</l>
  <l>durchaus studiert mit heißem Bemüh'n.</l>
</sp>
```

The intent declared with xml:lang is considered to apply to all attributes and content of the element where it is specified, unless overridden with an instance of xml:lang on another element within that content.

A simple declaration for xml:lang might take the form

```
xml:lang   NMTOKEN   #IMPLIED
```

but specific default values may also be given, if appropriate. In a collection of French poems for English students, with glosses and notes in English, the xml:lang attribute might be declared this way:

```
<!ATTLIST poem    xml:lang NMTOKEN 'fr'>
<!ATTLIST gloss   xml:lang NMTOKEN 'en'>
<!ATTLIST note    xml:lang NMTOKEN 'en'>
```

3. *Logical Structures*

Each XML document contains one or more **elements**, the boundaries of which are either delimited by start-tags and end-tags, or, for empty elements, by an empty-element tag. Each element has a type, identified by name, sometimes called its "generic identifier" (GI), and may have a set of attribute specifications. Each attribute specification has a name and a value.

Element

```
[39]  element  ::=  EmptyElemTag

                  | STag content ETag  [ WFC: Element Type
                                         Match ]

                                       [ VC: Element Valid ]
```

This specification does not constrain the semantics, use, or (beyond syntax) names of the element types and attributes, except that names beginning with a match to `(('X'|'x')('M'|'m')('L'|'l'))` are reserved for standardization in this or future versions of this specification.

Well-Formedness Constraint: Element Type Match

The Name in an element's end-tag must match the element type in the start-tag.

Validity Constraint: Element Valid

An element is valid if there is a declaration matching element-decl where the Name matches the element type, and one of the following holds:

1. The declaration matches EMPTY and the element has no content.

2. The declaration matches children and the sequence of child elements belongs to the language generated by the regular expression in the content model, with optional white space (characters matching the nonterminal S) between each pair of child elements.

3. The declaration matches Mixed and the content consists of character data and child elements whose types match names in the content model.

4. The declaration matches ANY, and the types of any child elements have been declared.

3.1 Start-Tags, End-Tags, and Empty-Element Tags

The beginning of every non-empty XML element is marked by a **start-tag**.

Start-tag

```
[40]  STag      ::=  '<' Name (S Attribute)*    [ WFC: Unique Att
                     S? '>'                       Spec ]

[41]  Attribute ::=  Name Eq AttValue           [ VC: Attribute
                                                   Value Type ]

                                                [ WFC: No External
                                                   Entity
                                                   References ]

                                                [ WFC: No < in At-
                                                   tribute Values ]
```

The `Name` in the start- and end-tags gives the element's **type**. The `Name-AttValue` pairs are referred to as the **attribute specifications** of the element, with the `Name` in each pair referred to as the **attribute name** and the content of the `AttValue` (the text between the ' or " delimiters) as the **attribute value**.

Well-Formedness Constraint: Unique Att Spec
No attribute name may appear more than once in the same start-tag or empty-element tag.

Validity Constraint: Attribute Value Type
The attribute must have been declared; the value must be of the type declared for it. (For attribute types, see "3.3 Attribute-List Declarations".)

Well-Formedness Constraint: No External Entity References
Attribute values cannot contain direct or indirect entity references to external entities.

Well-Formedness Constraint: No < in Attribute Values

The replacement text of any entity referred to directly or indirectly in an attribute value (other than "<") must not contain a <.

An example of a start-tag:

```
<termdef id="dt-dog" term="dog">
```

The end of every element that begins with a start-tag must be marked by an **end-tag** containing a name that echoes the element's type as given in the start-tag:

End-tag

[42]   ETag   ::=   '</' Name S? '>'

An example of an end-tag:

```
</termdef>
```

The text between the start-tag and end-tag is called the element's **content**:

Content of Elements

[43]   content   ::=   (element | CharData | Reference | CDSect | PI
                       | Comment)*

If an element is **empty**, it must be represented either by a start-tag immediately followed by an end-tag or by an empty-element tag. An **empty-element tag** takes a special form:

Tags for Empty Elements

[44]   EmptyElemTag   ::=   '<' Name (S Attribute)*   [WFC: Unique
                            S? '/>'   Att Spec]

Empty-element tags may be used for any element which has no content, whether or not it is declared using the keyword EMPTY. For interoperability, the empty-element tag must be used, and can only be used, for elements which are declared EMPTY.

Examples of empty elements:

```
<IMG align="left"
 src="http://www.w3.org/Icons/WWW/w3c_home" />
<br></br>
<br/>
```

3.2 Element Type Declarations

The element structure of an XML document may, for validation purposes, be constrained using element type and attribute-list declarations. An element type declaration constrains the element's content.

Element type declarations often constrain which element types can appear as children of the element. At user option, an XML processor may issue a warning when a declaration mentions an element type for which no declaration is provided, but this is not an error.

An **element type declaration** takes the form:

Element Type Declaration

```
[45]  elementdecl  ::=  '<!ELEMENT' S Name S
                        contentspec S? '>'      [ VC: Unique Ele-
                                                  ment Type Decla-
                                                  ration ]

[46]  contentspec  ::=  'EMPTY' | 'ANY' |
                        Mixed | children
```

---

where the Name gives the element type being declared.

Validity Constraint: Unique Element Type Declaration

No element type may be declared more than once.
Examples of element type declarations:

```
<!ELEMENT br EMPTY>
<!ELEMENT p (#PCDATA|emph)* >
```

```
<!ELEMENT %name.para; %content.para; >
<!ELEMENT container ANY>
```

3.2.1   Element Content

An element type has **element content** when elements of that type must contain only child elements (no character data), optionally separated by white space (characters matching the nonterminal S). In this case, the constraint includes a content model, a simple grammar governing the allowed types of the child elements and the order in which they are allowed to appear. The grammar is built on content particles (cps), which consist of names, choice lists of content particles, or sequence lists of content particles:

Element-content Models

[47]	children	::=	(choice | seq) ('?' | '*' | '+')?
[48]	cp	::=	(Name | choice | seq) ('?' | '*' | '+')?
[49]	choice	::=	'(' S? cp (S? '|' S? cp)* [VC: Proper S? ')' Group/PE Nesting]
[50]	seq	::=	'(' S? cp (S? ',' S? cp)* [VC: Proper S? ')' Group/PE Nesting]

---

where each Name is the type of an element which may appear as a child. Any content particle in a choice list may appear in the element content at the location where the choice list appears in the grammar; content particles occurring in a sequence list must each appear in the element content in the order given in the list. The optional character following a name or list governs whether the element or the content particles in the list may occur one or more (+), zero or more (*), or zero or one times (?). The absence of such an operator means that the element or content particle must appear exactly once. This syntax and meaning are identical to those used in the productions in this specification.

The content of an element matches a content model if and only if it is possible to trace out a path through the content model, obeying the sequence, choice, and repetition operators and matching each element in the content against an element type in the content model. For compatibility, it is an error if an element in the document can match more than one occurrence of an element type in the content model. For more information, see "E. Deterministic Content Models".

Validity Constraint: Proper Group/PE Nesting

Parameter-entity replacement text must be properly nested with parenthetized groups. That is to say, if either of the opening or closing parentheses in a `choice`, `seq`, or `Mixed` construct is contained in the replacement text for a parameter entity, both must be contained in the same replacement text. For interoperability, if a parameter-entity reference appears in a `choice`, `seq`, or `Mixed` construct, its replacement text should not be empty, and neither the first nor last non-blank character of the replacement text should be a connector (| or ,).

Examples of element-content models:

```
<!ELEMENT spec (front, body, back?)>
<!ELEMENT div1 (head, (p | list | note)*, div2*)>
<!ELEMENT dictionary-body (%div.mix; |
%dict.mix;)*>
```

3.2.2   Mixed Content

An element type has **mixed content** when elements of that type may contain character data, optionally interspersed with child elements. In this case, the types of the child elements may be constrained, but not their order or their number of occurrences:

Mixed-content Declaration

```
[51]  Mixed  ::=  '(' S? '#PCDATA' (S? '|' S? Name)* S? ')*'
               | '(' S? '#PCDATA' S? ')'   [ VC: Proper Group/
                                             PE Nesting ]

                                           [ VC: No Duplicate
                                             Types ]
```

---

where the Names give the types of elements that may appear as children.

Validity Constraint: No Duplicate Type

The same name must not appear more than once in a single mixed-content declaration.

Examples of mixed content declarations:

```
<!ELEMENT p (#PCDATA|a|ul|b|i|em)*>
<!ELEMENT p (#PCDATA | %font; | %phrase; |
  %special; | %form;)* >
<!ELEMENT b (#PCDATA)>
```

3.3   Attribute-List Declarations

Attributes are used to associate name-value pairs with elements. Attribute specifications may appear only within start-tags and empty-element tags; thus, the productions used to recognize them appear in "3.1 Start-Tags, End-Tags, and Empty-Element Tags". Attribute-list declarations may be used:

- To define the set of attributes pertaining to a given element type.

- To establish type constraints for these attributes.

- To provide default values for attributes.

Attribute-list declarations specify the name, data type, and default value (if any) of each attribute associated with a given element type:

Attribute-list Declaration

```
[52]  AttlistDecl  ::=  '<!ATTLIST' S Name AttDef* S? '>'
[53]  AttDef       ::=  S Name S AttType S DefaultDecl
```

The Name in the AttlistDecl rule is the type of an element. At user option, an XML processor may issue a warning if attributes are declared for an element type not itself declared, but this is not an error. The `Name` in the `AttDef` rule is the name of the attribute.

When more than one `AttlistDecl` is provided for a given element type, the contents of all those provided are merged. When more than one definition is provided for the same attribute of a given element type, the first declaration is binding and later declarations are ignored. For interoperability, writers of DTDs may choose to provide at most one attribute-list declaration for a given element type, at most one attribute definition for a given attribute name, and at least one attribute definition in each attribute-list declaration. For interoperability, an XML processor may at user option issue a warning when more than one attribute-list declaration is provided for a given element type, or more than one attribute definition is provided for a given attribute, but this is not an error.

3.3.1 Attribute Types

XML attribute types are of three kinds: a string type, a set of tokenized types, and enumerated types. The string type may take any literal string as a value; the tokenized types have varying lexical and semantic constraints, as noted:

Attribute Types

```
[54]  AttType       ::=  StringType | TokenizedType |
                         EnumeratedType

[55]  StringType    ::=  'CDATA'

[56]  TokenizedType ::=  'ID'        [ VC: ID ]

                                     [ VC: One ID per Element
                                     Type ]

                                     [ VC: ID Attribute
                                     Default ]

                       | 'IDREF'     [ VC: IDREF ]

                       | 'IDREFS'    [ VC: IDREF ]

                       | 'ENTITY'    [ VC: Entity Name ]
```

```
|  'ENTITIES'   [ VC: Entity Name ]
|  'NMTOKEN'    [ VC: Name Token ]
|  'NMTOKENS'   [ VC: Name Token ]
```

Validity Constraint: ID

Values of type `ID` must match the `Name` production. A name must not appear more than once in an XML document as a value of this type; i.e., ID values must uniquely identify the elements which bear them.

Validity Constraint: One ID per Element Type

No element type may have more than one ID attribute specified.

Validity Constraint: ID Attribute Default

An ID attribute must have a declared default of `#IMPLIED` or `#RE-QUIRED`.

Validity Constraint: IDREF

Values of type `IDREF` must match the `Name` production, and values of type `IDREFS` must match `Names`; each `Name` must match the value of an ID attribute on some element in the XML document; i.e. `IDREF` values must match the value of some ID attribute.

Validity Constraint: Entity Name

Values of type `ENTITY` must match the `Name` production, values of type `ENTITIES` must match `Names`; each `Name` must match the name of an unparsed entity declared in the DTD.

Validity Constraint: Name Token

Values of type `NMTOKEN` must match the `Nmtoken` production; values of type `NMTOKENS` must match Nmtokens.

Enumerated attributes can take one of a list of values provided in the declaration. There are two kinds of enumerated types:

Enumerated Attribute Types

```
[57]  EnumeratedType   ::=  NotationType | Enumeration
[58]  NotationType     ::=  'NOTATION' S '(' S?
                            Name (S? '|' S? Name)   [ VC: Notation
                            * S? ')'                  Attributes ]
[59]  Enumeration      ::=  '(' S? Nmtoken (S? '|'  [ VC: Enumera-
                            S? Nmtoken)* S? ')'       tion ]
```

A NOTATION attribute identifies a notation, declared in the DTD with associated system and/or public identifiers, to be used in interpreting the element to which the attribute is attached.

Validity Constraint: Notation Attributes

Values of this type must match one of the notation names included in the declaration; all notation names in the declaration must be declared.

Validity Constraint: Enumeration

Values of this type must match one of the Nmtoken tokens in the declaration.

For interoperability, the same Nmtoken should not occur more than once in the enumerated attribute types of a single element type.

3.3.2 Attribute Defaults

An attribute declaration provides information on whether the attribute's presence is required, and if not, how an XML processor should react if a declared attribute is absent in a document.

Attribute Defaults

```
[60]  DefaultDecl  ::=  '#REQUIRED' | '#IMPLIED'
                        | (('#FIXED' S)?  [ VC: Required
                        AttValue)           Attribute ]

                                          [ VC: Attribute Default
                                            Legal ]
```

```
[ WFC: No < in At-
tribute Values ]
[ VC: Fixed Attribute
Default ]
```

In an attribute declaration, #REQUIRED means that the attribute must always be provided, #IMPLIED that no default value is provided. If the declaration is neither #REQUIRED nor #IMPLIED, then the AttValue value contains the declared **default** value; the #FIXED keyword states that the attribute must always have the default value. If a default value is declared, when an XML processor encounters an omitted attribute, it is to behave as though the attribute were present with the declared default value.

Validity Constraint: Required Attribute

If the default declaration is the keyword #REQUIRED, then the attribute must be specified for all elements of the type in the attribute-list declaration.

Validity Constraint: Attribute Default Legal

The declared default value must meet the lexical constraints of the declared attribute type.

Validity Constraint: Fixed Attribute Default

If an attribute has a default value declared with the #FIXED keyword, instances of that attribute must match the default value.

Examples of attribute-list declarations:

```
<!ATTLIST termdef
        id      ID       #REQUIRED
        name    CDATA    #IMPLIED>
<!ATTLIST list
        type    (bullets|ordered|glossary)   "ordered">
<!ATTLIST form
        method  CDATA    #FIXED "POST">
```

3.3.3 Attribute-Value Normalization

Before the value of an attribute is passed to the application or checked for validity, the XML processor must normalize it as follows:

- a character reference is processed by appending the referenced character to the attribute value

- an entity reference is processed by recursively processing the replacement text of the entity

- a whitespace character (#x20, #xD, #xA, #x9) is processed by appending #x20 to the normalized value, except that only a single #x20 is appended for a "#xD#xA" sequence that is part of an external parsed entity or the literal entity value of an internal parsed entity

- other characters are processed by appending them to the normalized value

If the declared value is not CDATA, then the XML processor must further process the normalized attribute value by discarding any leading and trailing space (#x20) characters, and by replacing sequences of space (#x20) characters by a single space (#x20) character.

All attributes for which no declaration has been read should be treated by a non-validating parser as if declared CDATA.

3.4 Conditional Sections

Conditional sections are portions of the document type declaration external subset which are included in, or excluded from, the logical structure of the DTD based on the keyword which governs them.

Conditional Section

```
[61]  conditionalSect      ::=  includeSect | ignoreSect
[62]  includeSect          ::=  '<![' S? 'INCLUDE' S? '['
                                 extSubsetDecl ']]>'
[63]  ignoreSect           ::=  '<![' S? 'IGNORE' S? '['
                                 ignoreSectContents* ']]>'
[64]  ignoreSectContents   ::=  Ignore ('<![' ignoreSectContents
                                 ']]>' Ignore)*
[65]  Ignore               ::=  Char* - (Char* ('<![' | ']]>')
                                 Char*)
```

Like the internal and external DTD subsets, a conditional section may contain one or more complete declarations, comments, processing instructions, or nested conditional sections, intermingled with white space.

If the keyword of the conditional section is INCLUDE, then the contents of the conditional section are part of the DTD. If the keyword of the conditional section is IGNORE, then the contents of the conditional section are not logically part of the DTD. Note that for reliable parsing, the contents of even ignored conditional sections must be read in order to detect nested conditional sections and ensure that the end of the outermost (ignored) conditional section is properly detected. If a conditional section with a keyword of IN-CLUDE occurs within a larger conditional section with a keyword of IGNORE, both the outer and the inner conditional sections are ignored.

If the keyword of the conditional section is a parameter-entity reference, the parameter entity must be replaced by its content before the processor decides whether to include or ignore the conditional section.

An example:

```
<!ENTITY % draft 'INCLUDE' >
<!ENTITY % final 'IGNORE' >
```

```
<![%draft;[
<!ELEMENT book (comments*, title, body, supple-
ments?)>
]]>
<![%final;[
<!ELEMENT book (title, body, supplements?)>
]]>
```

4. *Physical Structures*

An XML document may consist of one or many storage units. These are called **entities**; they all have **content** and are all (except for the document entity, see below, and the external DTD subset) identified by **name**. Each XML document has one entity called the document entity, which serves as the starting point for the XML processor and may contain the whole document.

Entities may be either parsed or unparsed. A **parsed entity's** contents are referred to as its replacement text; this text is considered an integral part of the document.

An **unparsed entity** is a resource whose contents may or may not be text, and if text, may not be XML. Each unparsed entity has an associated notation, identified by name. Beyond a requirement that an XML processor make the identifiers for the entity and notation available to the application, XML places no constraints on the contents of unparsed entities.

Parsed entities are invoked by name using entity references; unparsed entities by name, given in the value of ENTITY or ENTITIES attributes.

General entities are entities for use within the document content. In this specification, general entities are sometimes referred to with the unqualified term *entity* when this leads to no ambiguity. Parameter entities are parsed entities for use within the DTD. These two types of entities use different forms of reference and are recognized in different contexts. Furthermore, they occupy different namespaces; a parameter entity and a general entity with the same name are two distinct entities.

4.1   Character and Entity References

A **character reference** refers to a specific character in the ISO/IEC 10646 character set, for example one not directly accessible from available input devices.

Character Reference

```
[66]  CharRef  ::=   '&#' [0-9]+ ';'

                 | '&#x' [0-9a-fA-F]+ ';'   [ WFC: Legal
                                               Character ]
```

Well-Formedness Constraint: Legal Character

Characters referred to using character references must match the production for Char.

If the character reference begins with "&#x", the digits and letters up to the terminating ; provide a hexadecimal representation of the character's code point in ISO/IEC 10646. If it begins just with "&#", the digits up to the terminating ; provide a decimal representation of the character's code point.

An **entity reference** refers to the content of a named entity. References to parsed general entities use ampersand (&) and semicolon (;) as delimiters. **Parameter-entity references** use percent-sign (%) and semicolon (;) as delimiters.

Entity Reference

```
[67]  Reference   ::=   EntityRef | CharRef
[68]  EntityRef   ::=   '&' Name ';'         [ WFC: Entity Declared ]

                                             [ VC: Entity Declared ]

                                             [ WFC: Parsed Entity ]

                                             [ WFC: No Recursion ]
[69]  PEReference  ::=   '%' Name ';'        [ VC: Entity Declared ]

                                             [ WFC: No Recursion ]

                                             [ WFC: In DTD ]
```

Well-Formedness Constraint: Entity Declared

In a document without any DTD, a document with only an internal DTD subset which contains no parameter entity references, or a document with "`standalone='yes'`", the `Name` given in the entity reference must match that in an entity declaration, except that well-formed documents need not declare any of the following entities: `amp`, `lt`, `gt`, `apos`, `quot`. The declaration of a parameter entity must precede any reference to it. Similarly, the declaration of a general entity must precede any reference to it which appears in a default value in an attribute-list declaration. Note that if entities are declared in the external subset or in external parameter entities, a non-validating processor is not obligated to read and process their declarations; for such documents, the rule that an entity must be declared is a well-formedness constraint only if standalone='yes'.

Validity Constraint: Entity Declared

In a document with an external subset or external parameter entities with "`standalone='no'`", the `Name` given in the entity reference must match that in an entity declaration. For interoperability, valid documents should declare the entities `amp`, `lt`, `gt`, `apos`, `quot`, in the form specified in "4.6 Predefined Entities". The declaration of a parameter entity must precede any reference to it. Similarly, the declaration of a general entity must precede any reference to it which appears in a default value in an attribute-list declaration.

Well-Formedness Constraint: Parsed Entity

An entity reference must not contain the name of an unparsed entity. Unparsed entities may be referred to only in attribute values declared to be of type `ENTITY` or `ENTITIES`.

Well-Formedness Constraint: No Recursion

A parsed entity must not contain a recursive reference to itself, either directly or indirectly.

Well-Formedness Constraint: In DTD

Parameter-entity references may only appear in the DTD.

Examples of character and entity references:

```
Type <key>less-than</key> (&#x3C;) to save options.
This document was prepared on &docdate; and
is classified &security-level;.
```

Example of a parameter-entity reference:

```
<!-- declare the parameter entity "ISOLat2"... -->
<!ENTITY % ISOLat2
        SYSTEM "http://www.xml.com/iso/isolat2-
xml.entities" >
<!-- ... now reference it. -->
%ISOLat2;
```

4.2   Entity Declarations

Entities are declared thus:

Entity Declaration

[70]	EntityDecl	::=	GEDecl | PEDecl
[71]	GEDecl	::=	'<!ENTITY' S Name S EntityDef S? '>'
[72]	PEDecl	::=	'<!ENTITY' S '%' S Name S PEDef S? '>'
[73]	EntityDef	::=	EntityValue | (ExternalID NDataDecl?)
[74]	PEDef	::=	EntityValue | ExternalID

The Name identifies the entity in an entity reference or, in the case of an unparsed entity, in the value of an ENTITY or ENTITIES attribute. If the same entity is declared more than once, the first declaration encountered is binding; at user option, an XML processor may issue a warning if entities are declared multiple times.

4.2.1   Internal Entities

If the entity definition is an EntityValue, the defined entity is called an **internal entity**. There is no separate physical storage object, and the content of the entity is given in the declaration. Note that some processing of entity and character references in the literal entity value may be required to produce the correct replacement text: see "4.5 Construction of Internal Entity Replacement Text".

An internal entity is a parsed entity.

Example of an internal entity declaration:

```
<!ENTITY Pub-Status "This is a pre-release of the
specification.">
```

4.2.2   External Entities

If the entity is not internal, it is an **external entity**, declared as follows:

External Entity Declaration

```
[75]   ExternalID  ::=  'SYSTEM' S SystemLiteral
                      | 'PUBLIC' S PubidLiteral S SystemLiteral
[76]   NDataDecl  ::=  S 'NDATA' S Name  [ VC: Notation Declared ]
```

If the NDataDecl is present, this is a general unparsed entity; otherwise it is a parsed entity.

Validity Constraint: Notation Declared

The Name must match the declared name of a notation.

The SystemLiteral is called the entity's **system identifier**. It is a URI, which may be used to retrieve the entity. Note that the hash mark (#) and fragment identifier frequently used with URIs are not, formally, part of the URI itself; an XML processor may signal an error if a fragment identifier is given as part of a system identifier. Unless otherwise provided by information outside the scope of this specification (e.g. a special XML element type defined by a particular DTD, or a processing instruction defined by a particular application specification), relative URIs are relative to the location of the resource within which the entity declaration occurs. A URI might thus be relative to the document entity, to the entity containing the external DTD subset, or to some other external parameter entity.

An XML processor should handle a non-ASCII character in a URI by representing the character in UTF-8 as one or more bytes, and then escaping these bytes with the URI escaping mechanism (i.e., by converting each byte to %HH, where HH is the hexadecimal notation of the byte value).

In addition to a system identifier, an external identifier may include a **public identifier**. An XML processor attempting to retrieve the entity's content may use the public identifier to try to generate an alternative URI. If the processor is unable to do so, it must use the URI specified in the system literal. Before a match is attempted, all strings of white space in the public identifier must be normalized to single space characters (#x20), and leading and trailing white space must be removed.

Examples of external entity declarations:

```
<!ENTITY open-hatch
         SYSTEM "http://www.textuality.com/boilerplate/
           OpenHatch.xml">
<!ENTITY open-hatch
         PUBLIC "-//Textuality//TEXT Standard open-hatch
           boilerplate//EN"
         "http://www.textuality.com/boilerplate/Open-
Hatch.xml">
<!ENTITY hatch-pic
         SYSTEM "../grafix/OpenHatch.gif"
         NDATA gif >
```

4.3   Parsed Entities

4.3.1   The Text Declaration

External parsed entities may each begin with a **text declaration**.

Text Declaration

[77]   TextDecl   ::=   '<?xml' VersionInfo? EncodingDecl S? '?>'

The text declaration must be provided literally, not by reference to a parsed entity. No text declaration may appear at any position other than the beginning of an external parsed entity.

4.3.2   Well-Formed Parsed Entities

The document entity is well-formed if it matches the production labeled `document`. An external general parsed entity is well-formed if it matches the production labeled `extParsedEnt`. An external parameter entity is well-formed if it matches the production labeled `extPE`.

Well-Formed External Parsed Entity

```
[78]   extParsedEnt   ::=   TextDecl? content

[79]   extPE          ::=   TextDecl? extSubsetDecl
```

An internal general parsed entity is well-formed if its replacement text matches the production labeled `content`. All internal parameter entities are well-formed by definition.

A consequence of well-formedness in entities is that the logical and physical structures in an XML document are properly nested; no start-tag, end-tag, empty-element tag, element, comment, processing instruction, character reference, or entity reference can begin in one entity and end in another.

4.3.3   Character Encoding in Entities

Each external parsed entity in an XML document may use a different encoding for its characters. All XML processors must be able to read entities in either UTF-8 or UTF-16.

Entities encoded in UTF-16 must begin with the Byte Order Mark described by ISO/IEC 10646 Annex E and Unicode Appendix B (the ZERO WIDTH NO-BREAK SPACE character, #xFEFF). This is an encoding signature, not part of either the markup or the character data of the XML document. XML processors must be able to use this character to differentiate between UTF-8 and UTF-16 encoded documents.

Although an XML processor is required to read only entities in the UTF-8 and UTF-16 encodings, it is recognized that other encodings are used around the world, and it may be desired for XML processors to read entities that use them. Parsed entities which are stored in an encoding other than UTF-8 or UTF-16 must begin with a text declaration containing an encoding declaration:

Encoding Declaration

```
[80]   EncodingDecl   ::=   S 'encoding' Eq ('"' EncName '"' |
                            "'" EncName "'" )

[81]   EncName        ::=   [A-Za-z] ([A-Za-z0-9._]   /* Encoding
                            | '-')*                     name con-
                                                        tains only
                                                        Latin char-
                                                        acters */
```

In the document entity, the encoding declaration is part of the XML declaration. The EncName is the name of the encoding used.

In an encoding declaration, the values "UTF-8", "UTF-16", "ISO-10646-UCS-2", and "ISO-10646-UCS-4" should be used for the various encodings and transformations of Unicode / ISO/IEC 10646, the values "ISO-8859-1", "ISO-8859-2",... "ISO-8859-9" should be used for the parts of ISO 8859, and the values "ISO-2022-JP", "Shift_JIS", and "EUC-JP" should be used for the various encoded forms of JIS X-0208-1997. XML processors may recognize other encodings; it is recommended that character encodings registered (as *charsets*) with the Internet Assigned Numbers Authority [IANA], other than those just listed, should be referred to using their registered names. Note that these registered names are defined to be case-insensitive, so processors wishing to match against them should do so in a case-insensitive way.

In the absence of information provided by an external transport protocol (e.g. HTTP or MIME), it is an error for an entity including an encoding declaration to be presented to the XML processor in an encoding other than that named in the declaration, for an encoding declaration to occur other than at the beginning of an external entity, or for an entity which begins with neither a Byte Order Mark nor an encoding declaration to use an encoding other than UTF-8. Note that since ASCII is a subset of UTF-8, ordinary ASCII entities do not strictly need an encoding declaration.

It is a fatal error when an XML processor encounters an entity with an encoding that it is unable to process.

Examples of encoding declarations:

```
<?xml encoding='UTF-8'?>
<?xml encoding='EUC-JP'?>
```

4.4 XML Processor Treatment of Entities and References

The table below summarizes the contexts in which character references, entity references, and invocations of unparsed entities might appear and the required behavior of an XML processor in each case. The labels in the leftmost column describe the recognition context:

Reference in Content

as a reference anywhere after the start-tag and before the end-tag of an element; corresponds to the nonterminal `content`.

Reference in Attribute Value

as a reference within either the value of an attribute in a start-tag, or a default value in an attribute declaration; corresponds to the nonterminal `AttValue`.

Occurs as Attribute Value

as a `Name`, not a reference, appearing either as the value of an attribute which has been declared as type `ENTITY`, or as one of the space-separated tokens in the value of an attribute which has been declared as type `ENTITIES`.

Reference in Entity Value

as a reference within a parameter or internal entity's literal entity value in the entity's declaration; corresponds to the nonterminal `EntityValue`.

Reference in DTD

as a reference within either the internal or external subsets of the DTD, but outside of an `EntityValue` or `AttValue`.

			Entity Type		
	Parameter	Internal General	External Parsed General	Unparsed	*Character*
Reference in Content	Not recognized	Included	Included if validating	Forbidden	Included
Reference in Attribute Value	Not recognized	Included in literal	Forbidden	Forbidden	Included
Occurs as Attribute Value	Not recognized	Not	Forbidden recognized	Forbidden	Notify
Reference in Entity Value	Included in literal	Bypassed	Bypassed	Forbidden	Included
Reference in DTD	Included as PE	Forbidden	Forbidden	Forbidden	Forbidden

4.4.1   Not Recognized

Outside the DTD, the % character has no special significance; thus, what would be parameter entity references in the DTD are not recognized as markup in content. Similarly, the names of unparsed entities are not recognized except when they appear in the value of an appropriately declared attribute.

4.4.2   Included

An entity is **included** when its replacement text is retrieved and processed, in place of the reference itself, as though it were part of the document at the location the reference was recognized. The replacement text may contain both character data and (except for parameter entities) markup, which must be recognized in the usual way, except that the replacement text of entities used to escape markup delimiters (the entities `amp`, `lt`, `gt`, `apos`, `quot`) is always treated as data. (The string "`AT&amp;T;`" expands to "`AT&T;`" and the remaining ampersand is not recognized as an entity-reference delimiter.) A character reference is **included** when the indicated character is processed in place of the reference itself.

4.4.3   Included If Validating

When an XML processor recognizes a reference to a parsed entity, in order to validate the document, the processor must include its replacement text. If the entity is external, and the processor is not attempting to validate the XML document, the processor may, but need not, include the entity's replacement text. If a non-validating parser does not include the replacement text, it must inform the application that it recognized, but did not read, the entity.

This rule is based on the recognition that the automatic inclusion provided by the SGML and XML entity mechanism, primarily designed to support modularity in authoring, is not necessarily appropriate for other applications, in particular document browsing. Browsers, for example, when encountering an external parsed entity reference, might choose to provide a visual indication of the entity's presence and retrieve it for display only on demand.

4.4.4   Forbidden

The following are forbidden, and constitute fatal errors:

- the appearance of a reference to an unparsed entity.

- the appearance of any character or general-entity reference in the DTD except within an `EntityValue` or `AttValue`.

- a reference to an external entity in an attribute value.

4.4.5 Included in Literal

When an entity reference appears in an attribute value, or a parameter entity reference appears in a literal entity value, its replacement text is processed in place of the reference itself as though it were part of the document at the location the reference was recognized, except that a single or double quote character in the replacement text is always treated as a normal data character and will not terminate the literal. For example, this is well-formed:

```
<!ENTITY % YN '"Yes"' >
<!ENTITY WhatHeSaid "He said &YN;" >
```

while this is not:

```
<!ENTITY EndAttr "27'" >
<element attribute='a-&EndAttr;>
```

4.4.6 Notify

When the name of an unparsed entity appears as a token in the value of an attribute of declared type ENTITY or ENTITIES, a validating processor must inform the application of the system and public (if any) identifiers for both the entity and its associated notation.

4.4.7 Bypassed

When a general entity reference appears in the EntityValue in an entity declaration, it is bypassed and left as is.

4.4.8 Included as PE

Just as with external parsed entities, parameter entities need only be included if validating. When a parameter-entity reference is recognized in the DTD and included, its replacement text is enlarged by the attachment of one leading and one following space (#x20) character; the intent is to constrain the replacement text of parameter entities to contain an integral number of grammatical tokens in the DTD.

4.5   Construction of Internal Entity Replacement Text

In discussing the treatment of internal entities, it is useful to distinguish two forms of the entity's value. The **literal entity value** is the quoted string actually present in the entity declaration, corresponding to the non-terminal EntityValue. The **replacement text** is the content of the entity, after replacement of character references and parameter-entity references.

The literal entity value as given in an internal entity declaration (EntityValue) may contain character, parameter-entity, and general-entity references. Such references must be contained entirely within the literal entity value. The actual replacement text that is included as described above must contain the *replacement text* of any parameter entities referred to, and must contain the character referred to, in place of any character references in the literal entity value; however, general-entity references must be left as-is, unexpanded. For example, given the following declarations:

```
<!ENTITY % pub    "&#xc9;ditions Gallimard" >
<!ENTITY   rights "All rights reserved" >
<!ENTITY   book   "La Peste: Albert Camus,
&#xA9; 1947 %pub;. &rights;" >
```

then the replacement text for the entity "book" is:

```
La Peste: Albert Camus,
© 1947 Éditions Gallimard. &rights;
```

The general-entity reference "&rights;" would be expanded should the reference "&book;" appear in the document's content or an attribute value.

These simple rules may have complex interactions; for a detailed discussion of a difficult example, see "D. Expansion of Entity and Character References".

4.6 Predefined Entities

Entity and character references can both be used to **escape** the left angle bracket, ampersand, and other delimiters. A set of general entities (amp, lt, gt, apos, quot) is specified for this purpose. Numeric character references may also be used; they are expanded immediately when recognized and must be treated as character data, so the numeric character references "<" and "&" may be used to escape < and & when they occur in character data.

All XML processors must recognize these entities whether they are declared or not. For interoperability, valid XML documents should declare these entities, like any others, before using them. If the entities in question are declared, they must be declared as internal entities whose replacement text is the single character being escaped or a character reference to that character, as shown below.

```
<!ENTITY lt      "&#38;#60;">
<!ENTITY gt      "&#62;">
<!ENTITY amp     "&#38;#38;">
<!ENTITY apos    "&#39;">
<!ENTITY quot    "&#34;">
```

Note that the < and & characters in the declarations of "lt" and "amp" are doubly escaped to meet the requirement that entity replacement be well-formed.

4.7 Notation Declarations

Notations identify by name the format of unparsed entities, the format of elements which bear a notation attribute, or the application to which a processing instruction is addressed.

Notation declarations provide a name for the notation, for use in entity and attribute-list declarations and in attribute specifications, and an external identifier for the notation which may allow an XML processor or its client application to locate a helper application capable of processing data in the given notation.

Notation Declarations

[82]	NotationDecl	::=	'<!NOTATION' S Name S (ExternalID |
			PublicID) S? '>'
[83]	PublicID	::=	'PUBLIC' S PubidLiteral

XML processors must provide applications with the name and external identifier(s) of any notation declared and referred to in an attribute value, attribute definition, or entity declaration. They may additionally resolve the external identifier into the system identifier, file name, or other information needed to allow the application to call a processor for data in the notation described. (It is not an error, however, for XML documents to declare and refer to notations for which notation-specific applications are not available on the system where the XML processor or application is running.)

4.8 Document Entity

The **document entity** serves as the root of the entity tree and a starting-point for an XML processor. This specification does not specify how the document entity is to be located by an XML processor; unlike other entities, the document entity has no name and might well appear on a processor input stream without any identification at all.

5. *Conformance*

5.1 Validating and Non-Validating Processors

Conforming XML processors fall into two classes: validating and non-validating.

Validating and non-validating processors alike must report violations of this specification's well-formedness constraints in the content of the document entity and any other parsed entities that they read.

Validating processors must report violations of the constraints expressed by the declarations in the DTD, and failures to fulfill the validity constraints given in this specification. To accomplish this, validating XML processors must read and process the entire DTD and all external parsed entities referenced in the document.

Non-validating processors are required to check only the document entity, including the entire internal DTD subset, for well-formedness. While they are not required to check the document for validity, they are required to **process** all the declarations they read in the internal DTD subset and in any parameter entity that they read, up to the first reference to a parameter entity that they do *not* read; that is to say, they must use the information in those declarations to normalize attribute values, include the replacement text of internal entities, and supply default attribute values. They must not process entity declarations or attribute-list declarations encountered after a reference to a parameter entity that is not read, since the entity may have contained overriding declarations.

5.2 Using XML Processors

The behavior of a validating XML processor is highly predictable; it must read every piece of a document and report all well-formedness and validity violations. Less is required of a non-validating processor; it need not read any part of the document other than the document entity. This has two effects that may be important to users of XML processors:

- Certain well-formedness errors, specifically those that require reading external entities, may not be detected by a non-validating processor. Examples include the constraints entitled Entity Declared, Parsed Entity, and No Recursion, as well as some of the cases described as forbidden in "4.4 XML Processor Treatment of Entities and References".

- The information passed from the processor to the application may vary, depending on whether the processor reads parameter and external entities. For example, a non-validating processor may not normalize attribute values, include the replacement text of internal entities, or supply default attribute values, where doing so depends on having read declarations in external or parameter entities.

For maximum reliability in interoperating between different XML processors, applications which use non-validating processors should not rely on any behaviors not required of such processors. Applications which require facilities such as the use of default attributes or internal entities which are declared in external entities should use validating XML processors.

6. *Notation*

The formal grammar of XML is given in this specification using a simple Extended Backus-Naur Form (EBNF) notation. Each rule in the grammar defines one symbol, in the form

```
symbol ::= expression
```

Symbols are written with an initial capital letter if they are defined by a regular expression, or with an initial lower case letter otherwise. Literal strings are quoted.

Within the expression on the right-hand side of a rule, the following expressions are used to match strings of one or more characters:

#xN

where N is a hexadecimal integer, the expression matches the character in ISO/IEC 10646 whose canonical (UCS-4) code value, when interpreted as an unsigned binary number, has the value indicated. The number of leading zeros in the #xN form is insignificant; the number of leading zeros in the corresponding code value is governed by the character encoding in use and is not significant for XML.

[a-zA-Z], [#xN-#xN]

matches any character with a value in the range(s) indicated (inclusive).

[^a-z], [^#xN-#xN]

matches any character with a value *outside* the range indicated.

[^abc], [^#xN#xN#xN]

matches any character with a value not among the characters given.

"string"

matches a literal string matching that given inside the double quotes.

'string'

matches a literal string matching that given inside the single quotes.

These symbols may be combined to match more complex patterns as follows, where A and B represent simple expressions:

(expression)

expression is treated as a unit and may be combined as described in this list.

A?

matches A or nothing; optional A.

A B

matches A followed by B.

A | B

matches A or B but not both.

A - B

matches any string that matches A but does not match B.

A+

matches one or more occurrences of A.

A*

matches zero or more occurrences of A.

Other notations used in the productions are:

/* ... */

comment.

[wfc: ...]

well-formedness constraint; this identifies by name a constraint on well-formed documents associated with a production.

[vc: ...]

validity constraint; this identifies by name a constraint on valid documents associated with a production.

Appendices

A. References

A.1 Normative References

IANA

(Internet Assigned Numbers Authority) *Official Names for Character Sets*, ed. Keld Simonsen et al. See ftp://ftp.isi.edu/in-notes/iana/assignments/character-sets.

IETF RFC 1766

IETF (Internet Engineering Task Force). *RFC 1766: Tags for the Identification of Languages*, ed. H. Alvestrand. 1995.

ISO 639

(International Organization for Standardization). *ISO 639:1988 (E). Code for the representation of names of languages.* [Geneva]: International Organization for Standardization, 1988.

ISO 3166

(International Organization for Standardization). *ISO 3166-1:1997 (E). Codes for the representation of names of countries and their subdivisions — Part 1: Country codes* [Geneva]: International Organization for Standardization, 1997.

ISO/IEC 10646

ISO (International Organization for Standardization). *ISO/IEC 10646-1993 (E). Information technology — Universal Multiple-Octet Coded Character Set (UCS) — Part 1: Architecture and Basic Multilingual Plane.* [Geneva]: International Organization for Standardization, 1993 (plus amendments AM 1 through AM 7).

Unicode

The Unicode Consortium. *The Unicode Standard, Version 2.0.* Reading, Mass.: Addison-Wesley Developers Press, 1996.

A.2 Other References

Aho/Ullman

Aho, Alfred V., Ravi Sethi, and Jeffrey D. Ullman. *Compilers: Principles, Techniques, and Tools.* Reading: Addison-Wesley, 1986, rpt. corr. 1988.

Berners-Lee et al.

Berners-Lee, T., R. Fielding, and L. Masinter. *Uniform Resource Identifiers (URI): Generic Syntax and Semantics.* 1997. (Work in progress; see updates to RFC1738.)

Brüggemann-Klein

Brüggemann-Klein, Anne. *Regular Expressions into Finite Automata.* Extended abstract in I. Simon, Hrsg., LATIN 1992, S.

97-98. Springer-Verlag, Berlin 1992. Full Version in Theoretical Computer Science 120: 197-213, 1993.

Brüggemann-Klein and Wood

Brüggemann-Klein, Anne, and Derick Wood. *Deterministic Regular Languages*. Universität Freiburg, Institut für Informatik, Bericht 38, Oktober 1991.

Clark

James Clark. Comparison of SGML and XML. See http://www.w3.org/TR/NOTE-sgml-xml-971215.

IETF RFC1738

IETF (Internet Engineering Task Force). *RFC 1738: Uniform Resource Locators (URL)*, ed. T. Berners-Lee, L. Masinter, M. McCahill. 1994.

IETF RFC1808

IETF (Internet Engineering Task Force). *RFC 1808: Relative Uniform Resource Locators*, ed. R. Fielding. 1995.

IETF RFC2141

IETF (Internet Engineering Task Force). *RFC 2141: URN Syntax*, ed. R. Moats. 1997.

ISO 8879

ISO (International Organization for Standardization). *ISO 8879:1986(E). Information processing — Text and Office Systems — Standard Generalized Markup Language (SGML)*. First edition — 1986-10-15. [Geneva]: International Organization for Standardization, 1986.

ISO/IEC 10744

ISO (International Organization for Standardization). *ISO/IEC 10744-1992 (E). Information technology — Hypermedia/Time-based Structuring Language (HyTime)*. [Geneva]: International Organization for Standardization, 1992. *Extended Facilities Annexe.* [Geneva]: International Organization for Standardization, 1996.

B. Character Classes

Following the characteristics defined in the Unicode standard, characters are classed as base characters (among others, these contain the alphabetic characters of the Latin alphabet, without diacritics), ideographic characters, and combining characters (among others, this class contains most diacritics); these classes combine to form the class of letters. Digits and extenders are also distinguished.

Characters

```
[84]  Letter    ::=  BaseChar | Ideographic
[85]  BaseChar  ::=  #x0041-#x005A] | [#x0061-#x007A] | [#x00C0-#x00D6] |
                     [#x00D8-#x00F6] | [#x00F8-#x00FF] | [#x0100-#x0131] |
                     [#x0134-#x013E] | [#x0141-#x0148] | [#x014A-#x017E] |
                     [#x0180-#x01C3] | [#x01CD-#x01F0] | [#x01F4-#x01F5] |
                     [#x01FA-#x0217] | [#x0250-#x02A8] | [#x02BB-#x02C1] |
                     #x0386 | [#x0388-#x038A] | #x038C | [#x038E-#x03A1] |
                     [#x03A3-#x03CE] | [#x03D0-#x03D6] | #x03DA | #x03DC |
                     #x03DE | #x03E0 | [#x03E2-#x03F3] | [#x0401-#x040C] |
                     [#x040E-#x044F] | [#x0451-#x045C] | [#x045E-#x0481] |
                     [#x0490-#x04C4] | [#x04C7-#x04C8] | [#x04CB-#x04CC] |
                     [#x04D0-#x04EB] | [#x04EE-#x04F5] | [#x04F8-#x04F9] |
                     [#x0531-#x0556] | #x0559 | [#x0561-#x0586] | [#x05D0-
                     #x05EA] | [#x05F0-#x05F2] | [#x0621-#x063A] | [#x0641-
                     #x064A] | [#x0671-#x06B7] | [#x06BA-#x06BE] |
                     [#x06C0-#x06CE] | [#x06D0-#x06D3] | #x06D5 | [#x06E5-
                     #x06E6] | [#x0905-#x0939] | #x093D | [#x0958-#x0961] |
                     [#x0985-#x098C] | [#x098F-#x0990] | [#x0993-#x09A8] |
                     [#x09AA-#x09B0] | #x09B2 | [#x09B6-#x09B9] | [#x09DC-
                     #x09DD] | [#x09DF-#x09E1] | [#x09F0-#x09F1] | [#x0A05-
                     #x0A0A] | [#x0A0F-#x0A10] | [#x0A13-#x0A28] |
                     [#x0A2A-#x0A30] | [#x0A32-#x0A33] | [#x0A35-#x0A36] |
                     [#x0A38-#x0A39] | [#x0A59-#x0A5C] | #x0A5E | [#x0A72-
                     #x0A74] | [#x0A85-#x0A8B] | #x0A8D | [#x0A8F-#x0A91] |
                     [#x0A93-#x0AA8] | [#x0AAA-#x0AB0] | [#x0AB2-#x0AB3] |
                     [#x0AB5-#x0AB9] | #x0ABD | #x0AE0 | [#x0B05-#x0B0C] |
```

```
[#x0B0F-#x0B10] | [#x0B13-#x0B28] | [#x0B2A-#x0B30] |
[#x0B32-#x0B33] | [#x0B36-#x0B39] | #x0B3D | [#x0B5C-
#x0B5D] | [#x0B5F-#x0B61] | [#x0B85-#x0B8A] | [#x0B8E-
#x0B90] | [#x0B92-#x0B95] | [#x0B99-#x0B9A] | #x0B9C |
[#x0B9E-#x0B9F] | [#x0BA3-#x0BA4] | [#x0BA8-#x0BAA] |
[#x0BAE-#x0BB5] | [#x0BB7-#x0BB9] | [#x0C05-#x0C0C] |
[#x0C0E-#x0C10] | [#x0C12-#x0C28] | [#x0C2A-#x0C33] |
[#x0C35-#x0C39] | [#x0C60-#x0C61] | [#x0C85-#x0C8C] |
[#x0C8E-#x0C90] | [#x0C92-#x0CA8] | [#x0CAA-#x0CB3] |
[#x0CB5-#x0CB9] | #x0CDE | [#x0CE0-#x0CE1] | [#x0D05-
#x0D0C] | [#x0D0E-#x0D10] | [#x0D12-#x0D28] | [#x0D2A-
#x0D39] | [#x0D60-#x0D61] | [#x0E01-#x0E2E] | #x0E30 |
[#x0E32-#x0E33] | [#x0E40-#x0E45] | [#x0E81-#x0E82] |
#x0E84 | [#x0E87-#x0E88] | #x0E8A | #x0E8D | [#x0E94-
#x0E97] | [#x0E99-#x0E9F] | [#x0EA1-#x0EA3] | #x0EA5 |
#x0EA7 | [#x0EAA-#x0EAB] | [#x0EAD-#x0EAE] | #x0EB0 |
[#x0EB2-#x0EB3] | #x0EBD | [#x0EC0-#x0EC4] | [#x0F40-
#x0F47] | [#x0F49-#x0F69] | [#x10A0-#x10C5] | [#x10D0-
#x10F6] | #x1100 | [#x1102-#x1103] | [#x1105-#x1107] |
#x1109 | [#x110B-#x110C] | [#x110E-#x1112] | #x113C |
#x113E | #x1140 | #x114C | #x114E | #x1150 | [#x1154-
#x1155] | #x1159 | [#x115F-#x1161] | #x1163 | #x1165 |
#x1167 | #x1169 | [#x116D-#x116E] | [#x1172-#x1173] |
#x1175 | #x119E | #x11A8 | #x11AB | [#x11AE-#x11AF] |
[#x11B7-#x11B8] | #x11BA | [#x11BC-#x11C2] | #x11EB |
#x11F0 | #x11F9 | [#x1E00-#x1E9B] | [#x1EA0-#x1EF9] |
[#x1F00-#x1F15] | [#x1F18-#x1F1D] | [#x1F20-#x1F45] |
[#x1F48-#x1F4D] | [#x1F50-#x1F57] | #x1F59 | #x1F5B |
#x1F5D | [#x1F5F-#x1F7D] | [#x1F80-#x1FB4] | [#x1FB6-
#x1FBC] | #x1FBE | [#x1FC2-#x1FC4] | [#x1FC6-#x1FCC] |
[#x1FD0-#x1FD3] | [#x1FD6-#x1FDB] | [#x1FE0-#x1FEC] |
[#x1FF2-#x1FF4] | [#x1FF6-#x1FFC] | #x2126 | [#x212A-
#x212B] | #x212E | [#x2180-#x2182] | [#x3041-#x3094] |
[#x30A1-#x30FA] | [#x3105-#x312C] | [#xAC00-#xD7A3]
```

```
[86]   Ideographic    ::=   [#x4E00-#x9FA5] | #x3007 | [#x3021-#x3029]
[87]   CombiningChar  ::=   [#x0300-#x0345] | [#x0360-#x0361] | [#x0483-
                           #x0486] | [#x0591-#x05A1] | [#x05A3-#x05B9] |
                           [#x05BB-#x05BD] | #x05BF | [#x05C1-#x05C2] |
                           #x05C4 | [#x064B-#x0652] | #x0670 | [#x06D6-
                           #x06DC] | [#x06DD-#x06DF] | [#x06E0-#x06E4] |
```

```
                    [#x06E7-#x06E8] | [#x06EA-#x06ED] | [#x0901-
                    #x0903] | #x093C | [#x093E-#x094C] | #x094D |
                    [#x0951-#x0954] | [#x0962-#x0963] | [#x0981-
                    #x0983] | #x09BC | #x09BE | #x09BF | [#x09C0-
                    #x09C4] | [#x09C7-#x09C8] | [#x09CB-#x09CD] |
                    #x09D7 | [#x09E2-#x09E3] | #x0A02 | #x0A3C |
                    #x0A3E | #x0A3F | [#x0A40-#x0A42] | [#x0A47-
                    #x0A48] | [#x0A4B-#x0A4D] | [#x0A70-#x0A71] |
                    [#x0A81-#x0A83] | #x0ABC | [#x0ABE-#x0AC5] |
                    [#x0AC7-#x0AC9] | [#x0ACB-#x0ACD] | [#x0B01-
                    #x0B03] | #x0B3C | [#x0B3E-#x0B43] | [#x0B47-
                    #x0B48] | [#x0B4B-#x0B4D] | [#x0B56-#x0B57] |
                    [#x0B82-#x0B83] | [#x0BBE-#x0BC2] | [#x0BC6-
                    #x0BC8] | [#x0BCA-#x0BCD] | #x0BD7 | [#x0C01-
                    #x0C03] | [#x0C3E-#x0C44] | [#x0C46-#x0C48] |
                    [#x0C4A-#x0C4D] | [#x0C55-#x0C56] | [#x0C82-
                    #x0C83] | [#x0CBE-#x0CC4] | [#x0CC6-#x0CC8] |
                    [#x0CCA-#x0CCD] | [#x0CD5-#x0CD6] | [#x0D02-
                    #x0D03] | [#x0D3E-#x0D43] | [#x0D46-#x0D48] |
                    [#x0D4A-#x0D4D] | #x0D57 | #x0E31 | [#x0E34-
                    #x0E3A] | [#x0E47-#x0E4E] | #x0EB1 | [#x0EB4
                    #x0EB9] | [#x0EBB-#x0EBC] | [#x0EC8-#x0ECD] |
                    [#x0F18-#x0F19] | #x0F35 | #x0F37 | #x0F39 |
                    #x0F3E | #x0F3F | [#x0F71-#x0F84] | [#x0F86-
                    #x0F8B] | [#x0F90-#x0F95] | #x0F97 | [#x0F99-
                    #x0FAD] | [#x0FB1-#x0FB7] | #x0FB9 |
                    [#x20D0-#x20DC] | #x20E1 | [#x302A-#x302F] |
                    #x3099 | #x309A

[88]  Digit          ::=  [#x0030-#x0039] | [#x0660-#x0669] | [#x06F0-
                    #x06F9] | [#x0966-#x096F] | [#x09E6-#x09EF] |
                    [#x0A66-#x0A6F] | [#x0AE6-#x0AEF] | [#x0B66-
                    #x0B6F] | [#x0BE7-#x0BEF] | [#x0C66-#x0C6F] |
                    [#x0CE6-#x0CEF] | [#x0D66-#x0D6F] | [#x0E50-
                    #x0E59] | [#x0ED0-#x0ED9] | [#x0F20-#x0F29]

[89]  Extender       ::=  #x00B7 | #x02D0 | #x02D1 | #x0387 | #x0640 |
#x0E46 | #x0EC6 | #x3005 | [#x3031-#x3035] | [#x309D-#x309E] | [#x30FC-
#x30FE]
```

The character classes defined here can be derived from the Unicode character database as follows:

- Name start characters must have one of the categories Ll, Lu, Lo, Lt, Nl.

- Name characters other than Name-start characters must have one of the categories Mc, Me, Mn, Lm, or Nd.

- Characters in the compatibility area (i.e. with character code greater than #xF900 and less than #xFFFE) are not allowed in XML names.

- Characters which have a font or compatibility decomposition (i.e. those with a "compatibility formatting tag" in field 5 of the database — marked by field 5 beginning with a "<") are not allowed.

- The following characters are treated as name-start characters rather than name characters, because the property file classifies them as Alphabetic: [#x02BB-#x02C1], #x0559, #x06E5, #x06E6.

- Characters #x20DD-#x20E0 are excluded (in accordance with Unicode, section 5.14).

- Character #x00B7 is classified as an extender, because the property list so identifies it.

- Character #x0387 is added as a name character, because #x00B7 is its canonical equivalent.

- Characters ':' and '_' are allowed as name-start characters.

- Characters '-' and '.' are allowed as name characters.

C. XML and SGML (Non-Normative)

XML is designed to be a subset of SGML, in that every valid XML document should also be a conformant SGML document. For a detailed comparison of the additional restrictions that XML places on documents beyond those of SGML, see [Clark].

D. Expansion of Entity and Character References (Non-Normative)

This appendix contains some examples illustrating the sequence of entity- and character-reference recognition and expansion, as specified in "4.4 XML Processor Treatment of Entities and References".
If the DTD contains the declaration

```
<!ENTITY example "<p>An ampersand (&#38;#38;) may
be escaped numerically (&#38;#38;#38;) or with a
general entity(&amp;amp;).</p>" >
```

then the XML processor will recognize the character references when it parses the entity declaration, and resolve them before storing the following string as the value of the entity "example":

```
<p>An ampersand (&#38;) may be escaped
numerically (&#38;#38;) or with a general entity
(&amp;amp;).</p>
```

A reference in the document to "&example;" will cause the text to be reparsed, at which time the start- and end-tags of the "p" element will be recognized and the three references will be recognized and expanded, resulting in a "p" element with the following content (all data, no delimiters or markup):

```
An ampersand (&) may be escaped
numerically (&#38;) or with a general entity
(&amp;).
```

A more complex example will illustrate the rules and their effects fully. In the following example, the line numbers are solely for reference.

```
1 <?xml version='1.0'?>
2 <!DOCTYPE test [
3 <!ELEMENT test (#PCDATA) >
4 <!ENTITY % xx '&#37;zz;'>
5 <!ENTITY % zz '&#60;!ENTITY tricky "error-prone" >' >
6 %xx;
```

```
7 ]>
8 <test>This sample shows a &tricky; method.</test>
```

This produces the following:

- in line 4, the reference to character 37 is expanded immediately, and the parameter entity "xx" is stored in the symbol table with the value "%zz;". Since the replacement text is not rescanned, the reference to parameter entity "zz" is not recognized. (And it would be an error if it were, since "zz" is not yet declared.)

- in line 5, the character reference "<" is expanded immediately and the parameter entity "zz" is stored with the replacement text "<!ENTITY tricky "error-prone" >", which is a well-formed entity declaration.

- in line 6, the reference to "xx" is recognized, and the replacement text of "xx" (namely "%zz;") is parsed. The reference to "zz" is recognized in its turn, and its replacement text ("<!ENTITY tricky "error-prone" >") is parsed. The general entity "tricky" has now been declared, with the replacement text "error-prone".

- in line 8, the reference to the general entity "tricky" is recognized, and it is expanded, so the full content of the "test" element is the self-describing (and ungrammatical) string *This sample shows a error-prone method.*

E. Deterministic Content Models (Non-Normative)

For compatibility, it is required that content models in element type declarations be deterministic.

SGML requires deterministic content models (it calls them "unambiguous"); XML processors built using SGML systems may flag non-deterministic content models as errors.

For example, the content model ((b, c) | (b, d)) is non-deterministic, because given an initial b the parser cannot know which b in the model is being matched without looking ahead to see which element follows the b. In this case, the two references to b can be collapsed into a single reference, making the model read (b, (c | d)). An initial b now clearly matches only a single name in the content model. The parser doesn't need to look ahead to see what follows; either c or d would be accepted.

More formally: a finite state automaton may be constructed from the content model using the standard algorithms, e.g. algorithm 3.5 in section 3.9 of Aho, Sethi, and Ullman [Aho/Ullman]. In many such algorithms, a follow set is constructed for each position in the regular expression (i.e., each leaf node in the syntax tree for the regular expression); if any position has a follow set in which more than one following position is labeled with the same element type name, then the content model is in error and may be reported as an error.

Algorithms exist which allow many but not all non-deterministic content models to be reduced automatically to equivalent deterministic models; see Brüggemann-Klein 1991 [Brüggemann-Klein].

F. Autodetection of Character Encodings (Non-Normative)

The XML encoding declaration functions as an internal label on each entity, indicating which character encoding is in use. Before an XML processor can read the internal label, however, it apparently has to know what character encoding is in use—which is what the internal label is trying to indicate. In the general case, this is a hopeless situation. It is not entirely hopeless in XML, however, because XML limits the general case in two ways: each implementation is assumed to support only a finite set of character encodings, and the XML encoding declaration is restricted in position and content in order to make it feasible to autodetect the character encoding in use in each entity in normal cases. Also, in many cases other sources of information are available in addition to the XML data stream itself. Two cases may be distinguished, depending on whether the XML entity is presented to the processor without, or with, any accompanying (external) information. We consider the first case first.

Because each XML entity not in UTF-8 or UTF-16 format *must* begin with an XML encoding declaration, in which the first characters must be '<?xml', any conforming processor can detect, after two to four octets of input, which of the following cases apply. In reading this list, it may help to know that in UCS-4, '<' is "#x0000003C" and '?' is "#x0000003F", and the Byte Order Mark required of UTF-16 data streams is "#xFEFF".

- 00 00 00 3C: UCS-4, big-endian machine (1234 order)

- 3C 00 00 00: UCS-4, little-endian machine (4321 order)

- 00 00 3C 00: UCS-4, unusual octet order (2143)

- 00 3C 00 00: UCS-4, unusual octet order (3412)

- FE FF: UTF-16, big-endian

- FF FE: UTF-16, little-endian

- 00 3C 00 3F: UTF-16, big-endian, no Byte Order Mark (and thus, strictly speaking, in error)

- 3C 00 3F 00: UTF-16, little-endian, no Byte Order Mark (and thus, strictly speaking, in error)

- 3C 3F 78 6D: UTF-8, ISO 646, ASCII, some part of ISO 8859, Shift-JIS, EUC, or any other 7-bit, 8-bit, or mixed-width encoding which ensures that the characters of ASCII have their normal positions, width, and values; the actual encoding declaration must be read to detect which of these applies, but since all of these encodings use the same bit patterns for the ASCII characters, the encoding declaration itself may be read reliably

- 4C 6F A7 94: EBCDIC (in some flavor; the full encoding declaration must be read to tell which code page is in use)

- other: UTF-8 without an encoding declaration, or else the data stream is corrupt, fragmentary, or enclosed in a wrapper of some kind

This level of autodetection is enough to read the XML encoding declaration and parse the character-encoding identifier, which is still necessary to distinguish the individual members of each family of encodings (e.g. to tell UTF-8 from 8859, and the parts of 8859 from each other, or to distinguish the specific EBCDIC code page in use, and so on).

Because the contents of the encoding declaration are restricted to ASCII characters, a processor can reliably read the entire encoding declaration as soon as it has detected which family of encodings is in use. Since in practice, all widely used character encodings fall into one of the categories above, the XML encoding declaration allows reasonably reliable in-band labeling of character encodings, even when external sources of information at the operating-system or transport-protocol level are unreliable.

Once the processor has detected the character encoding in use, it can act appropriately, whether by invoking a separate input routine for each case, or by calling the proper conversion function on each character of input.

Like any self-labeling system, the XML encoding declaration will not work if any software changes the entity's character set or encoding without updating the encoding declaration. Implementors of character-encoding routines should be careful to ensure the accuracy of the internal and external information used to label the entity.

The second possible case occurs when the XML entity is accompanied by encoding information, as in some file systems and some network protocols. When multiple sources of information are available, their relative priority and the preferred method of handling conflict should be specified as part of the higher-level protocol used to deliver XML. Rules for the relative priority of the internal label and the MIME-type label in an external header, for example, should be part of the RFC document defining the text/xml and application/xml MIME types. In the interests of interoperability, however, the following rules are recommended.

- If an XML entity is in a file, the Byte-Order Mark and encoding-declaration PI are used (if present) to determine the character encoding. All other heuristics and sources of information are solely for error recovery.

- If an XML entity is delivered with a MIME type of text/xml, then the `charset` parameter on the MIME type determines the character encoding method; all other heuristics and sources of information are solely for error recovery.

- If an XML entity is delivered with a MIME type of application/xml, then the Byte-Order Mark and encoding-declaration PI are used (if present) to determine the character encoding. All other heuristics and sources of information are solely for error recovery.

These rules apply only in the absence of protocol-level documentation; in particular, when the MIME types text/xml and application/xml are defined, the recommendations of the relevant RFC will supersede these rules.

G. W3C XML Working Group (Non-Normative)

This specification was prepared and approved for publication by the W3C XML Working Group (WG). WG approval of this specification does not necessarily imply that all WG members voted for its approval. The current and former members of the XML WG are:

Jon Bosak, Sun (Chair); James Clark (Technical Lead); Tim Bray, Textuality and Netscape (XML Co-editor); Jean Paoli, Microsoft (XML Co-editor); C. M. Sperberg-McQueen, U. of Ill. (XML Co-editor); Dan Connolly, W3C (W3C Liaison); Paula Angerstein, Texcel; Steve DeRose, INSO; Dave Hollander, HP; Eliot Kimber, ISOGEN; Eve Maler, ArborText; Tom Magliery, NCSA; Murray Maloney, Muzmo and Grif; Makoto Murata, Fuji Xerox Information Systems; Joel Nava, Adobe; Conleth O'Connell, Vignette; Peter Sharpe, SoftQuad; John Tigue, DataChannel

Appendix B
Document Object Model (Core) Level 1

Editors

Mike Champion, ArborText (from November 20, 1997)

Steve Byrne, JavaSoft (until November 19, 1997)

Gavin Nicol, Inso EPS

Lauren Wood, SoftQuad, Inc.

Table of contents

1.1.   *Overview of the DOM Core Interfaces*

This section defines a minimal set of objects and interfaces for accessing and manipulating document objects. The functionality specified in this section (the *Core* functionality) should be sufficient to allow software developers and web script authors to access and manipulate parsed HTML and XML content inside conforming products. The DOM Core API also allows population of a Document object using only DOM API calls; creating the skeleton Document and saving it persistently is left to the product that implements the DOM API.

1.1.1.   The DOM Structure Model

The DOM presents documents as a hierarchy of Node objects that also implement other, more specialized interfaces. Some types of nodes may have child nodes of various types, and others are leaf nodes that cannot have anything below them in the document structure. The node types, and which node types they may have as children, are as follows:

- Document -- Element (maximum of one), ProcessingInstruction, Comment, DocumentType

- DocumentFragment -- Element, ProcessingInstruction, Comment, Text, CDATASection, EntityReference

- DocumentType -- no children

- EntityReference -- Element, ProcessingInstruction, Comment, Text, CDATASection, EntityReference

- Element -- Element, Text, Comment, ProcessingInstruction, CDATASection, EntityReference

- `Attr` -- `Text, EntityReference`

- `ProcessingInstruction` -- no children

- `Comment` -- no children

- `Text` -- no children

- `CDATASection` -- no children

- `Entity` -- `Element, ProcessingInstruction, Comment, Text, CDATASection, EntityReference`

- `Notation` -- no children

The DOM also specifies a `NodeList` interface to handle ordered lists of `Node`s, such as the children of a `Node`, or the elements returned by the `Element.getElementsByTagName` method, and also a `NamedNodeMap` interface to handle unordered sets of nodes referenced by their name attribute, such as the attributes of an `Element`. `NodeLists` and `NamedNodeMaps` in the DOM are "live", that is, changes to the underlying document structure are reflected in all relevant `NodeLists` and `NamedNodeMaps`. For example, if a DOM user gets a `NodeList` object containing the children of an `Element`, then subsequently adds more children to that element (or removes children, or modifies them), those changes are automatically reflected in the `NodeList` without further action on the user's part. Likewise changes to a `Node` in the tree are reflected in all references to that `Node` in `NodeLists` and `NamedNodeMaps`.

1.1.2. Memory Management

Most of the APIs defined by this specification are *interfaces* rather than classes. That means that an actual implementation need only expose methods with the defined names and specified operation, not actually implement classes that correspond directly to the interfaces. This allows the DOM APIs to be implemented as a thin veneer on top of legacy applications with their own data structures, or on top of newer applications with different class hierarchies. This also means that ordinary constructors (in the Java or C++ sense) cannot be used to create DOM objects, since the underlying objects to be constructed may have little relationship to the DOM interfaces. The conventional solution to this in object-oriented design is to define *factory* methods that create instances of objects that implement the various interfaces. In the DOM Level 1, objects implementing some interface "X" are created by a "createX()" method on the Document interface; this is because all DOM objects live in the context of a specific Document.

The DOM Level 1 API does *not* define a standard way to create DOMImplementation or Document objects; actual DOM implementations must provide some proprietary way of bootstrapping these DOM interfaces, and then all other objects can be built from the Create methods on Document (or by various other convenience methods).

The Core DOM APIs are designed to be compatible with a wide range of languages, including both general-user scripting languages and the more challenging languages used mostly by professional programmers. Thus, the DOM APIs need to operate across a variety of memory management philosophies, from language platforms that do not expose memory management to the user at all, through those (notably Java) that provide explicit constructors but provide an automatic garbage collection mechanism to automatically reclaim unused memory, to those (especially C/C++) that generally require the programmer to explicitly allocate object memory, track where it is used, and explicitly free it for re-use. To ensure a consistent API across these platforms, the DOM does not address memory management issues at all, but instead leaves these for the implementation. Neither of the explicit language bindings devised by the DOM Working Group (for ECMAScript and Java) require any memory management methods, but DOM bindings for other languages (especially C or C++) probably will require such support. These extensions will be the responsibility of those adapting the DOM API to a specific language, not the DOM WG.

1.1.3. Naming Conventions

While it would be nice to have attribute and method names that are short, informative, internally consistent, and familiar to users of similar APIs, the names also should not clash with the names in legacy APIs supported by DOM implementations. Furthermore, both OMG IDL and `ECMAScript` have significant limitations in their ability to disambiguate names from different namespaces that makes it difficult to avoid naming conflicts with short, familiar names. So, DOM names tend to be long and quite descriptive in order to be unique across all environments.

The Working Group has also attempted to be internally consistent in its use of various terms, even though these may not be common distinctions in other APIs. For example, we use the method name "remove" when the method changes the structural model, and the method name "delete" when the method gets rid of something inside the structure model. The thing that is deleted is not returned. The thing that is removed may be returned, when it makes sense to return it.

1.1.4. Inheritance vs Flattened Views of the API

The DOM Core APIs present two somewhat different sets of interfaces to an XML/HTML document; one presenting an "object oriented" approach with a hierarchy of inheritance, and a "simplified" view that allows all manipulation to be done via the `Node` interface without requiring casts (in Java and other C-like languages) or query interface calls in COM environments. These operations are fairly expensive in Java and COM, and the DOM may be used in performance-critical environments, so we allow significant functionality using just the `Node` interface. Because many other users will find the inheritance hierarchy easier to understand than the "everything is a `Node`" approach to the DOM, we also support the full higher-level interfaces for those who prefer a more object-oriented API.

In practice, this means that there is a certain amount of redundancy in the API. The Working Group considers the "inheritance" approach the primary view of the API, and the full set of functionality on Node to be "extra" functionality that users may employ, but that does not eliminate the need for methods on other interfaces that an object-oriented analysis would dictate. (Of course, when the O-O analysis yields an attribute or method that is identical to one on the Node interface, we don't specify a completely redundant one). Thus, even though there is a generic nodeName attribute on the Node interface, there is still a tagName attribute on the Element interface; these two attributes must contain the same value, but the Working Group considers it worthwhile to support both, given the different constituencies the DOM API must satisfy.

1.1.5. The DOMString type

To ensure interoperability, the DOM specifies the DOMString type as follows:

- A DOMString is a sequence of 16-bit quantities. This may be expressed in IDL terms as:

  ```
  typedef sequence<unsigned short> DOMString;
  ```

- Applications must encode DOMString using UTF-16 (defined in Appendix C.3 of [UNICODE] and Amendment 1 of [ISO-10646]). The UTF-16 encoding was chosen because of its widespread industry practice. Please note that for both HTML and XML, the document character set (and therefore the notation of numeric character references) is based on UCS-4. A single numeric character reference in a source document may therefore in some cases correspond to two array positions in a DOMString (a high surrogate and a low surrogate). *Note: Even though the DOM defines the name of the string type to be DOMString, bindings may used different names. For, example for Java,* `DOMString` *is bound to the* `String` *type because it also uses UTF-16 as its encoding.*

Note:*As of August 1998, the OMG IDL specification included a* `wstring` *type. However, that definition did not meet the interoperability criteria of the DOM API since it relied on encoding negotiation to decide the width of a character.*

1.1.6. Case sensitivity in the DOM

The DOM has many interfaces that imply string matching. HTML processors generally assume an uppercase (less often, lowercase) normalization of names for such things as elements, while XML is explicitly case sensitive. For the purposes of the DOM, string matching takes place on a character code by character code basis, on the 16 bit value of a `DOMString`. As such, the DOM assumes that any normalizations will take place in the processor, *before* the DOM structures are built.

This then raises the issue of exactly what normalizations occur. The W3C I18N working group is in the process of defining exactly which normalizations are necessary for applications implementing the DOM.

1.2. *Fundamental Interfaces*

The interfaces within this section are considered *fundamental*, and must be fully implemented by all conforming implementations of the DOM, including all HTML DOM implementations.

Exception *DOMException*

DOM operations only raise exceptions in "exceptional" circumstances, i.e., when an operation is impossible to perform (either for logical reasons, because data is lost, or because the implementation has become unstable). In general, DOM methods return specific error values in ordinary processing situation, such as out-of-bound errors when using `NodeList`.

Implementations may raise other exceptions under other circumstances. For example, implementations may raise an implementation-dependent exception if a `null` argument is passed.

Some languages and object systems do not support the concept of exceptions. For such systems, error conditions may be indicated using native error reporting mechanisms. For some bindings, for example, methods may return error codes similar to those listed in the corresponding method descriptions.

IDL Definition

```
    exception DOMException {
  unsigned short    code;
};


// ExceptionCode
const unsigned short    INDEX_SIZE_ERR      = 1;
const unsigned short    DOMSTRING_SIZE_ERR = 2;
const unsigned short    HIERARCHY_REQUEST_ERR = 3;
const unsigned short    WRONG_DOCUMENT_ERR = 4;
const unsigned short    INVALID_CHARACTER_ERR = 5;
const unsigned short    NO_DATA_ALLOWED_ERR = 6;
const unsigned short    NO_MODIFICATION_ALLOWED_ERR = 7;
const unsigned short    NOT_FOUND_ERR       = 8;
const unsigned short    NOT_SUPPORTED_ERR   = 9;
const unsigned short    INUSE_ATTRIBUTE_ERR = 10;
```

Definition group *ExceptionCode*

An integer indicating the type of error generated.

Defined Constants

INDEX_SIZE_ERR

If index or size is negative, or greater than the allowed value

DOMSTRING_SIZE_ERR

If the specified range of text does not fit into a DOMString

HIERARCHY_REQUEST_ERR

If any node is inserted somewhere it doesn't belong

WRONG_DOCUMENT_ERR

If a node is used in a different document than the one that created it (that doesn't support it)

INVALID_CHARACTER_ERR

If an invalid character is specified, such as in a name.

NO_DATA_ALLOWED_ERR

If data is specified for a node which does not support data

NO_MODIFICATION_ALLOWED_ERR

If an attempt is made to modify an object where modifications are not allowed

NOT_FOUND_ERR

If an attempt was made to reference a node in a context where it does not exist

NOT_SUPPORTED_ERR

If the implementation does not support the type of object requested

INUSE_ATTRIBUTE_ERR

If an attempt is made to add an attribute that is already inuse elsewhere

Interface *DOMImplementation*

The `DOMImplementation` interface provides a number of methods for performing operations that are independent of any particular instance of the document object model.

The DOM Level 1 does not specify a way of creating a document instance, and hence document creation is an operation specific to an implementation. Future Levels of the DOM specification are expected to provide methods for creating documents directly.

IDL Definition

```
interface DOMImplementation {
  boolean                    hasFeature(in DOMString
    feature,
                                  in DOMString
    version);
};
```

Methods

`hasFeature`

Test if the DOM implementation implements a specific feature.

Parameters

`feature`

The package name of the feature to test. In Level 1, the legal values are "HTML" and "XML" (case-insensitive).

`version`

This is the version number of the package name to test. In Level 1, this is the string "1.0". If the version is not specified, supporting any version of the feature will cause the method to return `true`.

Return Value

`true`   if the feature is implemented in the specified version, `false` otherwise.

This method raises no exceptions.

Interface *DocumentFragment*

`DocumentFragment`   is a "lightweight" or "minimal" `Document` object. It is very common to want to be able to extract a portion of a document's tree or to create a new fragment of a document. Imagine implementing a user command like cut or rearranging a document by moving fragments around. It is desirable to have an object which can hold such fragments and it is quite natural to use a Node for this purpose. While it is true that a `Document` object could fulfil this role, a `Document` object can potentially be a heavyweight object, depending on the underlying implementation. What is really needed for this is a very lightweight object. `DocumentFragment` is such an object.

Furthermore, various operations — such as inserting nodes as children of another `Node` — may take `DocumentFragment` objects as arguments; this results in all the child nodes of the `DocumentFragment` being moved to the child list of this node.

The children of a `DocumentFragment` node are zero or more nodes representing the tops of any sub-trees defining the structure of the document. `DocumentFragment` nodes do not need to be well-formed XML documents (although they do need to follow the rules imposed upon well-formed XML parsed entities, which can have multiple top nodes). For example, a `DocumentFragment` might have only one child and that child node could be a `Text` node. Such a structure model represents neither an HTML document nor a well-formed XML document.

When a `DocumentFragment` is inserted into a `Document` (or indeed any other `Node` that may take children) the children of the `DocumentFragment` and not the `DocumentFragment` itself are inserted into the `Node`. This makes the `DocumentFragment` very useful when the user wishes to create nodes that are siblings; the `DocumentFragment` acts as the parent of these nodes so that the user can use the standard methods from the `Node` interface, such as `insertBefore()` and `appendChild()`.

IDL Definition

```
interface DocumentFragment : Node {
};
```

Interface *Document*

The `Document` interface represents the entire HTML or XML document. Conceptually, it is the root of the document tree, and provides the primary access to the document's data.

Since elements, text nodes, comments, processing instructions, etc. cannot exist outside the context of a `Document`, the `Docu-`

ment interface also contains the factory methods needed to create these objects. The `Node` objects created have a `ownerDocument` attribute which associates them with the `Document` within whose context they were created.

IDL Definition

```
interface Document : Node {
    readonly attribute  DocumentType            doctype;
    readonly attribute  DOMImplementation       implementation;
    readonly attribute  Element                 documentElement;
    Element                     createElement(in DOMString tagName)
                                            raises(DOMException);
    DocumentFragment            createDocumentFragment();
    Text                        createTextNode(in DOMString data);
    Comment                     createComment(in DOMString data);
    CDATASection                createCDATASection(in DOMString data)
                                            raises(DOMExcep-
tion);
    ProcessingInstruction       createProcessingInstruction(in DOM-
String target,
                                                    in DOM-
String data)

raises(DOMException);
    Attr                        createAttribute(in DOMString name)
                                            raises(DOMException);
    EntityReference             createEntityReference(in DOMString
name)
                                                    raises(DOMEx-
ception);
    NodeList                    getElementsByTagName(in DOMString
tagname);
};
```

Attributes

`doctype`

The Document Type Declaration (see `DocumentType`) associated with this document. For HTML documents as well as XML documents without a document type declaration this returns `null`. The DOM Level 1 does not support editing the Document Type Declaration, therefore `docType` cannot be altered in any way.

`implementation`

The `DOMImplementation` object that handles this document. A DOM application may use objects from multiple implementations.

`documentElement`

This is a convenience attribute that allows direct access to the child node that is the root element of the document. For HTML documents, this is the element with the tagName "HTML".

Methods

`createElement`

Creates an element of the type specified. Note that the instance returned implements the Element interface, so attributes can be specified directly on the returned object.

Parameters

`tagName`   The name of the element type to instantiate. For XML, this is case-sensitive. For HTML, the `tagName` parameter may be provided in any case, but it must be mapped to the canonical uppercase form by the DOM implementation.

Return Value

A new `Element` object.

Exceptions

`DOMException`

INVALID_CHARACTER_ERR: Raised if the specified name contains an invalid character.

`createDocumentFragment`

Creates an empty `DocumentFragment` object.

Return Value

> A new `DocumentFragment`.

> This method has no parameters.
> This method raises no exceptions.

`createTextNode`

> Creates a `Text` node given the specified string.

Parameters

> `data`   The data for the node.

Return Value

> The new `Text` object.

> This method raises no exceptions.

`createComment`

> Creates a `Comment` node given the specified string.

Parameters

> `data`   The data for the node.

Return Value

> The new `Comment` object.

> This method raises no exceptions.

`createCDATASection`

> Creates a `CDATASection` node whose value is the specified string.

Parameters

> `data`   The data for the `CDATASection` contents.

Return Value

> The new `CDATASection` object.

Exceptions

`DOMException`

> NOT_SUPPORTED_ERR: Raised if this document is an HTML document.

`createProcessingInstruction`

> Creates a `ProcessingInstruction` node given the specified name and data strings.

Parameters

`target`   The target part of the processing instruction.
`data`   The data for the node.

Return Value

> The new `ProcessingInstruction` object.

Exceptions

`DOMException`

> INVALID_CHARACTER_ERR: Raised if an invalid character is specified.
>
> NOT_SUPPORTED_ERR: Raised if this document is an HTML document.

`createAttribute`

> Creates an `Attr` of the given name. Note that the `Attr` instance can then be set on an `Element` using the `setAttribute` method.

Parameters

`name`   The name of the attribute.

Return Value

> A new `Attr` object.

Exceptions

`DOMException`

> INVALID_CHARACTER_ERR: Raised if the specified name contains an invalid character.

`createEntityReference`

Creates an EntityReference object.

Parameters

`name`   The name of the entity to reference.

Return Value

The new `EntityReference` object.

Exceptions

`DOMException`

INVALID_CHARACTER_ERR: Raised if the specified name contains an invalid character.

NOT_SUPPORTED_ERR: Raised if this document is an HTML document.

`getElementsByTagName`

Returns a `NodeList` of all the `Elements` with a given tag name in the order in which they would be encountered in a preorder traversal of the `Document` tree.

Parameters

`tagname`   The name of the tag to match on. The special value "*" matches all tags.

Return Value

A new `NodeList` object containing all the matched `Elements`. This method raises no exceptions.

Interface *Node*

The `Node` interface is the primary datatype for the entire Document Object Model. It represents a single node in the document tree. While all objects implementing the `Node` interface expose methods for dealing with children, not all objects implementing the `Node` interface may have children. For example, `Text` nodes may not have children, and adding children to such nodes results in a `DOMException` being raised.

The attributes `nodeName`, `nodeValue` and `attributes` are included as a mechanism to get at node information without casting down to the specific derived interface. In cases where there is no obvious mapping of these attributes for a specific `nodeType` (e.g., `nodeValue` for an Element or `attributes` for a Comment), this returns `null`. Note that the specialized interfaces may contain additional and more convenient mechanisms to get and set the relevant information.

IDL Definition

```
interface Node {
  // NodeType
  const unsigned short      ELEMENT_NODE          = 1;
  const unsigned short      ATTRIBUTE_NODE        = 2;
  const unsigned short      TEXT_NODE             = 3;
  const unsigned short      CDATA_SECTION_NODE    = 4;
  const unsigned short      ENTITY_REFERENCE_NODE = 5;
  const unsigned short      ENTITY_NODE           = 6;
  const unsigned short      PROCESSING_INSTRUCTION_NODE = 7;
  const unsigned short      COMMENT_NODE          = 8;
  const unsigned short      DOCUMENT_NODE         = 9;
  const unsigned short      DOCUMENT_TYPE_NODE    = 10;
  const unsigned short      DOCUMENT_FRAGMENT_NODE = 11;
  const unsigned short      NOTATION_NODE         = 12;

  readonly attribute  DOMString                nodeName;
          attribute  DOMString                nodeValue;
                                                     //
raises(DOMException) on setting
                                                     //
raises(DOMException) on retrieval
  readonly attribute  unsigned short           nodeType;
  readonly attribute  Node                     parentNode;
  readonly attribute  NodeList                 childNodes;
  readonly attribute  Node                     firstChild;
  readonly attribute  Node                     lastChild;
  readonly attribute  Node                     previousSibling;
  readonly attribute  Node                     nextSibling;
  readonly attribute  NamedNodeMap             attributes;
  readonly attribute  Document                 ownerDocument;
  Node                      insertBefore(in Node newChild,
                                         in Node refChild)
                                         raises(DOMException);
```

```
Node                    replaceChild(in Node newChild,
                                     in Node oldChild)
                                    raises(DOMException);
Node                    removeChild(in Node oldChild)
                                    raises(DOMException);
Node                    appendChild(in Node newChild)
                                    raises(DOMException);
boolean                 hasChildNodes();
Node                    cloneNode(in boolean deep);
};
```

Definition group *Node Type*

An integer indicating which type of node this is.

Defined Constants

ELEMENT_NODE

The node is a `Element`.

ATTRIBUTE_NODE

The node is an `Attr`.

TEXT_NODE

The node is a `Text` node.

CDATA_SECTION_NODE

The node is a `CDATASection`.

ENTITY_REFERENCE_NODE

The node is an `EntityReference`.

ENTITY_NODE

The node is an `Entity`.

PROCESSING_INSTRUCTION_NODE

The node is a `ProcessingInstruction`.

COMMENT_NODE

The node is a `Comment`.

DOCUMENT_NODE

The node is a `Document`.

DOCUMENT_TYPE_NODE

The node is a `DocumentType`.

DOCUMENT_FRAGMENT_NODE

The node is a `DocumentFragment`.

NOTATION_NODE

The node is a `Notation`.

The values of `nodeName`, `nodeValue`, and `attributes` vary according to the node type as follows:

nodeName	*nodeValue*	*attributes*	
Element	tagName	null	NamedNodeMap
Attr	name of attribute	value of attribute	null
Text	#text	content of the text node	null
CDATASection	#cdata-section	content of the CDATA Section	null
EntityReference	name of entity referenced	null	null
Entity	entity name	null	null
ProcessingInstruction	target	entire content excluding the target	null
Comment	#comment	content of the comment	null
Document	#document	null	null
DocumentType	document type name	null	null
DocumentFragment	#document-fragment	null	null
Notation	notation name	null	null

Attributes

nodeName

> The name of this node, depending on its type; see the table above.

nodeValue

> The value of this node, depending on its type; see the table above.

Exceptions on setting

DOMException

> NO_MODIFICATION_ALLOWED_ERR: Raised when the node is readonly.

Exceptions on retrieval

DOMException

> DOMSTRING_SIZE_ERR: Raised when it would return more characters than fit in a DOMString variable on the implementation platform.

nodeType

> A code representing the type of the underlying object, as defined above.

parentNode

> The parent of this node. All nodes, except Document, DocumentFragment, and Attr may have a parent. However, if a node has just been created and not yet added to the tree, or if it has been removed from the tree, this is null.

childNodes

> A NodeList that contains all children of this node. If there are no children, this is a NodeList containing no nodes. The content of the returned NodeList is "live" in the sense that, for instance, changes to the children of the node object that it was created from are immediately reflected in the nodes returned by the NodeList accessors; it is not a static snapshot of the content

of the node. This is true for every `NodeList`, including the ones returned by the `getElementsByTagName` method.

`firstChild`

The first child of this node. If there is no such node, this returns `null`.

`lastChild`

The last child of this node. If there is no such node, this returns `null`.

`previousSibling`

The node immediately preceding this node. If there is no such node, this returns `null`.

`nextSibling`

The node immediately following this node. If there is no such node, this returns `null`.

`attributes`

A `NamedNodeMap` containing the attributes of this node (if it is an `Element`) or `null` otherwise.

`ownerDocument`

The `Document` object associated with this node. This is also the `Document` object used to create new nodes. When this node is a `Document` this is `null`.

Methods

`insertBefore`

Inserts the node `newChild` before the existing child node refChild. If `refChild` is `null`, insert `newChild` at the end of the list of children.

If `newChild` is a `DocumentFragment` object, all of its children are inserted, in the same order, before `refChild`. If the new-Child is already in the tree, it is first removed.

Parameters

newChild   The node to insert.

refChild   The reference node, i.e., the node before which the new node must be inserted.

Return Value

The node being inserted.

Exceptions

DOMException

HIERARCHY_REQUEST_ERR: Raised if this node is of a type that does not allow children of the type of the newChild node, or if the node to insert is one of this node's ancestors.

WRONG_DOCUMENT_ERR: Raised if newChild was created from a different document than the one that created this node.

NO_MODIFICATION_ALLOWED_ERR: Raised if this node is readonly.

NOT_FOUND_ERR: Raised if refChild is not a child of this node.

replaceChild

Replaces the child node oldChild with newChild in the list of children, and returns the oldChild node. If the newChild is already in the tree, it is first removed.

Parameters

newChild   The new node to put in the child list.

oldChild   The node being replaced in the list.

Return Value

The node replaced.

Exceptions

DOMException

> HIERARCHY_REQUEST_ERR: Raised if this node is of a type that does not allow children of the type of the newChild node, or it the node to put in is one of this node's ancestors.

> WRONG_DOCUMENT_ERR: Raised if newChild was created from a different document than the one that created this node.

> NO_MODIFICATION_ALLOWED_ERR: Raised if this node is readonly.

> NOT_FOUND_ERR: Raised if oldChild is not a child of this node.

removeChild

> Removes the child node indicated by oldChild from the list of children, and returns it.

Parameters

> oldChild   The node being removed.

Return Value

> The node removed.

Exceptions

DOMException

> NO_MODIFICATION_ALLOWED_ERR: Raised if this node is readonly.

> NOT_FOUND_ERR: Raised if oldChild is not a child of this node.

appendChild

> Adds the node newChild to the end of the list of children of this node. If the newChild is already in the tree, it is first removed.

Parameters

newChild   The node to add.

If it is a DocumentFragment object, the entire contents of the document fragment are moved into the child list of this node

Return Value

The node added.

Exceptions

DOMException

HIERARCHY_REQUEST_ERR: Raised if this node is of a type that does not allow children of the type of the newChild node, or if the node to append is one of this node's ancestors.

WRONG_DOCUMENT_ERR: Raised if newChild was created from a different document than the one that created this node.

NO_MODIFICATION_ALLOWED_ERR: Raised if this node is readonly.

hasChildNodes

This is a convenience method to allow easy determination of whether a node has any children.

Return Value

true if the node has any children, false if the node has no children.

This method has no parameters.

This method raises no exceptions.

cloneNode

Returns a duplicate of this node, i.e., serves as a generic copy constructor for nodes. The duplicate node has no parent (parentNode returns null.).

Cloning an Element copies all attributes and their values, including those generated by the XML processor to represent defaulted attributes, but this method does not copy any text it contains unless it is a deep clone, since the text is contained in a child `Text` node. Cloning any other type of node simply returns a copy of this node.

Parameters

`deep`   If `true`, recursively clone the subtree under the specified node; if `false`, clone only the node itself (and its attributes, if it is an `Element`).

Return Value

The duplicate node.

This method raises no exceptions.

Interface *NodeList*

The `NodeList` interface provides the abstraction of an ordered collection of nodes, without defining or constraining how this collection is implemented.

The items in the `NodeList` are accessible via an integral index, starting from 0.

IDL Definition

```
interface NodeList {
  Node                    item(in unsigned long index);
  readonly attribute  unsigned long        length;
};
```

Methods

`item`

Returns the `index`th item in the collection. If `index` is greater than or equal to the number of nodes in the list, this returns `null`.

Parameters

`index`   Index into the collection.

Return Value

The node at the `index`th position in the `NodeList`, or `null` if that is not a valid index.

This method raises no exceptions.

Attributes

`length`

> The number of nodes in the list. The range of valid child node indices is 0 to `length-1` inclusive.

Interface *NamedNodeMap*

> Objects implementing the `NamedNodeMap` interface are used to represent collections of nodes that can be accessed by name. Note that `NamedNodeMap` does not inherit from `NodeList`; `NamedNodeMaps` are not maintained in any particular order. Objects contained in an object implementing `NamedNodeMap` may also be accessed by an ordinal index, but this is simply to allow convenient enumeration of the contents of a `NamedNodeMap`, and does not imply that the DOM specifies an order to these Nodes.

IDL Definition

```
interface NamedNodeMap {
  Node                      getNamedItem(in DOMString name);
  Node                      setNamedItem(in Node arg)
                                  raises(DOMException);
  Node                    removeNamedItem(in DOMString name)
                                  raises(DOMException);
  Node                    item(in unsigned long index);
  readonly attribute  unsigned long      length;
};
```

Methods

`getNamedItem`

> Retrieves a node specified by name.

Parameters

`name`   Name of a node to retrieve.

Return Value

> A `Node` (of any type) with the specified name, or `null` if the specified name did not identify any node in the map.
>
> This method raises no exceptions.

`setNamedItem`

Adds a node using its `nodeName` attribute.

As the `nodeName` attribute is used to derive the name which the node must be stored under, multiple nodes of certain types (those that have a "special" string value) cannot be stored as the names would clash. This is seen as preferable to allowing nodes to be aliased.

Parameters

`arg` A node to store in a named node map. The node will later be accessible using the value of the `nodeName` attribute of the node. If a node with that name is already present in the map, it is replaced by the new one.

Return Value

If the new `Node` replaces an existing node with the same name the previously existing `Node` is returned, otherwise `null` is returned.

Exceptions

`DOMException`

WRONG_DOCUMENT_ERR: Raised if `arg` was created from a different document than the one that created the `NamedNodeMap`.

NO_MODIFICATION_ALLOWED_ERR: Raised if this `NamedNodeMap` is readonly.

INUSE_ATTRIBUTE_ERR: Raised if `arg` is an `Attr` that is already an attribute of another `Element` object. The DOM user must explicitly clone `Attr` nodes to re-use them in other elements.

`removeNamedItem`

Removes a node specified by name. If the removed node is an `Attr` with a default value it is immediately replaced.

Parameters

name   The name of a node to remove.

Return Value

The node removed from the map or `null` if no node with such a name exists.

Exceptions

DOMException

NOT_FOUND_ERR: Raised if there is no node named name in the map.

item

Returns the `index`th item in the map. If `index` is greater than or equal to the number of nodes in the map, this returns `null`.

Parameters

index   Index into the map.

Return Value

The node at the `index`th position in the `NamedNodeMap`, or `null` if that is not a valid index.

This method raises no exceptions.

Attributes

length

The number of nodes in the map. The range of valid child node indices is 0 to `length-1` inclusive.

Interface *CharacterData*

The `CharacterData` interface extends Node with a set of attributes and methods for accessing character data in the DOM. For clarity this set is defined here rather than on each object that uses these attributes and methods. No DOM objects correspond directly to `CharacterData`, though `Text` and others do inherit the interface from it. All `offsets` in this interface start from 0.

IDL Definition

```
interface CharacterData : Node {
        attribute  DOMString              data;
                                // raises(DOMException)
on setting
                                // raises(DOMException)
on retrieval
  readonly attribute  unsigned long       length;
  DOMString                    substringData(in unsigned long
offset,
                                in unsigned long
count)
                                raises(DOMExcep-
tion);
  void                    appendData(in DOMString arg)
                            raises(DOMExcep-
tion);
  void                    insertData(in unsigned long
offset,
                            in DOMString arg)
                            raises(DOMExcep-
tion);
  void                    deleteData(in unsigned long
offset,
                            in unsigned long
count)
                            raises(DOMExcep-
tion);
  void                    replaceData(in unsigned long
offset,
                            in unsigned long
count,
                            in DOMString arg)
                            raises(DOMExcep-
tion);
};
```

Attributes

data

> The character data of the node that implements this interface.
> The DOM implementation may not put arbitrary limits on the
> amount of data that may be stored in a CharacterData node.
> However, implementation limits may mean that the entirety of a

node's data may not fit into a single DOMString. In such cases, the user may call substringData to retrieve the data in appropriately sized pieces.

Exceptions on setting

DOMException

> NO_MODIFICATION_ALLOWED_ERR: Raised when the node is readonly.

Exceptions on retrieval

DOMException

> DOMSTRING_SIZE_ERR: Raised when it would return more characters than fit in a DOMString variable on the implementation platform.

length

> The number of characters that are available through data and the substringData method below. This may have the value zero, i.e., CharacterData nodes may be empty.

Methods

substringData

> Extracts a range of data from the node.

Parameters

offset   Start offset of substring to extract.

count   The number of characters to extract.

Return Value

> The specified substring. If the sum of offset and count exceeds the length, then all characters to the end of the data are returned.

Exceptions

DOMException

> INDEX_SIZE_ERR: Raised if the specified offset is negative or greater than the number of characters in data, or if the specified count is negative.

DOMSTRING_SIZE_ERR: Raised if the specified range of text does not fit into a DOMString.

`appendData`

Append the string to the end of the character data of the node. Upon success, data provides access to the concatenation of data and the DOMString specified.

Parameters

arg   The DOMString to append.

Exceptions

DOMException

NO_MODIFICATION_ALLOWED_ERR: Raised if this node is readonly.

This method returns nothing.

`insertData`

Insert a string at the specified character offset.

Parameters

offset   The character offset at which to insert.

arg   The DOMString to insert.

Exceptions

DOMException

INDEX_SIZE_ERR: Raised if the specified offset is negative or greater than the number of characters in data.

NO_MODIFICATION_ALLOWED_ERR: Raised if this node is readonly.

This method returns nothing.

`deleteData`

Remove a range of characters from the node. Upon success, data and length reflect the change.

Parameters

offset   The offset from which to remove characters.

count   The number of characters to delete. If the sum of off-set and count exceeds length then all characters from offset to the end of the data are deleted.

Exceptions

DOMException

INDEX_SIZE_ERR: Raised if the specified offset is negative or greater than the number of characters in data, or if the specified count is negative.

NO_MODIFICATION_ALLOWED_ERR: Raised if this node is readonly.

This method returns nothing.

replaceData

Replace the characters starting at the specified character offset with the specified string.

Parameters

offset   The offset from which to start replacing.

count   The number of characters to replace. If the sum of off-set and count exceeds length, then all characters to the end of the data are replaced (i.e., the effect is the same as a remove method call with the same range, followed by an append method invocation).

arg   The DOMString with which the range must be replaced.

Exceptions

DOMException

INDEX_SIZE_ERR: Raised if the specified offset is negative or greater than the number of characters in data, or if the specified count is negative.

NO_MODIFICATION_ALLOWED_ERR: Raised if this node is readonly.

This method returns nothing.

Interface *Attr*

The `Attr` interface represents an attribute in an `Element` object. Typically the allowable values for the attribute are defined in a document type definition.

`Attr` objects inherit the `Node` interface, but since they are not actually child nodes of the element they describe, the DOM does not consider them part of the document tree. Thus, the `Node` attributes `parentNode`, `previousSibling`, and `nextSibling` have a null value for `Attr` objects. The DOM takes the view that attributes are properties of elements rather than having a separate identity from the elements they are associated with; this should make it more efficient to implement such features as default attributes associated with all elements of a given type. Furthermore, `Attr` nodes may not be immediate children of a `Document-Fragment`. However, they can be associated with `Element` nodes contained within a `DocumentFragment`. In short, users and implementors of the DOM need to be aware that `Attr` nodes have some things in common with other objects inheriting the `Node` interface, but they also are quite distinct.

The attribute's effective value is determined as follows: if this attribute has been explicitly assigned any value, that value is the attribute's effective value; otherwise, if there is a declaration for this attribute, and that declaration includes a default value, then that default value is the attribute's effective value; otherwise, the attribute does not exist on this element in the structure model until it has been explicitly added. Note that the `nodeValue` attribute on the `Attr` instance can also be used to retrieve the string version of the attribute's value(s).

In XML, where the value of an attribute can contain entity references, the child nodes of the `Attr` node provide a representation in which entity references are not expanded. These child nodes may be either `Text` or `EntityReference` nodes. Because the attribute type may be unknown, there are no tokenized attribute values.

IDL Definition

```
interface Attr : Node {
    readonly attribute  DOMString        name;
    readonly attribute  boolean          specified;
             attribute  DOMString        value;
};
```

Attributes

`name`

> Returns the name of this attribute.

`specified`

> If this attribute was explicitly given a value in the original document, this is `true`; otherwise, it is `false`. Note that the implementation is in charge of this attribute, not the user. If the user changes the value of the attribute (even if it ends up having the same value as the default value) then the `specified` flag is automatically flipped to `true`. To re-specify the attribute as the default value from the DTD, the user must delete the attribute. The implementation will then make a new attribute available with `specified` set to `false` and the default value (if one exists).
>
> In summary:

> - If the attribute has an assigned value in the document then `specified` is `true`, and the value is the assigned value.
>
> - If the attribute has no assigned value in the document and has a default value in the DTD, then `specified` is `false`, and the value is the default value in the DTD.
>
> - If the attribute has no assigned value in the document and has a value of #IMPLIED in the DTD, then the attribute does not appear in the structure model of the document.

`value`

> On retrieval, the value of the attribute is returned as a string. Character and general entity references are replaced with their values.

On setting, this creates a `Text` node with the unparsed contents of the string.

Interface *Element*

By far the vast majority of objects (apart from text) that authors encounter when traversing a document are `Element` nodes. Assume the following XML document:

```
<elementExample id="demo">
  <subelement1/>
  <subelement2><subsubelement/></subelement2>
</elementExample>
```

When represented using DOM, the top node is an `Element` node for "elementExample", which contains two child `Element` nodes, one for "subelement1" and one for "subelement2". "subelement1" contains no child nodes.

Elements may have attributes associated with them; since the `Element` interface inherits from `Node`, the generic `Node` interface method `getAttributes` may be used to retrieve the set of all attributes for an element. There are methods on the `Element` interface to retrieve either an `Attr` object by name or an attribute value by name. In XML, where an attribute value may contain entity references, an `Attr` object should be retrieved to examine the possibly fairly complex sub-tree representing the attribute value. On the other hand, in HTML, where all attributes have simple string values, methods to directly access an attribute value can safely be used as a convenience.

IDL Definition

```
interface Element : Node {
  readonly attribute  DOMString                tagName;
  DOMString               getAttribute(in DOMString name);
  void                    setAttribute(in DOMString name,
                                       in DOMString value)
                                       raises(DOMException);
  void                    removeAttribute(in DOMString name)
```

```
                                              raises
                                              (DOMException);
Attr                          getAttributeNode(in DOMString name);
Attr                          setAttributeNode(in Attr newAttr)
                                              raises
                                              (DOMException);
Attr                          removeAttributeNode(in Attr oldAttr)
                                              raises
                                              (DOMException);
NodeList                      getElementsByTagName(in DOMString
                                              name);
void                          normalize();
};
```

Attributes

`tagName`

The name of the element. For example, in:

```
<elementExample id="demo">
        . . .
</elementExample> ,
```

`tagName` has the value `"elementExample"`. Note that this is case-preserving in XML, as are all of the operations of the DOM. The HTML DOM returns the `tagName` of an HTML element in the canonical uppercase form, regardless of the case in the source HTML document.

Methods

`getAttribute`

Retrieves an attribute value by name.

Parameters

`name`   The name of the attribute to retrieve.

Return Value

The `Attr` value as a string, or the empty string if that attribute does not have a specified or default value.

This method raises no exceptions.

`setAttribute`

Adds a new attribute. If an attribute with that name is already present in the element, its value is changed to be that of the value parameter. This value is a simple string, it is not parsed as it is being set. So any markup (such as syntax to be recognized as an entity reference) is treated as literal text, and needs to be appropriately escaped by the implementation when it is written out. In order to assign an attribute value that contains entity references, the user must create an `Attr` node plus any `Text` and `EntityReference` nodes, build the appropriate subtree, and use `setAttributeNode` to assign it as the value of an attribute.

Parameters

`name`   The name of the attribute to create or alter.

`value`   Value to set in string form.

Exceptions

`DOMException`

INVALID_CHARACTER_ERR: Raised if the specified name contains an invalid character.

NO_MODIFICATION_ALLOWED_ERR: Raised if this node is readonly.

This method returns nothing.

`removeAttribute`

Removes an attribute by name. If the removed attribute has a default value it is immediately replaced.

Parameters

`name`   The name of the attribute to remove.

Exceptions

`DOMException`

NO_MODIFICATION_ALLOWED_ERR: Raised if this node is readonly.

This method returns nothing.

`getAttributeNode`

Retrieves an `Attr` node by name.

Parameters

`name`   The name of the attribute to retrieve.

Return Value

The `Attr` node with the specified attribute name or `null` if there is no such attribute.

This method raises no exceptions.

`setAttributeNode`

Adds a new attribute. If an attribute with that name is already present in the element, it is replaced by the new one.

Parameters

`newAttr`   The `Attr` node to add to the attribute list.

Return Value

If the `newAttr` attribute replaces an existing attribute with the same name, the previously existing `Attr` node is returned, otherwise `null` is returned.

Exceptions

`DOMException`

WRONG_DOCUMENT_ERR: Raised if `newAttr` was created from a different document than the one that created the element.

NO_MODIFICATION_ALLOWED_ERR: Raised if this node is readonly.

INUSE_ATTRIBUTE_ERR: Raised if `newAttr` is already an attribute of another `Element` object. The DOM user must explicitly clone `Attr` nodes to re-use them in other elements.

`removeAttributeNode`

Removes the specified attribute.

Parameters

oldAttr   The Attr node to remove from the attribute list. If the removed Attr has a default value it is immediately replaced.

Return Value

The Attr node that was removed.

Exceptions

DOMException

NO_MODIFICATION_ALLOWED_ERR: Raised if this node is readonly.

NOT_FOUND_ERR: Raised if oldAttr is not an attribute of the element.

getElementsByTagName

Returns a NodeList of all descendant elements with a given tag name, in the order in which they would be encountered in a pre-order traversal of the Element tree.

Parameters

name   The name of the tag to match on. The special value "*" matches all tags.

Return Value

A list of matching Element nodes.

This method raises no exceptions.

normalize

Puts all Text nodes in the full depth of the sub-tree underneath this Element into a "normal" form where only markup (e.g., tags, comments, processing instructions, CDATA sections, and entity references) separates Text nodes, i.e., there are no adjacent Text nodes. This can be used to ensure that the DOM view of a document is the same as if it were saved and re-loaded, and is useful when operations (such as XPointer lookups) that depend on a particular document tree structure are to be used.

This method has no parameters.

This method returns nothing.

This method raises no exceptions.

Interface *Text*

The `Text` interface represents the textual content (termed character datain XML) of an `Element` or `Attr`. If there is no markup inside an element's content, the text is contained in a single object implementing the `Text` interface that is the only child of the element. If there is markup, it is parsed into a list of elements and `Text` nodes that form the list of children of the element.

When a document is first made available via the DOM, there is only one `Text` node for each block of text. Users may create adjacent `Text` nodes that represent the contents of a given element without any intervening markup, but should be aware that there is no way to represent the separations between these nodes in XML or HTML, so they will not (in general) persist between DOM editing sessions. The `normalize()` method on `Element` merges any such adjacent `Text` objects into a single node for each block of text; this is recommended before employing operations that depend on a particular document structure, such as navigation with `XPointers`.

IDL Definition

```
interface Text : CharacterData {
  Text                      splitText(in unsigned long offset)
                                    raises(DOMException);
};
```

Methods

`splitText`

Breaks this `Text` node into two Text nodes at the specified offset, keeping both in the tree as siblings. This node then only contains all the content up to the `offset` point. And a new `Text` node, which is inserted as the next sibling of this node, contains all the content at and after the `offset` point.

Parameters

offset   The offset at which to split, starting from 0.

Return Value

The new Text node.

Exceptions

DOMException

INDEX_SIZE_ERR: Raised if the specified offset is negative or greater than the number of characters in data.

NO_MODIFICATION_ALLOWED_ERR: Raised if this node is readonly.

Interface *Comment*

This represents the content of a comment, i.e., all the characters between the starting '<!–' and ending '–>'. Note that this is the definition of a comment in XML, and, in practice, HTML, although some HTML tools may implement the full SGML comment structure.

IDL Definition

```
interface Comment : CharacterData {
};
```

1.3. Extended Interfaces

The interfaces defined here form part of the DOM Level 1 Core specification, but objects that expose these interfaces will never be encountered in a DOM implementation that deals only with HTML. As such, HTML-only DOM implementations do not need to have objects that implement these interfaces.

Interface *CDATASection*

CDATA sections are used to escape blocks of text containing characters that would otherwise be regarded as markup. The only delimiter that is recognized in a CDATA section is the "]]>" string that ends the CDATA section. CDATA sections can not be nested. The primary purpose is for including material such as XML fragments, without needing to escape all the delimiters.

The DOMString attribute of the Text node holds the text that is contained by the CDATA section. Note that this *may* contain characters that need to be escaped outside of CDATA sections and that, depending on the character encoding ("charset") chosen for serialization, it may be impossible to write out some characters as part of a CDATA section.

The CDATASection interface inherits the CharacterData interface through the Text interface. Adjacent CDATASections nodes are not merged by use of the Element.normalize() method.

IDL Definition

```
interface CDATASection : Text {
};
```

Interface *DocumentType*

Each Document has a doctype attribute whose value is either null or a DocumentType object. The DocumentType interface in the DOM Level 1 Core provides an interface to the list of entities that are defined for the document, and little else because the effect of namespaces and the various XML scheme efforts on DTD representation are not clearly understood as of this writing.

The DOM Level 1 doesn't support editing DocumentType nodes.

IDL Definition

```
interface DocumentType : Node {
  readonly attribute  DOMString        name;
  readonly attribute  NamedNodeMap     entities;
  readonly attribute  NamedNodeMap     notations;
};
```

Attributes

name

The name of DTD; i.e., the name immediately following the DOCTYPE keyword.

entities

A `NamedNodeMap` containing the general entities, both external and internal, declared in the DTD. Duplicates are discarded. For example in:

```
<!DOCTYPE ex SYSTEM "ex.dtd" [
  <!ENTITY foo "foo">
  <!ENTITY bar "bar">
  <!ENTITY % baz "baz">
]>
<ex/>
```

the interface provides access to `foo` and `bar` but not `baz`. Every node in this map also implements the `Entity` interface.

The DOM Level 1 does not support editing entities, therefore `entities` cannot be altered in any way.

notations

A `NamedNodeMap` containing the notations declared in the DTD. Duplicates are discarded. Every node in this map also implements the `Notation` interface.

The DOM Level 1 does not support editing notations, therefore `notations` cannot be altered in any way.

Interface *Notation*

This interface represents a notation declared in the DTD. A notation either declares, by name, the format of an unparsed entity (see section 4.7 of the XML 1.0 specification), or is used for formal declaration of Processing Instruction targets (see section 2.6 of the XML 1.0 specification). The `nodeName` attribute inherited from `Node` is set to the declared name of the notation.

The DOM Level 1 does not support editing `Notation` nodes; they are therefore readonly.

A `Notation` node does not have any parent.

IDL Definition

```
interface Notation : Node {
  readonly attribute  DOMString          publicId;
  readonly attribute  DOMString          systemId;
};
```

Attributes

`publicId`

> The public identifier of this notation. If the public identifier was not specified, this is `null`.

`systemId`

> The system identifier of this notation. If the system identifier was not specified, this is `null`.

Interface *Entity*

> This interface represents an entity, either parsed or unparsed, in an XML document. Note that this models the entity itself *not* the entity declaration. `Entity` declaration modeling has been left for a later Level of the DOM specification.

> The `nodeName` attribute that is inherited from `Node` contains the name of the entity.

> An XML processor may choose to completely expand entities before the structure model is passed to the DOM; in this case there will be no `EntityReference` nodes in the document tree.

> XML does not mandate that a non-validating XML processor read and process entity declarations made in the external subset or declared in external parameter entities. This means that parsed entities declared in the external subset need not be expanded by some classes of applications, and that the replacement value of the entity may not be available. When the replacement value is available, the corresponding `Entity` node's child list represents the structure of that replacement text. Otherwise, the child list is empty.

> The resolution of the children of the `Entity` (the replacement value) may be lazily evaluated; actions by the user (such as calling the `childNodes` method on the `Entity` Node) are assumed to trigger the evaluation.

> The DOM Level 1 does not support editing `Entity` nodes; if a user wants to make changes to the contents of an `Entity`, every

related `EntityReference` node has to be replaced in the structure model by a clone of the `Entity`'s contents, and then the desired changes must be made to each of those clones instead. All the descendants of an `Entity` node are readonly.

An `Entity` node does not have any parent.

IDL Definition
```
interface Entity : Node {
    readonly attribute  DOMString        publicId;
    readonly attribute  DOMString        systemId;
    readonly attribute  DOMString        notationName;
};
```

Attributes
`publicId`

> The public identifier associated with the entity, if specified. If the public identifier was not specified, this is `null`.

`systemId`

> The system identifier associated with the entity, if specified. If the system identifier was not specified, this is `null`.

`notationName`

> For unparsed entities, the name of the notation for the entity. For parsed entities, this is `null`.

Interface *EntityReference*

> `EntityReference` objects may be inserted into the structure model when an entity reference is in the source document, or when the user wishes to insert an entity reference. Note that character references and references to predefined entities are considered to be expanded by the HTML or XML processor so that characters are represented by their Unicode equivalent rather than by an entity reference. Moreover, the XML processor may completely expand references to entities while building the structure model, instead of providing `EntityReference` objects. If it does provide such objects, then for a given `EntityReference` node, it may be that there is no `Entity` node representing the refer-

enced entity; but if such an `Entity` exists, then the child list of the `EntityReference` node is the same as that of the `Entity` node. As with the `Entity` node, all descendants of the `EntityReference` are readonly.

The resolution of the children of the `EntityReference` (the replacement value of the referenced `Entity`) may be lazily evaluated; actions by the user (such as calling the `childNodes` method on the `EntityReference` node) are assumed to trigger the evaluation.

IDL Definition

```
interface EntityReference : Node {
};
```

Interface *ProcessingInstruction*

The `ProcessingInstruction` interface represents a "processing instruction", used in XML as a way to keep processor-specific information in the text of the document.

IDL Definition

```
interface ProcessingInstruction : Node {
  readonly attribute  DOMString                target;
           attribute  DOMString                data;
                                       // raises(DOMException)
on setting
};
```

Attributes

`target`

The target of this processing instruction. XML defines this as being the first token following the markup that begins the processing instruction.

`data`

The content of this processing instruction. This is from the first non white space character after the target to the character immediately preceding the `?>`.

Exceptions on setting

```
DOMException
```

NO_MODIFICATION_ALLOWED_ERR: Raised when the node is readonly.

Copyright Notice

When space permits, inclusion of the full text of this **NOTICE** should be provided. In addition, credit shall be attributed to the copyright holders for any software, documents, or other items or products that you create pursuant to the implementation of the contents of this document, or any portion thereof.

No right to create modifications or derivatives is granted pursuant to this license.

THIS DOCUMENT IS PROVIDED "AS IS," AND COPYRIGHT HOLDERS MAKE NO REPRESENTATIONS OR WARRANTIES, EXPRESS OR IMPLIED, INCLUDING, BUT NOT LIMITED TO, WARRANTIES OF MERCHANTABILITY, FITNESS FOR A PARTICULAR PURPOSE, NON-INFRINGEMENT, OR TITLE; THAT THE CONTENTS OF THE DOCUMENT ARE SUITABLE FOR ANY PURPOSE; NOR THAT THE IMPLEMENTATION OF SUCH CONTENTS WILL NOT INFRINGE ANY THIRD PARTY PATENTS, COPYRIGHTS, TRADEMARKS OR OTHER RIGHTS.

COPYRIGHT HOLDERS WILL NOT BE LIABLE FOR ANY DIRECT, INDIRECT, SPECIAL OR CONSEQUENTIAL DAMAGES ARISING OUT OF ANY USE OF THE DOCUMENT OR THE PERFORMANCE OR IMPLEMENTATION OF THE CONTENTS THEREOF.

The name and trademarks of copyright holders may NOT be used in advertising or publicity pertaining to this document or its contents without specific, written prior permission. Title to copyright in this document will at all times remain with copyright holders.

Appendix C
SAX Interfaces

A

addAttribute(String, String, String). Method in class `org.xml.sax.helpers.Attribute-ListImpl`
   Adds an attribute to an attribute list.
AttributeListImpl(). Constructor for class `org.xml.sax.helpers.AttributeListImpl`.
   Creates an empty attribute list.
AttributeListImpl(AttributeList). Constructor for class `org.xml.sax.helpers.Attribute-ListImpl`.
   Constructs a persistent copy of an existing attribute list.

C

characters(char[], int, int). Method in class `org.xml.sax.HandlerBase`.
   Receives notification of character data inside an element.
characters(char[], int, int). Method in interface `org.xml.sax.DocumentHandler`.
   Receives notification of character data.
clear(). Method in class `org.xml.sax.helpers.AttributeListImpl`.
   Clears the attribute list.

E

endDocument(). Method in class `org.xml.sax.HandlerBase`.
   Receives notification of the end of the document.

endDocument(). Method in interface `org.xml.sax.DocumentHandler`.
   Receives notification of the end of a document.
endElement(String). Method in class `org.xml.sax.HandlerBase.`
   Receives notification of the end of an element.
endElement(String). Method in interface `org.xml.sax.DocumentHandler.`
   Receives notification of the end of an element.
error(SAXParseException). Method in class `org.xml.sax.HandlerBase.`
   Receives notification of a recoverable parser error.
error(SAXParseException). Method in interface `org.xml.sax.ErrorHandler.`
   Receives notification of a recoverable error.

▋ F

fatalError(SAXParseException). Method in class `org.xml.sax.HandlerBase.`
   Reports a fatal XML parsing error.
fatalError(SAXParseException). Method in interface `org.xml.sax.ErrorHandler.`
   Receives notification of a non-recoverable error.

▋ G

getByteStream(). Method in class `org.xml.sax.InputSource.`
   Gets the byte stream for this input source.
getCharacterStream(). Method in class `org.xml.sax.InputSource.`
   Gets the character stream for this input source.
getColumnNumber(). Method in class `org.xml.sax.helpers.LocatorImpl.`
   Returns the saved column number (1-based).
getColumnNumber(). Method in class `org.xml.sax.SAXParseException.`
   Returns the column number of the end of the text where the exception occurred.
getColumnNumber(). Method in interface `org.xml.sax.Locator.`
   Returns the column number where the current document event ends.
getEncoding(). Method in class `org.xml.sax.InputSource.`
   Gets the character encoding for a byte stream or URI.
getException(). Method in class `org.xml.sax.SAXException.`
   Returns the embedded exception, if any.
getLength(). Method in class `org.xml.sax.helpers.AttributeListImpl.`
   Returns the number of attributes in the list.
getLength(). Method in interface `org.xml.sax.AttributeList.`
   Returns the number of attributes in this list.
getLineNumber(). Method in class `org.xml.sax.helpers.LocatorImpl.`
   Returns the saved line number (1-based).
getLineNumber(). Method in class `org.xml.sax.SAXParseException.`
   Returns the line number of the end of the text where the exception occurred.

getLineNumber(). Method in interface org.xml.sax.Locator.
Returns the line number where the current document event ends.
getMessage(). Method in class org.xml.sax.SAXException.
Returns a detail message for this exception.
getName(int). Method in class org.xml.sax.helpers.AttributeListImpl.
Gets the name of an attribute (by position).
getName(int). Method in interface org.xml.sax.AttributeList.
Returns the name of an attribute in this list (by position).
getPublicId(). Method in class org.xml.sax.helpers.LocatorImpl.
Returns the saved public identifier.
getPublicId(). Method in class org.xml.sax.InputSource.
Gets the public identifier for this input source.
getPublicId(). Method in class org.xml.sax.SAXParseException.
Gets the public identifier of the entity where the exception occurred.
getPublicId(). Method in interface org.xml.sax.Locator.
Returns the public identifier for the current document event.
getSystemId(). Method in class org.xml.sax.helpers.LocatorImpl.
Returns the saved system identifier.
getSystemId(). Method in class org.xml.sax.InputSource.
Gets the system identifier for this input source.
getSystemId(). Method in class org.xml.sax.SAXParseException.
Gets the system identifier of the entity where the exception occurred.
getSystemId(). Method in interface org.xml.sax.Locator.
Returns the system identifier for the current document event.
getType(int). Method in class org.xml.sax.helpers.AttributeListImpl.
Gets the type of an attribute (by position).
getType(int). Method in interface org.xml.sax.AttributeList.
Returns the type of an attribute in the list (by position).
getType(String). Method in class org.xml.sax.helpers.AttributeListImpl.
Gets the type of an attribute (by name).
getType(String). Method in interface org.xml.sax.AttributeList.
Returns the type of an attribute in the list (by name).
getValue(int). Method in class org.xml.sax.helpers.AttributeListImpl.
Gets the value of an attribute (by position).
getValue(int). Method in interface org.xml.sax.AttributeList.
Returns the value of an attribute in the list (by position).
getValue(String). Method in class org.xml.sax.helpers.AttributeListImpl.
Gets the value of an attribute (by name).
getValue(String). Method in interface org.xml.sax.AttributeList.
Returns the value of an attribute in the list (by name).

HandlerBase(). Constructor for class org.xml.sax.HandlerBase.

I

ignorableWhitespace(char[], int, int). Method in class org.xml.sax.HandlerBase.
Receives notification of ignorable whitespace in element content.
ignorableWhitespace(char[], int, int). Method in interface org.xml.sax.Document-Handler.
Receives notification of ignorable whitespace in element content.
InputSource(). Constructor for class org.xml.sax.InputSource.
Is zero-argument default constructor.
InputSource(InputStream). Constructor for class org.xml.sax.InputSource.
Creates a new input source with a byte stream.
InputSource(Reader). Constructor for class org.xml.sax.InputSource.
Creates a new input source with a character stream.
InputSource(String). Constructor for class org.xml.sax.InputSource.
Creates a new input source with a system identifier.

 L

LocatorImpl(). Constructor for class org.xml.sax.helpers.LocatorImpl.
Is zero-argument constructor.
LocatorImpl(Locator). Constructor for class org.xml.sax.helpers.LocatorImpl.
Copies constructor.

 M

makeParser(). Static method in class org.xml.sax.helpers.ParserFactory.
Is private null constructor.
makeParser(String). Static method in class org.xml.sax.helpers.ParserFactory.
Creates a new SAX parser object using the class name provided.

 N

notationDecl(String, String, String). Method in class org.xml.sax.HandlerBase.
Receives notification of a notation declaration.
notationDecl(String, String, String). Method in interface org.xml.sax.DTDHandler.
Receives notification of a notation declaration event.

 P

parse(InputSource). Method in interface org.xml.sax.Parser.
Parses an XML document.

parse(String). Method in interface `org.xml.sax.Parser.`
  Parses an XML document from a system identifier (URI).
ParserFactory(). Constructor for class `org.xml.sax.helpers.ParserFactory.`
processingInstruction(String, String). Method in class `org.xml.sax.HandlerBase.`
  Receives notification of a processing instruction.
processingInstruction(String, String). Method in interface `org.xml.sax.Document-`
    `Handler.`
  Receives notification of a processing instruction.

▌ R

removeAttribute(String). Method in class `org.xml.sax.helpers.Attribute-`
    `ListImpl.`
  Removes an attribute from the list.
resolveEntity(String, String). Method in class `org.xml.sax.HandlerBase.`
  Resolves an external entity.
resolveEntity(String, String). Method in interface `org.xml.sax.EntityResolver.`
  Allows the application to resolve external entities.

▌ S

SAXException(Exception). Constructor for class `org.xml.sax.SAXException`.
  Creates a new SAXException wrapping an existing exception.
SAXException(String). Constructor for class `org.xml.sax.SAXException`.
  Creates a new SAXException.
SAXException(String, Exception). Constructor for class `org.xml.sax.SAXException.`
  Creates a new SAXException from an existing exception.
SAXParseException(String, Locator). Constructor for class `org.xml.sax.SAXParse-`
    `Exception.`
  Creates a new SAXParseException from a message and a Locator.
SAXParseException(String, Locator, Exception). Constructor for class
    `org.xml.sax.SAXParseException.`
  Wraps an existing exception in a SAXParseException.
SAXParseException(String, String, String, int, int). Constructor for class
    `org.xml.sax.SAXParseException.`
  Creates a new SAXParseException.
SAXParseException(String, String, String, int, int, Exception). Constructor for class
    `org.xml.sax.SAXParseException.`
  Creates a new SAXParseException with an embedded exception.
setAttributeList(AttributeList). Method in class `org.xml.sax.helpers.`
    `AttributeListImpl.`
  Sets the attribute list, discarding previous contents.

setByteStream(InputStream). Method in class `org.xml.sax.InputSource.`
Sets the byte stream for this input source.

setCharacterStream(Reader). Method in class `org.xml.sax.InputSource.`
Sets the character stream for this input source.

setColumnNumber(int). Method in class `org.xml.sax.helpers.LocatorImpl.`
Sets the column number for this locator (1-based).

setDocumentHandler(DocumentHandler). Method in interface
`org.xml.sax.Parser.`
Allows an application to register a document event handler.

setDocumentLocator(Locator). Method in class `org.xml.sax.HandlerBase.`
Receives a locator object for document events.

setDocumentLocator(Locator). Method in interface `org.xml.sax.Document-`
`Handler.`
Receives an object for locating the origin of SAX document events.

setDTDHandler(DTDHandler). Method in interface `org.xml.sax.Parser.`
Allows an application to register a DTD event handler.

setEncoding(String). Method in class `org.xml.sax.InputSource.`
Sets the character encoding, if known.

setEntityResolver(EntityResolver). Method in interface `org.xml.sax.Parser.`
Allows an application to register a custom entity resolver.

setErrorHandler(ErrorHandler). Method in interface `org.xml.sax.Parser.`
Allows an application to register an error event handler.

setLineNumber(int). Method in class `org.xml.sax.helpers.LocatorImpl.`
Sets the line number for this locator (1-based).

setLocale(Locale). Method in interface `org.xml.sax.Parser.`
Allows an application to request a locale for errors and warnings.

setPublicId(String). Method in class `org.xml.sax.helpers.LocatorImpl.`
Sets the public identifier for this locator.

setPublicId(String). Method in class `org.xml.sax.InputSource.`
Sets the public identifier for this input source.

setSystemId(String). Method in class `org.xml.sax.helpers.LocatorImpl.`
Sets the system identifier for this locator.

setSystemId(String). Method in class `org.xml.sax.InputSource.`
Sets the system identifier for this input source.

startDocument(). Method in class `org.xml.sax.HandlerBase.`
Receives notification of the beginning of the document.

startDocument(). Method in interface `org.xml.sax.DocumentHandler.`
Receives notification of the beginning of a document.

startElement(String, AttributeList). Method in class `org.xml.sax.HandlerBase.`
Receives notification of the start of an element.

startElement(String, AttributeList). Method in interface `org.xml.sax.Document-`
`Handler.`
Receives notification of the beginning of an element.

toString(). Method in class `org.xml.sax.`SAXException.
Converts this exception to a string.

unparsedEntityDecl(String, String, String, String). Method in class `org.xml.sax.-`
`HandlerBase`
Receives notification of an unparsed entity declaration.

unparsedEntityDecl(String, String, String, String). Method in interface `org.xml.-`
`sax.DTDHandler`
Receives notification of an unparsed entity declaration event.

warning(SAXParseException). Method in class `org.xml.sax.HandlerBase`
Receives notification of a parser warning.

warning(SAXParseException). Method in interface `org.xml.sax.ErrorHandler`
Receives notification of a warning.

Interface org.xml.sax.Parser

public interface **Parser**—Basic interface for SAX (Simple AP
for XML) parsers.

All SAX parsers must implement this basic interface: It allows applications to register handlers for different types of events and to initiate a parse from a URI, or a character stream.

All SAX parsers must also implement a zero-argument constructor (although other constructors are also allowed).

SAX parsers are reusable but not re-entrant: The application may reuse a parser object (possibly with a different input source) once the first parse has completed successfully, but it may not invoke the `parse()` methods recursively within a parse.

Version:

1.0

Author:

David Megginson (ak117@freenet.carleton.ca)

See Also:

EntityResolver, DTDHandler, Document-
Handler, ErrorHandler, HandlerBase, InputSource

Method Index

parse(InputSource)

Parses an XML document.

parse(String)

Parses an XML document from a system identifier (URI).

setDocumentHandler(DocumentHandler)

Allows an application to register a document event handler.

setDTDHandler(DTDHandler)

Allows an application to register a DTD event handler.

setEntityResolver(EntityResolver)

Allows an application to register a custom entity resolver.

setErrorHandler(ErrorHandler)

Allows an application to register an error event handler.

setLocale(Locale)

Allows an application to request a locale for errors and warnings.

Methods

setLocale

```
public abstract void setLocale(Locale locale)
throws SAX-Exception
```
Allows an application to request a locale for errors and warnings.

SAX parsers are not required to provide localization for errors and warnings; if they cannot support the requested locale, however, they must throw a SAX exception. Applications may not request a locale change in the middle of a parse.

Parameters:

locale—A Java locale object.

Throws: SAXException

Throws an exception (using the previous or default locale) if the requested locale is not supported.

See Also:

SAXException, SAXParseException

setEntityResolver

```
public abstract void setEntityResolver(EntityResolver
   resolver)
```

Allows an application to register a custom entity resolver.

If the application does not register an entity resolver, the SAX parser will resolve system identifiers and open connections to entities itself (this is the default behavior implemented in HandlerBase).

Applications may register a new or different entity resolver in the middle of a parse, and the SAX parser must begin using the new resolver immediately.

Parameters:

resolver—The object for resolving entities.

See Also:

EntityResolver, HandlerBase

setDTDHandler

```
public abstract void setDTDHandler(DTDHandler handler)
```

Allows an application to register a DTD event handler.

If the application does not register a DTD handler, all DTD events reported by the SAX parser will be silently ignored (this is the default behavior implemented by HandlerBase).

Applications may register a new or different handler in the middle of a parse, and the SAX parser must begin using the new handler immediately.

Parameters:

handler—The DTD handler.

See Also:

DTDHandler, HandlerBase

setDocumentHandler

```
public abstract void setDocumentHandler(DocumentHandler
   handler)
```

Allows an application to register a document event handler.

If the application does not register a document handler, all document events reported by the SAX parser will be silently ignored (this is the default behavior implemented by HandlerBase).

Applications may register a new or different handler in the middle of a parse, and the SAX parser must begin using the new handler immediately.

Parameters:

handler—The document handler.

See Also:

DocumentHandler, HandlerBase

setErrorHandler

```
public abstract void setErrorHandler(ErrorHandler handler)
```

Allows an application to register an error event handler.

If the application does not register an error event handler, all error events reported by the SAX parser will be silently ignored, except for `fatalError`, which will throw a `SAXException` (this is the default behavior implemented by `HandlerBase`).

Applications may register a new or different handler in the middle of a parse, and the SAX parser must begin using the new handler immediately.

Parameters:

handler—The error handler.

See Also:

ErrorHandler, SAXException, HandlerBase

parse

```
public abstract void parse(InputSource source) throws
    SAXException, IOException
```

Parses an XML document.

The application can use this method to instruct the SAX parser to begin parsing an XML document from any valid input source (a character stream, a byte stream, or a URI).

Applications may not invoke this method while a parse is in progress (they should create a new `Parser` instead for each additional XML document). Once a parse is complete, an application may reuse the same `Parser` object, possibly with a different input source.

Parameters:

source—The input source for the top-level of the XML document.

Throws: SAXException

Any SAX exception, possibly wrapping another exception.

Throws: IOException

An IO exception from the parser, possibly from a byte stream or character stream supplied by the application.

See Also:

InputSource, parse, setEntityResolver, setDTDHandler, setDocumentHandler, setErrorHandler

parse

```
public abstract void parse(String systemId) throws
    SAXException, IOException
```

Parses an XML document from a system identifier (URI).

This method is a shortcut for the common case of reading a document from a system identifier. It is the exact equivalent of the following:

```
parse(new InputSource(systemId));
```

If the system identifier is a URL, it must be fully resolved by the application before it is passed to the parser.

Parameters:

systemId—The system identifier (URL).

Throws: SAXException

Any SAX exception, possibly wrapping another exception.

Throws: IOException

An IO exception from the parser, possibly from a byte stream or character stream supplied by the application.

See Also:

parse

Interface org.xml.sax.AttributeList

public interface **AttributeList**—Interface for an element's attribute specifications.

The SAX parser implements this interface and passes an instance to the SAX application as the second argument of each startElement event.

The instance provided will return valid results only during the scope of the startElement invocation (to save it for future use, the application must make a copy: The AttributeListImpl helper class provides a convenient constructor for doing so).

An AttributeList includes only attributes that have been specified or defaulted: #IMPLIED attributes will not be included.

There are two ways for the SAX application to obtain information from the AttributeList. First, it can iterate through the entire list:

```
public void startElement (String name, AttributeList atts) {
  for (int i = 0; i < atts.getLength(); i++) {
    String name = atts.getName(i);
    String type = atts.getType(i);
    String value = atts.getValue(i);
    [...]
  }
}
```

(Note that the result of getLength() will be zero if there are no attributes.)

As an alternative, the application can request the value or type of specific attributes:

```
public void startElement (String name, AttributeList atts) {
  String identifier = atts.getValue("id");
  String label = atts.getValue("label");
  [...]
}
```

The `AttributeListImpl` helper class provides a convenience implementation for use by parser or application writers.

Version:

1.0

Author:

David Megginson (ak117@freenet.carleton.ca)

See Also:

`startElement`, `AttributeListImpl`

Method Index

getLength()

Returns the number of attributes in this list.

getName(int)

Returns the name of an attribute in this list (by position).

getType(int)

Returns the type of an attribute in the list (by position).

getType(String)

Returns the type of an attribute in the list (by name).

getValue(int)

Returns the value of an attribute in the list (by position).

getValue(String)

Returns the value of an attribute in the list (by name).

Methods

getLength

```
public abstract int getLength()
```

Returns the number of attributes in this list.

The SAX parser may provide attributes in any arbitrary order, regardless of the order in which they were declared or specified. The number of attributes may be zero.

Returns:

The number of attributes in the list.

getName

```
public abstract String getName(int i)
```

Returns the name of an attribute in this list (by position).

The names must be unique: The SAX parser will not include the same attribute twice. Attributes without values (those declared #IM-PLIED without a value specified in the start tag) will be omitted from the list.

If the attribute name has a namespace prefix, the prefix will still be attached.

Parameters:

i—The index of the attribute in the list (starting at 0).

Returns:

The name of the indexed attribute, or null if the index is out of range.

See Also:

getLength

getType

```
public abstract String getType(int i)
```

Returns the type of an attribute in the list (by position).

The attribute type is one of the strings `"CDATA"`, `"ID"`, `"IDREF"`, `"IDREFS"`, `"NMTOKEN"`, `"NMTOKENS"`, `"ENTITY"`, `"ENTITIES"`, or `"NOTATION"` (always in uppercase).

If the parser has not read a declaration for the attribute, or if the parser does not report attribute types, then it must return the value `"CDATA"` as stated in the XML 1.0 `Recommendation` (clause 3.3.3, "Attribute-Value Normalization").

For an enumerated attribute that is not a notation, the parser will report the type as `"NMTOKEN"`.

Parameters:

i—The index of the attribute in the list (starting at 0).

Returns:

The attribute type as a string, or null if the index is out of range.

See Also:

getLength, getType

getValue

```
public abstract String getValue(int i)
```

Returns the value of an attribute in the list (by position).

If the attribute value is a list of tokens (IDREFS, ENTITIES, or NMTOKENS), the tokens will be concatenated into a single string separated by whitespace.

Parameters:

i—The index of the attribute in the list (starting at 0).

Returns:

The attribute value as a string, or null if the index is out of range.

See Also:

getLength, getValue

getType

```
public abstract String getType(String name)
```

Returns the type of an attribute in the list (by name).

The return value is the same as the return value for getType(int).

If the attribute name has a namespace prefix in the document, the application must include the prefix here.

Parameters:

name—The name of the attribute.

Returns:

The attribute type as a string, or null if no such attribute exists.

See Also:

getType

getValue

```
public abstract String getValue(String name)
```

Returns the value of an attribute in the list (by name).

The return value is the same as the return value for getValue(int).

If the attribute name has a namespace prefix in the document, the application must include the prefix here.

Parameters:

i—The index of the attribute in the list.

Returns:

The attribute value as a string, or null if no such attribute exists.

See Also:

getValue

Interface org.xml.sax. DocumentHandler

public interface **DocumentHandler**—Receives notification of general document events.

This is the main interface that most SAX applications implement: If the application needs to be informed of basic parsing events, it implements this interface and registers an instance with the SAX parser using the setDocumentHandler method. The parser uses the instance to report basic document-related events like the start and end of elements and character data.

The order of events in this interface is very important, and it mirrors the order of information in the document itself. For example, all of an element's content (character data, processing instructions, and/or subelements) will appear, in order, between the startElement event and the corresponding endElement event.

Application writers who do not want to implement the entire interface can derive a class from HandlerBase, which implements the default functionality; parser writers can instantiate Handler-Base to obtain a default handler. The application can find the location of any document event using the Locator interface supplied by the Parser through the setDocumentLocator method.

Version:

1.0

Author:

David Megginson (ak117@freenet.carleton.ca)

See Also:

setDocumentHandler, Locator, HandlerBase

Method Index

characters(char[], int, int)

Receives notification of character data.

endDocument()

Receives notification of the end of a document.

endElement(String)

Receives notification of the end of an element.

ignorableWhitespace(char[], int, int)

Receives notification of ignorable whitespace in element content.

processingInstruction(String, String)

Receives notification of a processing instruction.

setDocumentLocator(Locator)

Receives an object for locating the origin of SAX document events.

startDocument()

Receives notification of the beginning of a document.

startElement(String, AttributeList)

Receives notification of the beginning of an element.

Methods

setDocumentLocator

```
public abstract void setDocumentLocator(Locator locator)
```

Receives an object for locating the origin of SAX document events.
SAX parsers are strongly encouraged (although not absolutely required) to supply a locator: If it does so, it must supply the locator to the application by invoking this method before invoking any of the other methods in the DocumentHandler interface.

The locator allows the application to determine the end position of any document-related event, even if the parser is not reporting an error. Typically, the application will use this information for reporting its own errors (such as character content that does not match an application's business rules). The information returned by the locator is probably not sufficient for use with a search engine.

Note that the locator will return correct information only during the invocation of the events in this interface. The application should not attempt to use it at any other time.

Parameters:

locator—An object that can return the location of any SAX document event.

See Also:

Locator

startDocument

```
public abstract void startDocument() throws SAXException
```

Receives notification of the beginning of a document.
The SAX parser will invoke this method only once, before any other methods in this interface or in DTDHandler (except for set-DocumentLocator).

Throws: `SAXException`

Any SAX exception, possibly wrapping another exception.

endDocument

```
public abstract void endDocument() throws SAXException
```

Receives notification of the end of a document.

The SAX parser will invoke this method only once, and it will be the last method invoked during the parse. The parser will not invoke this method until it has either abandoned parsing (because of an unrecoverable error) or reached the end of input.

Throws: SAXException

Any SAX exception, possibly wrapping another exception.

startElement

```
public abstract void startElement(String name,
                            AttributeList atts) throws
                         SAXException
```

Receives notification of the beginning of an element.

The `Parser` will invoke this method at the beginning of every element in the XML document; there will be a corresponding `endElement()` event for every `startElement()` event (even when the element is empty). All of the element's content will be reported, in order, before the corresponding `endElement()` event.

If the element name has a namespace prefix, the prefix will still be attached. Note that the attribute list provided will contain only attributes with explicit values (specified or defaulted): `#IMPLIED` attributes will be omitted.

Parameters:

name—The element type name.

atts—The attributes attached to the element, if any.

Throws: <u>SAXException</u>

Any SAX exception, possibly wrapping another exception.

See Also:

<u>endElement</u>, <u>AttributeList</u>

endElement

```
public abstract void endElement(String name) throws
    SAXException
```

Receives notification of the end of an element.

The SAX parser will invoke this method at the end of every element in the XML document; there will be a corresponding `startElement()` event for every `endElement()` event (even when the element is empty).

If the element name has a namespace prefix, the prefix will still be attached to the name.

Parameters:

name—The element type name.

Throws: SAXException

Any SAX exception, possibly wrapping another exception.

characters

```
public abstract void characters(char ch[],
                                int start,
                                int length) throws
                                    SAXException
```

Receives notification of character data.

The `Parser` will call this method to report each chunk of character data. SAX parsers may return all contiguous character data in a single chunk, or they may split it into several chunks; however, all of the characters in any single event must come from the same external entity, so that the `Locator` provides useful information.

The application must not attempt to read from the array outside the specified range.

Note that some parsers will report whitespace using the `ignorableWhitespace()` method rather than this one (validating parsers must do so).

Parameters:

ch—The characters from the XML document.

start—The start position in the array.

length—The number of characters to read from the array.

Throws: `SAXException`

Any SAX exception, possibly wrapping another exception.

See Also:

`ignorableWhitespace`, `Locator`

ignorableWhitespace

```
public abstract void ignorableWhitespace(char ch[],
                                int start,
                                int length) throws
                                    SAXException
```

Receives notification of ignorable whitespace in element content.

Validating `Parsers` must use this method to report each chunk of ignorable whitespace (see the W3C XML 1.0 recommendation, section 2.10): non-validating parsers may also use this method if they are capable of parsing and using content models.

SAX parsers may return all contiguous whitespace in a single chunk, or they may split it into several chunks; however, all of the characters in any single event must come from the same external entity, so that the `Locator` provides useful information.

The application must not attempt to read from the array outside the specified range.

Parameters:

ch—The characters from the XML document.

start—The start position in the array.

length—The number of characters to read from the array.

Throws: SAXException

Any SAX exception, possibly wrapping another exception.

See Also:

characters

processingInstruction

```
public abstract void processingInstruction(String target,
                                          String data)
                                     throws
                                          SAXException
```

Receives notification of a processing instruction.

The Parser will invoke this method once for each processing instruction found: Note that processing instructions may occur before or after the main document element.

A SAX parser should never report an XML declaration (XML 1.0, section 2.8) or a text declaration (XML 1.0, section 4.3.1) using this method.

Parameters:

target—The processing instruction target.

data—The processing instruction data, or null if none was supplied.

Throws: SAXException

Any SAX exception, possibly wrapping another exception.

Interface org.xml.sax.DTDHandler

public interface **DTDHandler**—Receives notification of basic DTD-related events.

If a SAX application needs information about notations and un-parsed entities, then the application implements this interface and registers an instance with the SAX parser using the parser's setDTD-Handler method. The parser uses the instance to report notation and unparsed entity declarations to the application.

The SAX parser may report these events in any order, regardless of the order in which the notations and unparsed entities were declared; however, all DTD events must be reported after the document handler's startDocument event and before the first startElement event.

It is up to the application to store the information for future use (perhaps in a hash table or object tree). If the application encounters attributes of type "NOTATION", "ENTITY", or "ENTITIES", it can use the information that it obtained through this interface to find the entity and/or notation corresponding with the attribute value.

The HandlerBase class provides a default implementation of this interface, which simply ignores the events.

Version:

1.0

Author:

David Megginson (ak117@freenet.carleton.ca)

See Also:

setDTDHandler, HandlerBase

Method Index

notationDecl(String, String, String)

Receives notification of a notation declaration event.

unparsedEntityDecl(String, String, String, String)

Receives notification of an unparsed entity declaration event.

Methods

notationDecl

```
public abstract void notationDecl(String name,
                                  String publicId,
                                  String systemId) throws
                            SAXException
```

Receives notification of a notation declaration event.

It is up to the application to record the notation for later reference, if necessary.

If a system identifier is present, and it is a URL, the SAX parser must resolve it fully before passing it to the application.

Parameters:

name—The notation name.

publicId—The notation's public identifier, or null if none was given.

systemId—The notation's system identifier, or null if none was given.

Throws: SAXException

Any SAX exception, possibly wrapping another exception.

See Also:

unparsedEntityDecl, AttributeList

unparsedEntityDecl

```
public abstract void unparsedEntityDecl(String name,
                                        String publicId,
                                        String systemId,
                                        String notationName)
                            throws
                                SAXException
```

Receives notification of an unparsed entity declaration event.

Note that the notation name corresponds to a notation reported by the `notationDecl()` event. It is up to the application to record the entity for later reference, if necessary.

If the system identifier is a URL, the parser must resolve it fully before passing it to the application.

Parameters:

name—The unparsed entity's name.

publicId—The entity's public identifier, or null if none was given.

systemId—The entity's system identifier (it must always have one).

notation—The name of the associated notation.

Throws: SAXException

Any SAX exception, possibly wrapping another exception.

See Also:

notationDecl, AttributeList

Interface org.xml.sax.EntityResolver

public interface **EntityResolver**—Basic interface for resolving entities.

If a SAX application needs to implement customized handling for external entities, it must implement this interface and register an instance with the SAX parser using the parser's `setEntityResolver` method.

The parser will then allow the application to intercept any external entities (including the external DTD subset and external parameter entities, if any) before including them.

Many SAX applications will not need to implement this interface, but it will especially be useful for applications that build XML documents from databases or other specialized input sources, or for applications that use URI types other than URLs.

The following resolver would provide the application with a special character stream for the entity with the system identifier `http://www.myhost.com/today`:

```
import org.xml.sax.EntityResolver;
import org.xml.sax.InputSource;
public class MyResolver implements EntityResolver {
   public InputSource resolveEntity (String publicId, String
systemId)
   {
     if (systemId.equals("http://www.myhost.com/today")) {
            // return a special input source
       MyReader reader = new MyReader();
       return new InputSource(reader);
     } else {
            // use the default behaviour
       return null;
     }
   }
}
```

The application can also use this interface to redirect system identifiers to local URIs or to look up replacements in a catalog (possibly by using the public identifier).

The `HandlerBase` class implements the default behavior for this interface, which is simply always to return null (to request that the parser use the default system identifier).

Version:

1.0

Author:

David Megginson (ak117@freenet.carleton.ca)

See Also:

<u>setEntityResolver</u>, <u>InputSource</u>, <u>Handler-Base</u>

Method Index

<u>**resolveEntity**</u>(String, String)
Allows the application to resolve external entities.

Methods

< resolveEntity

```
public abstract InputSource resolveEntity(String publicId,
                                          String systemId)
throws SAXException, IOException
```

Allows the application to resolve external entities.

The `Parser` will call this method before opening any external entity except the top-level document entity (including the external DTD subset, external entities referenced within the DTD, and external entities referenced within the document element): The application may request that the parser resolve the entity itself, that it use an alternative URI, or that it use an entirely different input source.

Application writers can use this method to redirect external system identifiers to secure and/or local URIs, to look up public identifiers in a catalogue, or to read an entity from a database or other input source (including, for example, a dialog box).

If the system identifier is a URL, the SAX parser must resolve it fully before reporting it to the application.

Parameters:

publicId—The public identifier of the external entity being referenced, or null if none was supplied.

systemId—The system identifier of the external entity being referenced.

Returns:

An `InputSource` object describing the new input source, or null to request that the parser open a regular URI connection to the system identifier.

Throws: `SAXException`

Any SAX exception, possibly wrapping another exception.

Throws: `IOException`

A Java-specific IO exception, possibly the result of creating a new `InputStream` or `Reader` for the `InputSource`.

See Also:

`InputSource`

Interface org.xml.sax.ErrorHandler

public interface **ErrorHandler**—Basic interface for SAX error handlers.

If a SAX application needs to implement customized error handling, it must implement this interface and then register an instance with the

SAX parser using the parser's `setErrorHandler` method. The parser will then report all errors and warnings through this interface.

The parser will use this interface instead of throwing an exception: It is up to the application whether to throw an exception for different types of errors and warnings. Note, however, that there is no requirement that the parser continue to provide useful information after a call to `fatalError` (in other words, a SAX driver class could catch an exception and report a `fatalError`).

The `HandlerBase` class provides a default implementation of this interface, ignoring warnings and recoverable errors and throwing a `SAXParseException` for fatal errors. An application may extend that class rather than implementing the complete interface itself.

Version:

1.0

Author:

David Megginson (`ak117@freenet.carleton.ca`)

See Also:

`setErrorHandler`, `SAXParseException`, `HandlerBase`

Method Index

error(`SAXParseException`)
Receives notification of a recoverable error.

fatalError(`SAXParseException`)
Receives notification of a non-recoverable error.

warning(`SAXParseException`)
Receives notification of a warning.

Methods

warning

```
public abstract void warning(SAXParseException exception)
   throws SAXException
```

Receives notification of a warning.

SAX parsers will use this method to report conditions that are not errors or fatal errors as defined by the XML 1.0 recommendation. The default behavior is to take no action.

The SAX parser must continue to provide normal parsing events after invoking this method: It should still be possible for the application to process the document through to the end.

Parameters:

exception—The warning information encapsulated in a SAX parse exception.

Throws: SAXException

Any SAX exception, possibly wrapping another exception.

See Also:

SAXParseException

error

```
public abstract void error(SAXParseException exception)
   throws SAXException
```

Receives notification of a recoverable error.

This corresponds to the definition of "error" in section 1.2 of the W3C XML 1.0 Recommendation. For example, a validating parser would use this callback to report the violation of a validity constraint. The default behavior is to take no action.

The SAX parser must continue to provide normal parsing events after invoking this method: It should still be possible for the application to process the document through to the end. If the application cannot do so, then the parser should report a fatal error even if the XML 1.0 Recommendation does not require it to do so.

Parameters:

exception—The error information encapsulated in a SAX parse exception.

Throws: SAXException

Any SAX exception, possibly wrapping another exception.

See Also:

SAXParseException

fatalError

```
public abstract void fatalError(SAXParseException exception)
  throws SAXException
```

Receives notification of a non-recoverable error.

This corresponds to the definition of "fatal error" in section 1.2 of the W3C XML 1.0 Recommendation. For example, a parser would use this callback to report the violation of a well-formedness constraint.

The application must assume that the document is unusable after the parser has invoked this method, and should continue (if at all) only for the sake of collecting addition error messages. In fact, SAX parsers are free to stop reporting any other events once this method has been invoked.

Parameters:

exception—The error information encapsulated in a SAX parse exception.

Throws: SAXException

Any SAX exception, possibly wrapping another exception.

See Also:

SAXParseException

Class org.xml.sax.HandlerBase

```
java.lang.Object
   |
   +—org.xml.sax.HandlerBase
```

public class **HandlerBase**
extends Object
implements <u>EntityResolver</u>, <u>DTDHandler</u>, <u>Document-Handler</u>, <u>ErrorHandler</u>—Default base class for handlers.

This class implements the default behaviour for four SAX interfaces: EntityResolver, DTDHandler, DocumentHandler, and ErrorHandler.

Application writers can extend this class when they need to implement only part of an interface; parser writers can instantiate this class to provide default handlers when the application has not supplied its own.

Note that the use of this class is optional.

Version:

1.0

Author:

David Megginson (`ak117@freenet.carleton.ca`)

See Also:

<u>EntityResolver</u>, <u>DTDHandler</u>, <u>Document-Handler</u>, <u>ErrorHandler</u>

Constructor Index

HandlerBase()

Method Index

characters(char[], int, int)

Receives notification of character data inside an element.

endDocument()

Receives notification of the end of the document.

endElement(String)

Receives notification of the end of an element.

error(SAXParseException)

Receives notification of a recoverable parser error.

fatalError(SAXParseException)

Reports a fatal XML parsing error.

ignorableWhitespace(char[], int, int)

Receives notification of ignorable whitespace in element content.

notationDecl(String, String, String)

Receives notification of a notation declaration.

processingInstruction(String, String)

Receives notification of a processing instruction.

resolveEntity(String, String)

Resolves an external entity.

setDocumentLocator(Locator)

Receives a Locator object for document events.

startDocument()

Receives notification of the beginning of the document.

startElement(String, AttributeList)

Receives notification of the start of an element.

unparsedEntityDecl(String, String, String, String)

Receives notification of an unparsed entity declaration.

warning(SAXParseException)

Receives notification of a parser warning.

Constructors

HandlerBase

```
public HandlerBase()
```

Methods

resolveEntity

```
public InputSource resolveEntity(String publicId,
                                 String systemId) throws
                             SAXException
```

Resolves an external entity.

Always returns null, so that the parser will use the system identifier provided in the XML document. This method implements the SAX default behavior: Application writers can override it in a subclass to do special translations such as catalog lookups or URI redirection.

Parameters:

publicId—The public identifier, or null if none is available.

systemId—The system identifier provided in the XML document.

Returns:

The new input source, or null to require the default behavior.

Throws: SAXException

Any SAX exception, possibly wrapping another exception.

See Also:

resolveEntity

notationDecl

```
public void notationDecl(String name,
                         String publicId,
                         String systemId)
```

Receives notification of a notation declaration.

By default, does nothing. Application writers may override this method in a subclass if they wish to keep track of the notations declared in a document.

> **Parameters:**
>
> name—The notation name.
>
> publicId—The notation public identifier, or null if not available.
>
> systemId—The notation system identifier.
>
> **See Also:**
>
> notationDecl

unparsedEntityDecl

```
public void unparsedEntityDecl(String name,
                               String publicId,
                               String systemId,
                               String notationName)
```

Receives notification of an unparsed entity declaration.

By default, does nothing. Application writers may override this method in a subclass to keep track of the unparsed entities declared in a document.

> **Parameters:**
>
> name—The entity name.

publicId—The entity public identifier, or null if not available.

systemId—The entity system identifier.

notationName—The name of the associated notation.

See Also:

unparsedEntityDecl

setDocumentLocator

```
public void setDocumentLocator(Locator locator)
```

Receives a `Locator` object for document events.

By default, does nothing. Application writers may override this method in a subclass if they wish to store the locator for use with other document events.

Parameters:

locator—A locator for all SAX document events.

See Also:

setDocumentLocator, Locator

startDocument

```
public void startDocument() throws SAXException
```

Receives notification of the beginning of the document.

By default, does nothing. Application writers may override this method in a subclass to take specific actions at the beginning of a document (such as allocating the root node of a tree or creating an output file).

Throws: SAXException

Any SAX exception, possibly wrapping another exception.

See Also:

startDocument

endDocument

```
public void endDocument() throws SAXException
```

Receives notification of the end of the document.

By default, does nothing. Application writers may override this method in a subclass to take specific actions at the beginning of a document (such as finalizing a tree or closing an output file).

Throws: SAXException

Any SAX exception, possibly wrapping another exception.

See Also:

endDocument

startElement

```
public void startElement(String name,
                         AttributeList attributes) throws
                    SAXException
```

Receives notification of the start of an element.

By default, does nothing. Application writers may override this method in a subclass to take specific actions at the start of each element (such as allocating a new tree node or writing output to a file).

Parameters:

name—The element type name.

attributes—The specified or defaulted attributes.

Throws: SAXException

Any SAX exception, possibly wrapping another exception.

See Also:

startElement

endElement

```
public void endElement(String name) throws SAXException
```

Receives notification of the end of an element.

By default, does nothing. Application writers may override this method in a subclass to take specific actions at the end of each element (such as finalizing a tree node or writing output to a file).

Parameters:

name—The element type name.

attributes—The specified or defaulted attributes.

Throws: <u>SAXException</u>

Any SAX exception, possibly wrapping another exception.

See Also:

<u>endElement</u>

characters

```
public void characters(char ch[],
                       int start,
                       int length) throws SAXException
```

Receives notification of character data inside an element.

By default, does nothing. Application writers may override this method to take specific actions for each chunk of character data (such as adding the data to a node or buffer, or printing it to a file).

Parameters:

ch—The characters.

start—The start position in the character array.

length—The number of characters to use from the character array.

Throws: <u>SAXException</u>

Any SAX exception, possibly wrapping another exception.

See Also:

<u>characters</u>

ignorableWhitespace

```
public void ignorableWhitespace(char ch[],
                                int start,
                                int length) throws
                                    SAXException
```

Receives notification of ignorable whitespace in element content.

By default, does nothing. Application writers may override this method to take specific actions for each chunk of ignorable white-space (such as adding data to a node or buffer, or printing it to a file).

Parameters:

ch—The whitespace characters.

start—The start position in the character array.

length—The number of characters to use from the character array.

Throws: SAXException

Any SAX exception, possibly wrapping another exception.

See Also:

ignorableWhitespace

processingInstruction

```
public void processingInstruction(String target,
                                  String data) throws
                                      SAXException
```

Receives notification of a processing instruction.

By default, does nothing. Application writers may override this method in a subclass to take specific actions for each processing in-struction, such as setting status variables or invoking other methods.

Parameters:

target—The processing instruction target.

data—The processing instruction data, or null if none is supplied.

Throws: `SAXException`

Any SAX exception, possibly wrapping another exception.

See Also:

`processingInstruction`

warning

```
public void warning(SAXParseException e) throws SAXException
```

Receives notification of a parser warning.

The default implementation does nothing. Application writers may override this method in a subclass to take specific actions for each warning, such as inserting the message in a log file or printing it to the console.

Parameters:

e—The warning information encoded as an exception.

Throws: `SAXException`

Any SAX exception, possibly wrapping another exception.

See Also:

`warning, SAXParseException`

error

```
public void error(SAXParseException e) throws SAXException
```

Receives notification of a recoverable parser error.

The default implementation does nothing. Application writers may override this method in a subclass to take specific actions for each error, such as inserting the message in a log file or printing it to the console.

Parameters:

e—The warning information encoded as an exception.

Throws: SAXException

Any SAX exception, possibly wrapping another exception.

See Also:

warning, SAXParseException

fatalError

```
public void fatalError(SAXParseException e) throws
    SAXException
```

Reports a fatal XML parsing error.

The default implementation throws a SAXParseException. Application writers may override this method in a subclass if they need to take specific actions for each fatal error (such as collecting all of the errors into a single report). In any case, the application must stop all regular processing when this method is invoked, since the document is no longer reliable, and the parser may no longer report parsing events.

Parameters:

e—The error information encoded as an exception.

Throws: SAXException

Any SAX exception, possibly wrapping another exception.

See Also:

fatalError, SAXParseException

Class org.xml.sax.InputSource

```
java.lang.Object
  |
  +—org.xml.sax.InputSource
```

public class **InputSource**

extends Object—A single input source for an XML entity.

This class allows a SAX application to encapsulate information about an input source in a single object, which may include a public identifier, a system identifier, a byte stream (possibly with a specified encoding), and/or a character stream.

There are two places that the application will deliver this input source to the parser: as the argument to the `Parser.parse` method, or as the return value of the `EntityResolver.resolveEntity` method.

The SAX parser will use the `InputSource` object to determine how to read XML input. If there is a character stream available, the parser will read that stream directly; if not, the parser will use a byte stream, if available. If neither a character stream nor a byte stream is available, the parser will attempt to open a URI connection to the resource identified by the system identifier.

An `InputSource` object belongs to the application. The SAX parser will never modify it in any way (it may modify a copy if necessary).

Version:

> 1.0

Author:

> David Megginson (ak117@freenet.carleton.ca)

See Also:

> parse, resolveEntity, InputStream, Reader

Constructor Index

InputSource ( )

Zero-argument default constructor.

InputSource(InputStream)

Creates a new input source with a byte stream.

InputSource(Reader)

Creates a new input source with a character stream.

InputSource(String)

Creates a new input source with a system identifier.

Method Index

getByteStream()

Gets the byte stream for this input source.

getCharacterStream()

Gets the character stream for this input source.

getEncoding()

Gets the character encoding for a byte stream or URI.

getPublicId()

Gets the public identifier for this input source.

getSystemId()

Gets the system identifier for this input source.

setByteStream(InputStream)

Sets the byte stream for this input source.

setCharacterStream(Reader)

Sets the character stream for this input source.

setEncoding(String)

Sets the character encoding, if known.

setPublicId(String)

Sets the public identifier for this input source.

setSystemId(String)

Sets the system identifier for this input source.

Constructors

InputSource

```
public InputSource()
```

Zero-argument default constructor.

See Also:

setPublicId, setSystemId, setByteStream, setCharacterStream, setEncoding

InputSource

```
public InputSource(String systemId)
```

Creates a new input source with a system identifier.
Applications may use setPublicId to include a public identifier as well, or setEncoding to specify the character encoding, if known. If the system identifier is a URL, it must be fullly resolved.

Parameters:

systemId—The system identifier (URI).

See Also:

setPublicId, setSystemId, setByteStream, setEncoding, setCharacterStream

InputSource

```
public InputSource(InputStream byteStream)
```

Creates a new input source with a byte stream.
Application writers may use setSystemId to provide a base for resolving relative URIs, setPublicId to include a public identifier, and/or setEncoding to specify the object's character encoding.

Parameters:

byteStream—The raw byte stream containing the document.

See Also:

`setPublicId`, `setSystemId`, `setEncoding`, `setByteStream`, `setCharacterStream`

InputSource

```
public InputSource(Reader characterStream)
```

Creates a new input source with a character stream.

Application writers may use `setSystemId()` to provide a base for resolving relative URIs, and `setPublicId` to include a public identifier.

The character stream will not include a byte order mark.

See Also:

`setPublicId`, `setSystemId`, `setByteStream`, `setCharacterStream`

Methods

setPublicId

```
public void setPublicId(String publicId)
```

Sets the public identifier for this input source.

The public identifier is always optional; if the application writer includes one, it will be provided as part of the location information.

Parameters:

publicId—The public identifier as a string.

See Also:

`getPublicId`, `getPublicId`, `getPublicId`

getPublicId

```
public String getPublicId()
```

Gets the public identifier for this input source.

Returns:

The public identifier, or null if none was supplied.

See Also:

setPublicId

setSystemId

```
public void setSystemId(String systemId)
```

Sets the system identifier for this input source.

The system identifier is optional if there is a byte stream or a character stream, but it is still useful to provide one, since the application can use it to resolve relative URIs and can include it in error messages and warnings (the parser will attempt to open a connection to the URI only if there is no byte stream or character stream specified).

If the application knows the character encoding of the object pointed to by the system identifier, it can register the encoding using the setEncoding method.

If the system ID is a URL, it must be fully resolved.

Parameters:

systemId—The system identifier as a string.

See Also:

setEncoding, getSystemId, getSystemId, getSystemId

getSystemId

```
public String getSystemId()
```

Gets the system identifier for this input source.

The getEncoding method will return the character encoding of the object pointed to, or null if unknown.

If the system ID is a URL, it will be fully resolved.

Returns:

The system identifier.

See Also:

setSystemId, getEncoding

setByteStream

```
public void setByteStream(InputStream byteStream)
```

Set the byte stream for this input source.

The SAX parser will ignore this if there is also a character stream specified, but it will use a byte stream in preference to opening a URI connection itself.

If the application knows the character encoding of the byte stream, it should set it with the setEncoding method.

Parameters:

byteStream—A byte stream containing an XML document or other entity.

See Also:

setEncoding, getByteStream, getEncoding, InputStream

getByteStream

```
public InputStream getByteStream()
```

Gets the byte stream for this input source.

The getEncoding method will return the character encoding for this byte stream, or null if unknown.

Returns:

The byte stream, or null if none was supplied.

See Also:

`getEncoding`, `setByteStream`

setEncoding

`public void setEncoding(String encoding)`

Sets the character encoding, if known.

The encoding must be a string acceptable for an XML encoding declaration (see section 4.3.3 of the XML 1.0 Recommendation).

This method has no effect when the application provides a character stream.

Parameters:

encoding—A string describing the character encoding.

See Also:

`setSystemId`, `setByteStream`, `getEncoding`

getEncoding

`public String getEncoding()`

Gets the character encoding for a byte stream or URI.

Returns:

The encoding, or null if none was supplied.

See Also:

`setByteStream`, `getSystemId`, `getByteStream`

setCharacterStream

`public void setCharacterStream(Reader characterStream)`

Sets the character stream for this input source.

If there is a character stream specified, the SAX parser will ignore any byte stream and will not attempt to open a URI connection to the system identifier.

Parameters:

characterStream—The character stream containing the XML document or other entity.

See Also:

getCharacterStream, Reader

getCharacterStream

```
public Reader getCharacterStream()
```

Gets the character stream for this input source.

Returns:

The character stream, or null if none was supplied.

See Also:

setCharacterStream

Interface org.xml.sax.Locator

public interface **Locator**—Interface for associating a SAX event with a document location.

If a SAX parser provides location information to the SAX application, it does so by implementing this interface and then passing an instance to the application using the document handler's setDocumentLocator method. The application can use the object to obtain the location of any other document handler event in the XML source document.

Note that the results returned by the object will be valid only during the scope of each document handler method: The application will receive unpredictable results if it attempts to use the locator at any other time.

SAX parsers are not required to supply a locator, but they are very strongly encouraged to do so. If the parser supplies a locator, it must do so before reporting any other document events. If no locator has been set by the time the application receives the `startDocument` event, the application should assume that a locator is not available.

Version:

1.0

Author:

David Megginson (`ak117@freenet.carleton.ca`)

See Also:

`setDocumentLocator`

Method Index

getColumnNumber()

Returns the column number where the current document event ends.

getLineNumber()

Returns the line number where the current document event ends.

getPublicId()

Returns the public identifier for the current document event.

getSystemId()

Returns the system identifier for the current document event.

Methods

getPublicId

```
public abstract String getPublicId()
```

Returns the public identifier for the current document event. This will be the public identifier.

Returns:

A string containing the public identifier, or null if none is available.

See Also:

getSystemId

getSystemId

```
public abstract String getSystemId()
```

Returns the system identifier for the current document event. If the system identifier is a URL, the parser must resolve it fully before passing it to the application.

Returns:

A string containing the system identifier, or null if none is available.

See Also:

getPublicId

getLineNumber

```
public abstract int getLineNumber()
```

Returns the line number where the current document event ends. Note that this is the line position of the first character after the text associated with the document event.

Returns:

The line number, or -1 if none is available.

See Also:

getColumnNumber

getColumnNumber

```
public abstract int getColumnNumber()
```

Returns the column number where the current document event ends. Note that this is the column number of the first character after the text associated with the document event. The first column in a line is position 1.

Returns:

The column number, or -1 if none is available.

See Also:

getLineNumber

Class org.xml.sax.SAXException

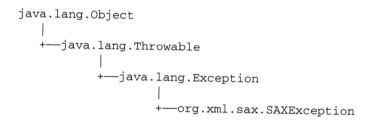

```
java.lang.Object
   |
   +—java.lang.Throwable
          |
          +—java.lang.Exception
                 |
                 +—org.xml.sax.SAXException
```

public class **SAXException**

extends Exception—Encapsulates a general SAX error or warning. This class can contain basic error or warning information from either the XML parser or the application: A parser writer or application writer can subclass it to provide additional functionality. SAX handlers may throw this exception or any exception subclassed from it.

If the application needs to pass through other types of exceptions, it must wrap those exceptions in a SAXException or an exception derived from a SAXException.

If the parser or application needs to include information about a specific location in an XML document, it should use the SAX-ParseException subclass.

Version:

1.0

Author:

David Megginson (ak117@freenet.carleton.ca)

See Also:

SAXParseException

Constructor Index

SAXException(Exception)

Creates a new SAXException wrapping an existing exception.

SAXException(String)

Creates a new SAXException.

SAXException(String, Exception)

Creates a new SAXException from an existing exception.

Method Index

getException()

Returns the embedded exception, if any.

<u>getMessage</u>()

Returns a detail message for this exception.

<u>toString</u>()

Converts this exception to a string.

Constructors

SAXException

```
public SAXException(String message)
```

Creates a new SAXException.

Parameters:

message—The error or warning message.

See Also:

<u>setLocale</u>

SAXException

```
public SAXException(Exception e)
```

Creates a new SAXException wrapping an existing exception. The existing exception will be embedded in the new one, and its message will become the default message for the SAXException.

Parameters:

e—The exception to be wrapped in a SAXException.

SAXException

```
public SAXException(String message,
                    Exception e)
```

Creates a new SAXException from an existing exception.

The existing exception will be embedded in the new one, but the new exception will have its own message.

Parameters:

message—The detail message.

e—The exception to be wrapped in a SAXException.

See Also:

setLocale

Methods

getMessage

```
public String getMessage()
```

Returns a detail message for this exception.

If there is an embedded exception, and if the SAXException has no detail message of its own, this method will return the detail message from the embedded exception.

Returns:

The error or warning message.

Overrides:

getMessage in class Throwable

See Also:

setLocale

getException

```
public Exception getException()
```

Returns the embedded exception, if any.

Returns:

The embedded exception, or null if there is none.

toString

```
public String toString()
```

Converts this exception to a string.

Returns:

A string version of this exception.

Overrides:

toString in class Throwable

Class org.xml.sax.SAXParseException

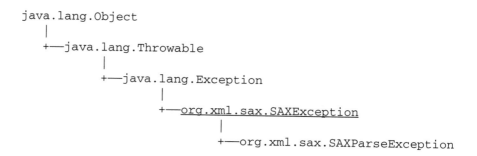

```
java.lang.Object
    |
    +—java.lang.Throwable
            |
            +—java.lang.Exception
                    |
                    +—org.xml.sax.SAXException
                            |
                            +—org.xml.sax.SAXParseException
```

public class **SAXParseException**

extends SAXException—Encapsulates an XML parse error or warning.

This exception will include information for locating the error in the original XML document. Note that although the application will receive a SAXParseException as the argument to the handlers in the ErrorHandler interface, the application is not actually required to throw the exception; instead, it can simply read the information in it and take a different action.

Since this exception is a subclass of SAXException, it inherits the ability to wrap another exception.

Version:

1.0

Author:

David Megginson (ak117@freenet.carleton.ca)

See Also:

SAXException, Locator, ErrorHandler

Constructor Index

SAXParseException(String, Locator)

Creates a new SAXParseException from a message and a Locator.

SAXParseException(String, Locator, Exception)

Wraps an existing exception in a SAXParseException.

SAXParseException(String, String, String, int, int)

Creates a new SAXParseException.

SAXParseException(String, String, String, int, int, Exception)

Creates a new SAXParseException with an embedded exception.

Method Index

getColumnNumber()

The column number of the end of the text where the exception occurred.

getLineNumber()

The line number of the end of the text where the exception occurred.

getPublicId()

Gets the public identifier of the entity where the exception occurred.

getSystemId()

Gets the system identifier of the entity where the exception occurred.

Constructors

SAXParseException

```
public SAXParseException(String message,
                         Locator locator)
```

Creates a new SAXParseException from a message and a Locator.

This constructor is especially useful when an application is creating its own exception from within a DocumentHandler callback.

Parameters:

message—The error or warning message.

locator—The locator object for the error or warning.

See Also:

Locator, setLocale

SAXParseException

```
public SAXParseException(String message,
                         Locator locator,
                         Exception e)
```

Wraps an existing exception in a SAXParseException.

This constructor is especially useful when an application is creating its own exception from within a DocumentHandler callback, and it needs to wrap an existing exception that is not a subclass of SAX-Exception.

Parameters:

message—The error or warning message, or null to use the message from the embedded exception.

locator—The locator object for the error or warning.

e—Any exception.

See Also:

Locator, setLocale

SAXParseException

```
public SAXParseException(String message,
                         String publicId,
                         String systemId,
                         int lineNumber,
                         int columnNumber)
```

Creates a new SAXParseException.

This constructor is most useful for parser writers.

If the system identifier is a URL, the parser must resolve it fully before creating the exception.

Parameters:

message—The error or warning message.

publicId—The public identifier of the entity that generated the error or warning.

systemId—The system identifier of the entity that generated the error or warning.

lineNumber—The line number of the end of the text that caused the error or warning.

columnNumber—The column number of the end of the text that caused the error or warning.

See Also:

`setLocale`

SAXParseException

```
public SAXParseException(String message,
                         String publicId,
                         String systemId,
                         int lineNumber,
                         int columnNumber,
                         Exception e)
```

Creates a new `SAXParseException` with an embedded exception. This constructor is most useful for parser writers who need to wrap an exception that is not a subclass of `SAXException`.

If the system identifier is a URL, the parser must resolve it fully before creating the exception.

Parameters:

message—The error or warning message, or null to use the message from the embedded exception.

publicId—The public identifier of the entity that generated the error or warning.

systemId—The system identifier of the entity that generated the error or warning.

lineNumber—The line number of the end of the text that caused the error or warning.

columnNumber—The column number of the end of the text that caused the error or warning.

e—Another exception to embed in this one.

See Also:

`setLocale`

Methods

getPublicId

```
public String getPublicId()
```

Gets the public identifier of the entity where the exception occurred.

Returns:

A string containing the public identifier, or null if none is available.

See Also:

getPublicId

getSystemId

```
public String getSystemId()
```

Gets the system identifier of the entity where the exception occurred.

If the system identifier is a URL, it will be resolved fully.

Returns:

A string containing the system identifier, or null if none is available.

See Also:

getSystemId

getLineNumber

```
public int getLineNumber()
```

The line number of the end of the text where the exception occurred.

Returns:

An integer representing the line number, or -1 if none is available.

See Also:

getLineNumber

getColumnNumber

```
public int getColumnNumber()
```

The column number of the end of the text where the exception occurred.

The first column in a line is position 1.

Returns:

An integer representing the column number, or -1 if none is available.

See Also:

getColumnNumber

Class org.xml.sax.helpers. AttributeListImpl

```
java.lang.Object
  |
  +—org.xml.sax.helpers.AttributeListImpl
```

public class **AttributeListImpl**
extends Object
implements AttributeList—Convenience implementation for AttributeList.

This class provides a convenience implementation of the SAX AttributeList class. This implementation is useful both for SAX parser writers, who can use it to provide attributes to the application, and for SAX application writers, who can use it to create a persistent copy of an element's attribute specifications:

```
private AttributeList myatts;
public void startElement (String name, AttributeList atts)
{
            // create a persistent copy of the attribute
               list
            // for use outside this method
   myatts = new AttributeListImpl(atts);
   [...]
}
```

Please note that SAX parsers are not required to use this class to provide an implementation of `AttributeList`; it is supplied only as an optional convenience. In particular, parser writers are encouraged to invent more efficient implementations.

Version:

1.0

Author:

David Megginson (ak117@freenet.carleton.ca)

See Also:

AttributeList, startElement

Constructor Index

AttributeListImpl()

Creates an empty attribute list.

AttributeListImpl(AttributeList)

Constructs a persistent copy of an existing attribute list.

Method Index

addAttribute(String, String, String)
Adds an attribute to an attribute list.

clear()
Clears the attribute list.

getLength()
Returns the number of attributes in the list.

getName(int)
Gets the name of an attribute (by position).

getType(int)
Gets the type of an attribute (by position).

getType(String)
Gets the type of an attribute (by name).

getValue(int)
Gets the value of an attribute (by position).

getValue(String)
Gets the value of an attribute (by name).

removeAttribute(String)
Removes an attribute from the list.

setAttributeList(AttributeList)
Sets the attribute list, discarding previous contents.

Constructors

AttributeListImpl

```
public AttributeListImpl()
```

Creates an empty attribute list.

This constructor is most useful for parser writers, who will use it to create a single, reusable attribute list that can be reset with the clear method between elements.

See Also:

addAttribute, clear

AttributeListImpl

```
public AttributeListImpl(AttributeList atts)
```

Constructs a persistent copy of an existing attribute list.

This constructor is most useful for application writers, who will use it to create a persistent copy of an existing attribute list.

Parameters:

atts—The attribute list to copy.

See Also:

startElement

Methods

setAttributeList

```
public void setAttributeList(AttributeList atts)
```

Sets the attribute list, discarding previous contents.

This method allows an application writer to reuse an attribute list easily.

Parameters:

atts—The attribute list to copy.

addAttribute

```
public void addAttribute(String name,
                         String type,
                         String value)
```

Adds an attribute to an attribute list.

This method is provided for SAX parser writers, to allow them to build up an attribute list incrementally before delivering it to the application.

Parameters:

name—The attribute name.

type—The attribute type (`"NMTOKEN"` for an enumeration).

value—The attribute value (must not be null).

See Also:

`removeAttribute, startElement`

removeAttribute

```
public void removeAttribute(String name)
```

Removes an attribute from the list.

SAX application writers can use this method to filter an attribute out of an `AttributeList`. Note that invoking this method will change the length of the attribute list and some of the attribute's indices.

If the requested attribute is not in the list, this is a no-op.

Parameters:

name—The attribute name.

See Also:

`addAttribute`

clear

```
public void clear()
```

Clears the attribute list.

SAX parser writers can use this method to reset the attribute list between `DocumentHandler.startElement` events. Normally, it will make sense to reuse the same `AttributeListImpl` object rather than allocating a new one each time.

See Also:

startElement

getLength

```
public int getLength()
```

Returns the number of attributes in the list.

Returns:

The number of attributes in the list.

See Also:

getLength

getName

```
public String getName(int i)
```

Gets the name of an attribute (by position).

Parameters:

i—The position of the attribute in the list.

Returns:

The attribute name as a string, or null if there is no attribute at that position.

See Also:

getName

getType

```
public String getType(int i)
```

Gets the type of an attribute (by position).

Parameters:

i—The position of the attribute in the list.

Returns:

The attribute type as a string ("NMTOKEN" for an enumeration, and "CDATA" if no declaration was read), or null if there is no attribute at that position.

See Also:

getType

getValue

```
public String getValue(int i)
```

Gets the value of an attribute (by position).

Parameters:

i—The position of the attribute in the list.

Returns:

The attribute value as a string, or null if there is no attribute at that position.

See Also:

getValue

getType

```
public String getType(String name)
```

Gets the type of an attribute (by name).

Parameters:
name—The attribute name.

Returns:
The attribute type as a string (`"NMTOKEN"` for an enumeration, and `"CDATA"` if no declaration was read).

See Also:
getType

getValue

```
public String getValue(String name)
```

Gets the value of an attribute (by name).

Parameters:
name—The attribute name.

See Also:
getValue

Class org.xml.sax.helpers.LocatorImpl

```
java.lang.Object
  |
  +—org.xml.sax.helpers.LocatorImpl
```

public class **LocatorImpl**
extends Object
implements <u>Locator</u>—Provides an optional convenience implementation of <code>Locator</code>.

This class is available mainly for application writers, who can use it to make a persistent snapshot of a locator at any point during a document parse:

```
Locator locator;
Locator startloc;
public void setLocator (Locator locator)
{
        // note the locator
   this.locator = locator;
}
public void startDocument ()
{
        // save the location of the start of the document
        // for future use.
   Locator startloc = new LocatorImpl(locator);
}
```

Normally, parser writers will not use this class, since it is more efficient to provide location information only when requested, rather than constantly updating a <code>Locator</code> object.

See Also:

<u>Locator</u>

Constructor Index

<u>LocatorImpl</u>()
Zero-argument constructor.

LocatorImpl(Locator)

Copy constructor.

Method Index

getColumnNumber()

Returns the saved column number (1-based).

getLineNumber()

Returns the saved line number (1-based).

getPublicId()

Returns the saved public identifier.

getSystemId()

Returns the saved system identifier.

setColumnNumber(int)

Sets the column number for this locator (1-based).

setLineNumber(int)

Sets the line number for this locator (1-based).

setPublicId(String)

Sets the public identifier for this locator.

setSystemId(String)

Sets the system identifier for this locator.

Constructors

LocatorImpl

```
public LocatorImpl()
```

Zero-argument constructor.

This will not normally be useful, since the main purpose of this class is to make a snapshot of an existing `Locator`.

LocatorImpl

```
public LocatorImpl(Locator locator)
```

Copy constructor.

Creates a persistent copy of the current state of a locator. When the original locator changes, this copy will still keep the original values (and it can be used outside the scope of `DocumentHandler` methods).

Parameters:

locator—The locator to copy.

Methods

getPublicId

```
public String getPublicId()
```

Returns the saved public identifier.

Returns:

The public identifier as a string, or null if none is available.

See Also:

getPublicId, setPublicId

getSystemId

```
public String getSystemId()
```

Returns the saved system identifier.

Returns:

The system identifier as a string, or null if none is | available.

See Also:

getSystemId, setSystemId

getLineNumber

```
public int getLineNumber()
```

Returns the saved line number (1-based).

Returns:

The line number as an integer, or -1 if none is available.

See Also:

getLineNumber, setLineNumber

getColumnNumber

```
public int getColumnNumber()
```

Returns the saved column number (1-based).

Returns:

The column number as an integer, or -1 if none is available.

See Also:

getColumnNumber, setColumnNumber

setPublicId

```
public void setPublicId(String publicId)
```

Sets the public identifier for this locator.

Parameters:

> publicId—The new public identifier, or null if none is available.

See Also:

> getPublicId

setSystemId

```
public void setSystemId(String systemId)
```

Sets the system identifier for this locator.

Parameters:

> systemId—The new system identifier, or null if none is available.

See Also:

> getSystemId

setLineNumber

```
public void setLineNumber(int lineNumber)
```

Sets the line number for this locator (1-based).

Parameters:

> lineNumber—The line number, or -1 if none is available.

See Also:

> getLineNumber

setColumnNumber

```
public void setColumnNumber(int columnNumber)
```

Sets the column number for this locator (1-based).

Parameters:

columnNumber—The column number, or -1 if none is available.

See Also:

getColumnNumber

Class org.xml.sax.helpers.ParserFactory

```
java.lang.Object
   |
   +—org.xml.sax.helpers.ParserFactory
```

public class **ParserFactory**
extends Object—Java-specific class for dynamically loading SAX parsers.

This class is not part of the platform-independent definition of SAX; it is an additional convenience class designed specifically for Java XML application writers. SAX applications can use the static methods in this class to allocate a SAX parser dynamically at run-time based either on the value of the org.xml.sax.parser system property or on a string containing the class name.

Note that the application still requires an XML parser that implements SAX.

Version:

1.0

Author:

David Megginson (ak117@freenet.carleton.ca)

See Also:

Parser, Class

Constructor Index

ParserFactory()

Method Index

makeParser ()
> Private null constructor.

makeParser (String)
> Creates a new SAX parser object using the class name provided.

Constructors

ParserFactory

```
public ParserFactory()
```

Methods

makeParser

```
public static Parser makeParser() throws ClassNotFoundExcep-
tion, IllegalAccessException, InstantiationException, Null-
PointerException, ClassCastException
```

Private null constructor. private ParserFactor () { } /** Creates a new SAX parser using the org.xml.sax.parser system property.

The named class must exist and must implement the org.xml.sax.Parser interface.

Throws: NullPointerException

There is no value for the `org.xml.sax.parser` system property.

Throws: `ClassNotFoundException`

The SAX parser class was not found (check your CLASS-PATH).

Throws: `IllegalAccessException`

The SAX parser class was found, but you do not have permission to load it.

Throws: `InstantiationException`

The SAX parser class was found but could not be instantiated.

Throws: `ClassCastException`

The SAX parser class was found and instantiated, but does not implement `org.xml.sax.Parser`.

See Also:

makeParser, Parser

makeParser

```
public static Parser makeParser(String className) throws
ClassNotFoundException, IllegalAccessException,
InstantiationException, ClassCastException
```

Creates a new SAX parser object using the class name provided. The named class must exist and must implement the `org.xml.sax.Parser` interface.

Parameters:

className—A string containing the name of the SAX parser class.

Throws: `ClassNotFoundException`

The SAX parser class was not found (check your CLASS-PATH).

Throws: `IllegalAccessException`

The SAX parser class was found, but you do not have permission to load it.

Throws: `InstantiationException`

The SAX parser class was found but could not be instantiated.

Throws: `ClassCastException`

The SAX parser class was found and instantiated, but does not implement `org.xml.sax.Parser`.

See Also:

`makeParser, Parser`

Appendix D
Java Language Binding

This appendix contains the complete Java binding for the Level 1 Document Object Model. The definitions are divided into Core and HTML.

The Java files are also available at http://www.w3.org/TR/REC-DOM-Level-1/java-binding.zip

D.1   Document Object Model Level 1 Core

```
public abstract class DOMException extends RuntimeException {
  public DOMException(short code, String message) {
    super(message);
    this.code = code;
  }
  public short    code;
  // ExceptionCode
  public static final short        INDEX_SIZE_ERR       = 1;
  public static final short        DOMSTRING_SIZE_ERR   = 2;
```

```
  public static final short          HIERARCHY_REQUEST_ERR = 3;
  public static final short          WRONG_DOCUMENT_ERR    = 4;
  public static final short          INVALID_CHARACTER_ERR = 5;
  public static final short          NO_DATA_ALLOWED_ERR   = 6;
  public static final short          NO_MODIFICATION_ALLOWED_ERR = 7;
  public static final short          NOT_FOUND_ERR         = 8;
  public static final short          NOT_SUPPORTED_ERR     = 9;
  public static final short          INUSE_ATTRIBUTE_ERR   = 10;

}

// ExceptionCode
public static final short          INDEX_SIZE_ERR        = 1;
public static final short          DOMSTRING_SIZE_ERR    = 2;
public static final short          HIERARCHY_REQUEST_ERR = 3;
public static final short          WRONG_DOCUMENT_ERR    = 4;
public static final short          INVALID_CHARACTER_ERR = 5;
public static final short          NO_DATA_ALLOWED_ERR   = 6;
public static final short          NO_MODIFICATION_ALLOWED_ERR = 7;
public static final short          NOT_FOUND_ERR         = 8;
public static final short          NOT_SUPPORTED_ERR     = 9;
public static final short          INUSE_ATTRIBUTE_ERR   = 10;

}

public interface DOMImplementation {
  public boolean                 hasFeature(String feature,
                                            String version);
}

public interface DocumentFragment extends Node {
}

public interface Document extends Node {
  public DocumentType        getDoctype();
  public DOMImplementation   getImplementation();
  public Element             getDocumentElement();
  public Element             createElement(String tagName)
                                          throws DOMException;
  public DocumentFragment    createDocumentFragment();
  public Text                createTextNode(String data);
  public Comment             createComment(String data);
  public CDATASection        createCDATASection(String data)
                                          throws DOMException;
  public ProcessingInstruction createProcessingInstruction(String tar-
get,
```

```
                                                    String
data)
                                                    throws
DOMException;
  public Attr            createAttribute(String name)
                                   throws DOMException;
  public EntityReference createEntityReference(String name)
                                        throws DOMException;
  public NodeList        getElementsByTagName(String tagname);
}

public interface Node {
  // NodeType
  public static final short        ELEMENT_NODE        = 1;
  public static final short        ATTRIBUTE_NODE      = 2;
  public static final short        TEXT_NODE           = 3;
  public static final short        CDATA_SECTION_NODE  = 4;
  public static final short        ENTITY_REFERENCE_NODE = 5;
  public static final short        ENTITY_NODE         = 6;
  public static final short        PROCESSING_INSTRUCTION_NODE = 7;
  public static final short        COMMENT_NODE        = 8;
  public static final short        DOCUMENT_NODE       = 9;
  public static final short        DOCUMENT_TYPE_NODE  = 10;
  public static final short        DOCUMENT_FRAGMENT_NODE = 11;
  public static final short        NOTATION_NODE       = 12;

  public String          getNodeName();
  public String          getNodeValue()
                                        throws DOMException;
  public void            setNodeValue(String nodeValue)
                                        throws DOMException;
  public short           getNodeType();
  public Node            getParentNode();
  public NodeList        getChildNodes();
  public Node            getFirstChild();
  public Node            getLastChild();
  public Node            getPreviousSibling();
  public Node            getNextSibling();
  public NamedNodeMap    getAttributes();
  public Document        getOwnerDocument();
  public Node            insertBefore(Node newChild,
                               Node refChild)
                               throws DOMException;
  public Node            replaceChild(Node newChild,
                               Node oldChild)
                               throws DOMException;
```

```
  public Node                   removeChild(Node oldChild)
                                        throws DOMException;
  public Node                   appendChild(Node newChild)
                                        throws DOMException;
  public boolean                hasChildNodes();
  public Node                   cloneNode(boolean deep);
}

public interface NodeList {
  public Node                   item(int index);
  public int                    getLength();
}

public interface NamedNodeMap {
  public Node                   getNamedItem(String name);
  public Node                   setNamedItem(Node arg)
                                        throws DOMException;
  public Node                   removeNamedItem(String name)
                                        throws DOMException;
  public Node                   item(int index);
  public int                    getLength();
}

public interface CharacterData extends Node {
  public String                 getData()
                                    throws DOMException;
  public void                   setData(String data)
                                    throws DOMException;
  public int                    getLength();
  public String                 substringData(int offset,
                                        int count)
                                    throws DOMException;
  public void                   appendData(String arg)
                                    throws DOMException;
  public void                   insertData(int offset,
                                        String arg)
                                    throws DOMException;
  public void                   deleteData(int offset,
                                        int count)
                                    throws DOMException;
  public void                   replaceData(int offset,
                                        int count,
                                        String arg)
                                    throws DOMException;
}
```

```
public interface Attr extends Node {
  public String             getName();
  public boolean            getSpecified();
  public String             getValue();
  public void               setValue(String value);
}

public interface Element extends Node {
  public String             getTagName();
  public String             getAttribute(String name);
  public void               setAttribute(String name,
                                         String value)
                                throws DOMException;
  public void               removeAttribute(String name)
                                   throws DOMException;
  public Attr               getAttributeNode(String name);
  public Attr               setAttributeNode(Attr newAttr)
                                   throws DOMException;
  public Attr               removeAttributeNode(Attr oldAttr)
                                   throws DOMException;
  public NodeList           getElementsByTagName(String name);
  public void               normalize();
}

public interface Text extends CharacterData {
  public Text               splitText(int offset)
                                throws DOMException;
}

public interface Comment extends CharacterData {
}

public interface CDATASection extends Text {
}

public interface DocumentType extends Node {
  public String             getName();
  public NamedNodeMap       getEntities();
  public NamedNodeMap       getNotations();
}

public interface Notation extends Node {
  public String             getPublicId();
  public String             getSystemId();
}
```

```
public interface Entity extends Node {
  public String              getPublicId();
  public String              getSystemId();
  public String              getNotationName();
}


public interface EntityReference extends Node {
}


public interface ProcessingInstruction extends Node {
  public String              getTarget();
  public String              getData();
  public void                setData(String data)
                                        throws DOMException;

}
```

D.2 | Document Object Model Level 1 HTML

```
public interface HTMLCollection {
  public int                 getLength();
  public Node                item(int index);
  public Node                namedItem(String name);
}


public interface HTMLDocument extends Document {
  public String              getTitle();
  public void                setTitle(String title);
  public String              getReferrer();
  public String              getDomain();
  public String              getURL();
  public HTMLElement         getBody();
  public void                setBody(HTMLElement body);
  public HTMLCollection      getImages();
  public HTMLCollection      getApplets();
  public HTMLCollection      getLinks();
  public HTMLCollection      getForms();
  public HTMLCollection      getAnchors();
  public String              getCookie();
  public void                setCookie(String cookie);
```

```
  public void            open();
  public void            close();
  public void            write(String text);
  public void            writeln(String text);
  public Element         getElementById(String elementId);
  public NodeList        getElementsByName(String elementName);
}

public interface HTMLElement extends Element {
  public String          getId();
  public void            setId(String id);
  public String          getTitle();
  public void            setTitle(String title);
  public String          getLang();
  public void            setLang(String lang);
  public String          getDir();
  public void            setDir(String dir);
  public String          getClassName();
  public void            setClassName(String className);
}

public interface HTMLHtmlElement extends HTMLElement {
  public String          getVersion();
  public void            setVersion(String version);
}

public interface HTMLHeadElement extends HTMLElement {
  public String          getProfile();
  public void            setProfile(String profile);
}

public interface HTMLLinkElement extends HTMLElement {
  public boolean         getDisabled();
  public void            setDisabled(boolean disabled);
  public String          getCharset();
  public void            setCharset(String charset);
  public String          getHref();
  public void            setHref(String href);
  public String          getHreflang();
  public void            setHreflang(String hreflang);
  public String          getMedia();
  public void            setMedia(String media);
  public String          getRel();
  public void            setRel(String rel);
  public String          getRev();
```

```
  public void              setRev(String rev);
  public String            getTarget();
  public void              setTarget(String target);
  public String            getType();
  public void              setType(String type);
}


public interface HTMLTitleElement extends HTMLElement {
  public String            getText();
  public void              setText(String text);
}


public interface HTMLMetaElement extends HTMLElement {
  public String            getContent();
  public void              setContent(String content);
  public String            getHttpEquiv();
  public void              setHttpEquiv(String httpEquiv);
  public String            getName();
  public void              setName(String name);
  public String            getScheme();
  public void              setScheme(String scheme);
}


public interface HTMLBaseElement extends HTMLElement {
  public String            getHref();
  public void              setHref(String href);
  public String            getTarget();
  public void              setTarget(String target);
}


public interface HTMLIsIndexElement extends HTMLElement {
  public HTMLFormElement   getForm();
  public String            getPrompt();
  public void              setPrompt(String prompt);
}


public interface HTMLStyleElement extends HTMLElement {
  public boolean           getDisabled();
  public void              setDisabled(boolean disabled);
  public String            getMedia();
  public void              setMedia(String media);
  public String            getType();
  public void              setType(String type);
}
```

```
public interface HTMLBodyElement extends HTMLElement {
  public String          getALink();
  public void            setALink(String aLink);
  public String          getBackground();
  public void            setBackground(String background);
  public String          getBgColor();
  public void            setBgColor(String bgColor);
  public String          getLink();
  public void            setLink(String link);
  public String          getText();
  public void            setText(String text);
  public String          getVLink();
  public void            setVLink(String vLink);
}

public interface HTMLFormElement extends HTMLElement {
  public HTMLCollection    getElements();
  public int               getLength();
  public String            getName();
  public void              setName(String name);
  public String            getAcceptCharset();
  public void              setAcceptCharset(String acceptCharset);
  public String            getAction();
  public void              setAction(String action);
  public String            getEnctype();
  public void              setEnctype(String enctype);
  public String            getMethod();
  public void              setMethod(String method);
  public String            getTarget();
  public void              setTarget(String target);
  public void              submit();
  public void              reset();
}

public interface HTMLSelectElement extends HTMLElement {
  public String            getType();
  public int               getSelectedIndex();
  public void              setSelectedIndex(int selectedIndex);
  public String            getValue();
  public void              setValue(String value);
  public int               getLength();
  public HTMLFormElement   getForm();
  public HTMLCollection    getOptions();
  public boolean           getDisabled();
  public void              setDisabled(boolean disabled);
```

```
  public boolean            getMultiple();
  public void               setMultiple(boolean multiple);
  public String             getName();
  public void               setName(String name);
  public int                getSize();
  public void               setSize(int size);
  public int                getTabIndex();
  public void               setTabIndex(int tabIndex);
  public void               add(HTMLElement element,
                                HTMLElement before);
  public void               remove(int index);
  public void               blur();
  public void               focus();
}

public interface HTMLOptGroupElement extends HTMLElement {
  public boolean            getDisabled();
  public void               setDisabled(boolean disabled);
  public String             getLabel();
  public void               setLabel(String label);
}

public interface HTMLOptionElement extends HTMLElement {
  public HTMLFormElement    getForm();
  public boolean            getDefaultSelected();
  public void               setDefaultSelected(boolean defaultSe-
lected);
  public String             getText();
  public int                getIndex();
  public void               setIndex(int index);
  public boolean            getDisabled();
  public void               setDisabled(boolean disabled);
  public String             getLabel();
  public void               setLabel(String label);
  public boolean            getSelected();
  public String             getValue();
  public void               setValue(String value);
}

public interface HTMLInputElement extends HTMLElement {
  public String             getDefaultValue();
  public void               setDefaultValue(String defaultValue);
  public boolean            getDefaultChecked();
  public void               setDefaultChecked(boolean defaultChecked);
  public HTMLFormElement    getForm();
```

```
public String            getAccept();
public void              setAccept(String accept);
public String            getAccessKey();
public void              setAccessKey(String accessKey);
public String            getAlign();
public void              setAlign(String align);
public String            getAlt();
public void              setAlt(String alt);
public boolean           getChecked();
public void              setChecked(boolean checked);
public boolean           getDisabled();
public void              setDisabled(boolean disabled);
public int               getMaxLength();
public void              setMaxLength(int maxLength);
public String            getName();
public void              setName(String name);
public boolean           getReadOnly();
public void              setReadOnly(boolean readOnly);
public String            getSize();
public void              setSize(String size);
public String            getSrc();
public void              setSrc(String src);
public int               getTabIndex();
public void              setTabIndex(int tabIndex);
public String            getType();
public String            getUseMap();
public void              setUseMap(String useMap);
public String            getValue();
public void              setValue(String value);
public void              blur();
public void              focus();
public void              select();
public void              click();
}

public interface HTMLTextAreaElement extends HTMLElement {
  public String            getDefaultValue();
  public void              setDefaultValue(String defaultValue);
  public HTMLFormElement   getForm();
  public String            getAccessKey();
  public void              setAccessKey(String accessKey);
  public int               getCols();
  public void              setCols(int cols);
  public boolean           getDisabled();
  public void              setDisabled(boolean disabled);
```

```
   public String          getName();
   public void            setName(String name);
   public boolean         getReadOnly();
   public void            setReadOnly(boolean readOnly);
   public int             getRows();
   public void            setRows(int rows);
   public int             getTabIndex();
   public void            setTabIndex(int tabIndex);
   public String          getType();
   public String          getValue();
   public void            setValue(String value);
   public void            blur();
   public void            focus();
   public void            select();
}


public interface HTMLButtonElement extends HTMLElement {
   public HTMLFormElement  getForm();
   public String           getAccessKey();
   public void             setAccessKey(String accessKey);
   public boolean          getDisabled();
   public void             setDisabled(boolean disabled);
   public String           getName();
   public void             setName(String name);
   public int              getTabIndex();
   public void             setTabIndex(int tabIndex);
   public String           getType();
   public String           getValue();
   public void             setValue(String value);
}


public interface HTMLLabelElement extends HTMLElement {
   public HTMLFormElement  getForm();
   public String           getAccessKey();
   public void             setAccessKey(String accessKey);
   public String           getHtmlFor();
   public void             setHtmlFor(String htmlFor);
}


public interface HTMLFieldSetElement extends HTMLElement {
   public HTMLFormElement  getForm();
}


public interface HTMLLegendElement extends HTMLElement {
   public HTMLFormElement  getForm();
```

```
  public String          getAccessKey();
  public void            setAccessKey(String accessKey);
  public String          getAlign();
  public void            setAlign(String align);
}

public interface HTMLUListElement extends HTMLElement {
  public boolean         getCompact();
  public void            setCompact(boolean compact);
  public String          getType();
  public void            setType(String type);
}

public interface HTMLOListElement extends HTMLElement {
  public boolean         getCompact();
  public void            setCompact(boolean compact);
  public int             getStart();
  public void            setStart(int start);
  public String          getType();
  public void            setType(String type);
}

public interface HTMLDListElement extends HTMLElement {
  public boolean         getCompact();
  public void            setCompact(boolean compact);
}

public interface HTMLDirectoryElement extends HTMLElement {
  public boolean         getCompact();
  public void            setCompact(boolean compact);
}

public interface HTMLMenuElement extends HTMLElement {
  public boolean         getCompact();
  public void            setCompact(boolean compact);
}

public interface HTMLLIElement extends HTMLElement {
  public String          getType();
  public void            setType(String type);
  public int             getValue();
  public void            setValue(int value);
}

public interface HTMLBlockquoteElement extends HTMLElement {
  public String          getCite();
```

```java
    public void                  setCite(String cite);
}

public interface HTMLDivElement extends HTMLElement {
    public String                getAlign();
    public void                  setAlign(String align);
}

public interface HTMLParagraphElement extends HTMLElement {
    public String                getAlign();
    public void                  setAlign(String align);
}

public interface HTMLHeadingElement extends HTMLElement {
    public String                getAlign();
    public void                  setAlign(String align);
}

public interface HTMLQuoteElement extends HTMLElement {
    public String                getCite();
    public void                  setCite(String cite);
}

public interface HTMLPreElement extends HTMLElement {
    public int                   getWidth();
    public void                  setWidth(int width);
}

public interface HTMLBRElement extends HTMLElement {
    public String                getClear();
    public void                  setClear(String clear);
}

public interface HTMLBaseFontElement extends HTMLElement {
    public String                getColor();
    public void                  setColor(String color);
    public String                getFace();
    public void                  setFace(String face);
    public String                getSize();
    public void                  setSize(String size);
}

public interface HTMLFontElement extends HTMLElement {
    public String                getColor();
    public void                  setColor(String color);
```

```
  public String             getFace();
  public void               setFace(String face);
  public String             getSize();
  public void               setSize(String size);
}

public interface HTMLHRElement extends HTMLElement {
  public String             getAlign();
  public void               setAlign(String align);
  public boolean            getNoShade();
  public void               setNoShade(boolean noShade);
  public String             getSize();
  public void               setSize(String size);
  public String             getWidth();
  public void               setWidth(String width);
}

public interface HTMLModElement extends HTMLElement {
  public String             getCite();
  public void               setCite(String cite);
  public String             getDateTime();
  public void               setDateTime(String dateTime);
}

public interface HTMLAnchorElement extends HTMLElement {
  public String             getAccessKey();
  public void               setAccessKey(String accessKey);
  public String             getCharset();
  public void               setCharset(String charset);
  public String             getCoords();
  public void               setCoords(String coords);
  public String             getHref();
  public void               setHref(String href);
  public String             getHreflang();
  public void               setHreflang(String hreflang);
  public String             getName();
  public void               setName(String name);
  public String             getRel();
  public void               setRel(String rel);
  public String             getRev();
  public void               setRev(String rev);
  public String             getShape();
  public void               setShape(String shape);
  public int                getTabIndex();
  public void               setTabIndex(int tabIndex);
```

```
    public String          getTarget();
    public void            setTarget(String target);
    public String          getType();
    public void            setType(String type);
    public void            blur();
    public void            focus();
}

public interface HTMLImageElement extends HTMLElement {
    public String          getLowSrc();
    public void            setLowSrc(String lowSrc);
    public String          getName();
    public void            setName(String name);
    public String          getAlign();
    public void            setAlign(String align);
    public String          getAlt();
    public void            setAlt(String alt);
    public String          getBorder();
    public void            setBorder(String border);
    public String          getHeight();
    public void            setHeight(String height);
    public String          getHspace();
    public void            setHspace(String hspace);
    public boolean         getIsMap();
    public void            setIsMap(boolean isMap);
    public String          getLongDesc();
    public void            setLongDesc(String longDesc);
    public String          getSrc();
    public void            setSrc(String src);
    public String          getUseMap();
    public void            setUseMap(String useMap);
    public String          getVspace();
    public void            setVspace(String vspace);
    public String          getWidth();
    public void            setWidth(String width);
}

public interface HTMLObjectElement extends HTMLElement {
    public HTMLFormElement getForm();
    public String          getCode();
    public void            setCode(String code);
    public String          getAlign();
    public void            setAlign(String align);
    public String          getArchive();
    public void            setArchive(String archive);
```

```
  public String          getBorder();
  public void            setBorder(String border);
  public String          getCodeBase();
  public void            setCodeBase(String codeBase);
  public String          getCodeType();
  public void            setCodeType(String codeType);
  public String          getData();
  public void            setData(String data);
  public boolean         getDeclare();
  public void            setDeclare(boolean declare);
  public String          getHeight();
  public void            setHeight(String height);
  public String          getHspace();
  public void            setHspace(String hspace);
  public String          getName();
  public void            setName(String name);
  public String          getStandby();
  public void            setStandby(String standby);
  public int             getTabIndex();
  public void            setTabIndex(int tabIndex);
  public String          getType();
  public void            setType(String type);
  public String          getUseMap();
  public void            setUseMap(String useMap);
  public String          getVspace();
  public void            setVspace(String vspace);
  public String          getWidth();
  public void            setWidth(String width);
}

public interface HTMLParamElement extends HTMLElement {
  public String          getName();
  public void            setName(String name);
  public String          getType();
  public void            setType(String type);
  public String          getValue();
  public void            setValue(String value);
  public String          getValueType();
  public void            setValueType(String valueType);
}

public interface HTMLAppletElement extends HTMLElement {
  public String          getAlign();
  public void            setAlign(String align);
  public String          getAlt();
}
```

```
  public void                 setAlt(String alt);
  public String               getArchive();
  public void                 setArchive(String archive);
  public String               getCode();
  public void                 setCode(String code);
  public String               getCodeBase();
  public void                 setCodeBase(String codeBase);
  public String               getHeight();
  public void                 setHeight(String height);
  public String               getHspace();
  public void                 setHspace(String hspace);
  public String               getName();
  public void                 setName(String name);
  public String               getObject();
  public void                 setObject(String object);
  public String               getVspace();
  public void                 setVspace(String vspace);
  public String               getWidth();
  public void                 setWidth(String width);
}


public interface HTMLMapElement extends HTMLElement {
  public HTMLCollection       getAreas();
  public String               getName();
  public void                 setName(String name);
}


public interface HTMLAreaElement extends HTMLElement {
  public String               getAccessKey();
  public void                 setAccessKey(String accessKey);
  public String               getAlt();
  public void                 setAlt(String alt);
  public String               getCoords();
  public void                 setCoords(String coords);
  public String               getHref();
  public void                 setHref(String href);
  public boolean              getNoHref();
  public void                 setNoHref(boolean noHref);
  public String               getShape();
  public void                 setShape(String shape);
  public int                  getTabIndex();
  public void                 setTabIndex(int tabIndex);
  public String               getTarget();
  public void                 setTarget(String target);
}
```

```
public interface HTMLScriptElement extends HTMLElement {
  public String              getText();
  public void                setText(String text);
  public String              getHtmlFor();
  public void                setHtmlFor(String htmlFor);
  public String              getEvent();
  public void                setEvent(String event);
  public String              getCharset();
  public void                setCharset(String charset);
  public boolean             getDefer();
  public void                setDefer(boolean defer);
  public String              getSrc();
  public void                setSrc(String src);
  public String              getType();
  public void                setType(String type);
}

public interface HTMLTableElement extends HTMLElement {
  public HTMLTableCaptionElement getCaption();
  public void                setCaption(HTMLTableCaptionElement cap-
tion);
  public HTMLTableSectionElement getTHead();
  public void                setTHead(HTMLTableSectionElement tHead);
  public HTMLTableSectionElement getTFoot();
  public void                setTFoot(HTMLTableSectionElement tFoot);
  public HTMLCollection      getRows();
  public HTMLCollection      getTBodies();
  public String              getAlign();
  public void                setAlign(String align);
  public String              getBgColor();
  public void                setBgColor(String bgColor);
  public String              getBorder();
  public void                setBorder(String border);
  public String              getCellPadding();
  public void                setCellPadding(String cellPadding);
  public String              getCellSpacing();
  public void                setCellSpacing(String cellSpacing);
  public String              getFrame();
  public void                setFrame(String frame);
  public String              getRules();
  public void                setRules(String rules);
  public String              getSummary();
  public void                setSummary(String summary);
  public String              getWidth();
  public void                setWidth(String width);
```

```
    public HTMLElement          createTHead();
    public void                 deleteTHead();
    public HTMLElement          createTFoot();
    public void                 deleteTFoot();
    public HTMLElement          createCaption();
    public void                 deleteCaption();
    public HTMLElement          insertRow(int index);
    public void                 deleteRow(int index);
}


public interface HTMLTableCaptionElement extends HTMLElement {
    public String               getAlign();
    public void                 setAlign(String align);
}


public interface HTMLTableColElement extends HTMLElement {
    public String               getAlign();
    public void                 setAlign(String align);
    public String               getCh();
    public void                 setCh(String ch);
    public String               getChOff();
    public void                 setChOff(String chOff);
    public int                  getSpan();
    public void                 setSpan(int span);
    public String               getVAlign();
    public void                 setVAlign(String vAlign);
    public String               getWidth();
    public void                 setWidth(String width);
}


public interface HTMLTableSectionElement extends HTMLElement {
    public String               getAlign();
    public void                 setAlign(String align);
    public String               getCh();
    public void                 setCh(String ch);
    public String               getChOff();
    public void                 setChOff(String chOff);
    public String               getVAlign();
    public void                 setVAlign(String vAlign);
    public HTMLCollection       getRows();
    public HTMLElement          insertRow(int index);
    public void                 deleteRow(int index);
}


public interface HTMLTableRowElement extends HTMLElement {
    public int                  getRowIndex();
```

```
    public void              setRowIndex(int rowIndex);
    public int               getSectionRowIndex();
    public void              setSectionRowIndex(int sectionRowIndex);
    public HTMLCollection    getCells();
    public void              setCells(HTMLCollection cells);
    public String            getAlign();
    public void              setAlign(String align);
    public String            getBgColor();
    public void              setBgColor(String bgColor);
    public String            getCh();
    public void              setCh(String ch);
    public String            getChOff();
    public void              setChOff(String chOff);
    public String            getVAlign();
    public void              setVAlign(String vAlign);
    public HTMLElement       insertCell(int index);
    public void              deleteCell(int index);
}

public interface HTMLTableCellElement extends HTMLElement {
    public int               getCellIndex();
    public void              setCellIndex(int cellIndex);
    public String            getAbbr();
    public void              setAbbr(String abbr);
    public String            getAlign();
    public void              setAlign(String align);
    public String            getAxis();
    public void              setAxis(String axis);
    public String            getBgColor();
    public void              setBgColor(String bgColor);
    public String            getCh();
    public void              setCh(String ch);
    public String            getChOff();
    public void              setChOff(String chOff);
    public int               getColSpan();
    public void              setColSpan(int colSpan);
    public String            getHeaders();
    public void              setHeaders(String headers);
    public String            getHeight();
    public void              setHeight(String height);
    public boolean           getNoWrap();
    public void              setNoWrap(boolean noWrap);
    public int               getRowSpan();
    public void              setRowSpan(int rowSpan);
    public String            getScope();
    public void              setScope(String scope);
```

```
  public String            getVAlign();
  public void              setVAlign(String vAlign);
  public String            getWidth();
  public void              setWidth(String width);
}

public interface HTMLFrameSetElement extends HTMLElement {
  public String            getCols();
  public void              setCols(String cols);
  public String            getRows();
  public void              setRows(String rows);
}

public interface HTMLFrameElement extends HTMLElement {
  public String            getFrameBorder();
  public void              setFrameBorder(String frameBorder);
  public String            getLongDesc();
  public void              setLongDesc(String longDesc);
  public String            getMarginHeight();
  public void              setMarginHeight(String marginHeight);
  public String            getMarginWidth();
  public void              setMarginWidth(String marginWidth);
  public String            getName();
  public void              setName(String name);
  public boolean           getNoResize();
  public void              setNoResize(boolean noResize);
  public String            getScrolling();
  public void              setScrolling(String scrolling);
  public String            getSrc();
  public void              setSrc(String src);
}

public interface HTMLIFrameElement extends HTMLElement {
  public String            getAlign();
  public void              setAlign(String align);
  public String            getFrameBorder();
  public void              setFrameBorder(String frameBorder);
  public String            getHeight();
  public void              setHeight(String height);
  public String            getLongDesc();
  public void              setLongDesc(String longDesc);
  public String            getMarginHeight();
  public void              setMarginHeight(String marginHeight);
  public String            getMarginWidth();
  public void              setMarginWidth(String marginWidth);
```

```
public String          getName();
public void            setName(String name);
public String          getScrolling();
public void            setScrolling(String scrolling);
public String          getSrc();
public void            setSrc(String src);
public String          getWidth();
public void            setWidth(String width);
}
```

Index

LICENSE AGREEMENT AND LIMITED WARRANTY

READ THE FOLLOWING TERMS AND CONDITIONS CAREFULLY BEFORE OPENING THIS SOFTWARE MEDIA PACKAGE. THIS LEGAL DOCUMENT IS AN AGREEMENT BETWEEN YOU AND PRENTICE-HALL, INC. (THE "COMPANY"). BY OPENING THIS SEALED SOFTWARE MEDIA PACKAGE, YOU ARE AGREEING TO BE BOUND BY THESE TERMS AND CONDITIONS. IF YOU DO NOT AGREE WITH THESE TERMS AND CONDITIONS, DO NOT OPEN THE SOFTWARE MEDIA PACKAGE. PROMPTLY RETURN THE UNOPENED SOFTWARE MEDIA PACKAGE AND ALL ACCOMPANYING ITEMS TO THE PLACE YOU OBTAINED THEM FOR A FULL REFUND OF ANY SUMS YOU HAVE PAID.

1.   **GRANT OF LICENSE:** In consideration of your payment of the license fee, which is part of the price you paid for this product, and your agreement to abide by the terms and conditions of this Agreement, the Company grants to you a nonexclusive right to use and display the copy of the enclosed software program (hereinafter the "SOFTWARE") on a single computer (i.e., with a single CPU) at a single location so long as you comply with the terms of this Agreement. The Company reserves all rights not expressly granted to you under this Agreement.

2.   **OWNERSHIP OF SOFTWARE:** You own only the magnetic or physical media (the enclosed software media) on which the SOFTWARE is recorded or fixed, but the Company retains all the rights, title, and ownership to the SOFTWARE recorded on the original software media copy(ies) and all subsequent copies of the SOFTWARE, regardless of the form or media on which the original or other copies may exist. This license is not a sale of the original SOFTWARE or any copy to you.

3.   **COPY RESTRICTIONS:** This SOFTWARE and the accompanying printed materials and user manual (the "Documentation") are the subject of copyright. You may <u>not</u> copy the Documentation or the SOFTWARE, except that you may make a single copy of the SOFTWARE for backup or archival purposes only. You may be held legally responsible for any copying or copyright infringement which is caused or encouraged by your failure to abide by the terms of this restriction.

4.   **USE RESTRICTIONS:** You may <u>not</u> network the SOFTWARE or otherwise use it on more than one computer or computer terminal at the same time. You may physically transfer the SOFTWARE from one computer to another provided that the SOFTWARE is used on only one computer at a time. You may <u>not</u> distribute copies of the SOFTWARE or Documentation to others. You may <u>not</u> reverse engineer, disassemble, decompile, modify, adapt, translate, or create derivative works based on the SOFTWARE or the Documentation without the prior written consent of the Company.

5.   **TRANSFER RESTRICTIONS:** The enclosed SOFTWARE is licensed only to you and may <u>not</u> be transferred to any one else without the prior written consent of the Company. Any unauthorized transfer of the SOFTWARE shall result in the immediate termination of this Agreement.

6.   **TERMINATION:** This license is effective until terminated. This license will terminate automatically without notice from the Company and become null and void if you fail to comply with any provisions or limitations of this license. Upon termination, you shall destroy the Documentation and all copies of the SOFTWARE. All provisions of this Agreement as to warranties, limitation of liability, remedies or damages, and our ownership rights shall survive termination.

7.   **MISCELLANEOUS:** This Agreement shall be construed in accordance with the laws of the United States of America and the State of New York and shall benefit the Company, its affiliates, and assignees.

8.   **LIMITED WARRANTY AND DISCLAIMER OF WARRANTY:** The Company warrants that the SOFTWARE, when properly used in accordance with the Documentation, will operate in substantial conformity with the description of the SOFTWARE set forth in the Documentation. The Company does not

warrant that the SOFTWARE will meet your requirements or that the operation of the SOFTWARE will be uninterrupted or error-free. The Company warrants that the media on which the SOFTWARE is delivered shall be free from defects in materials and workmanship under normal use for a period of thirty (30) days from the date of your purchase. Your only remedy and the Company's only obligation under these limited warranties is, at the Company's option, return of the warranted item for a refund of any amounts paid by you or replacement of the item. Any replacement of SOFTWARE or media under the warranties shall not extend the original warranty period. The limited warranty set forth above shall not apply to any SOFTWARE which the Company determines in good faith has been subject to misuse, neglect, improper installation, repair, alteration, or damage by you. EXCEPT FOR THE EXPRESSED WARRANTIES SET FORTH ABOVE, THE COMPANY DISCLAIMS ALL WARRANTIES, EXPRESS OR IMPLIED, INCLUDING WITHOUT LIMITATION, THE IMPLIED WARRANTIES OF MERCHANTABILITY AND FITNESS FOR A PARTICULAR PURPOSE. EXCEPT FOR THE EXPRESS WARRANTY SET FORTH ABOVE, THE COMPANY DOES NOT WARRANT, GUARANTEE, OR MAKE ANY REPRESENTATION REGARDING THE USE OR THE RESULTS OF THE USE OF THE SOFTWARE IN TERMS OF ITS CORRECTNESS, ACCURACY, RELIABILITY, CURRENTNESS, OR OTHERWISE.

IN NO EVENT, SHALL THE COMPANY OR ITS EMPLOYEES, AGENTS, SUPPLIERS, OR CONTRACTORS BE LIABLE FOR ANY INCIDENTAL, INDIRECT, SPECIAL, OR CONSEQUENTIAL DAMAGES ARISING OUT OF OR IN CONNECTION WITH THE LICENSE GRANTED UNDER THIS AGREEMENT, OR FOR LOSS OF USE, LOSS OF DATA, LOSS OF INCOME OR PROFIT, OR OTHER LOSSES, SUSTAINED AS A RESULT OF INJURY TO ANY PERSON, OR LOSS OF OR DAMAGE TO PROPERTY, OR CLAIMS OF THIRD PARTIES, EVEN IF THE COMPANY OR AN AUTHORIZED REPRESENTATIVE OF THE COMPANY HAS BEEN ADVISED OF THE POSSIBILITY OF SUCH DAMAGES. IN NO EVENT SHALL LIABILITY OF THE COMPANY FOR DAMAGES WITH RESPECT TO THE SOFTWARE EXCEED THE AMOUNTS ACTUALLY PAID BY YOU, IF ANY, FOR THE SOFTWARE.

SOME JURISDICTIONS DO NOT ALLOW THE LIMITATION OF IMPLIED WARRANTIES OR LIABILITY FOR INCIDENTAL, INDIRECT, SPECIAL, OR CONSEQUENTIAL DAMAGES, SO THE ABOVE LIMITATIONS MAY NOT ALWAYS APPLY. THE WARRANTIES IN THIS AGREEMENT GIVE YOU SPECIFIC LEGAL RIGHTS AND YOU MAY ALSO HAVE OTHER RIGHTS WHICH VARY IN ACCORDANCE WITH LOCAL LAW.

ACKNOWLEDGMENT

YOU ACKNOWLEDGE THAT YOU HAVE READ THIS AGREEMENT, UNDERSTAND IT, AND AGREE TO BE BOUND BY ITS TERMS AND CONDITIONS. YOU ALSO AGREE THAT THIS AGREEMENT IS THE COMPLETE AND EXCLUSIVE STATEMENT OF THE AGREEMENT BETWEEN YOU AND THE COMPANY AND SUPERSEDES ALL PROPOSALS OR PRIOR AGREEMENTS, ORAL, OR WRITTEN, AND ANY OTHER COMMUNICATIONS BETWEEN YOU AND THE COMPANY OR ANY REPRESENTATIVE OF THE COMPANY RELATING TO THE SUBJECT MATTER OF THIS AGREEMENT.

Should you have any questions concerning this Agreement or if you wish to contact the Company for any reason, please contact in writing at the address below.

Robin Short
Prentice Hall PTR
One Lake Street
Upper Saddle River, New Jersey 07458

About the CD-ROM

The CD-ROM contains the following files and programs:

Code Examples

DOMWalker—This is a simple example of how to traverse a DOM Document.

SAXTest—This is the example used in Chapter 2 that illustrated the events produced by SAX.

Sitemap—This is the example used in Chapter 2 to illustrate filtering using the DOM.

Seralization— This directory contains the source code to the example in Chapter 3 that illustrated transforming a Java object graph into an XML document.

XMLColumn—This directory contains the source code illustrated in Chapter 4 that implements reading and writing XML from a relational database that supports BLOB types.

JMS—This directory contains the example from Chapter 5 that illustrate the sending and receiving of XML messages using the Java Messaging Service (JMS).

JNDI — This directory contains the examples from Chapter 6 illustrating the use of an XML document as a data source for directory and naming.

DPG — This directory contains the examples from Chapter 7 illustrating a declarative processing runtime engine.

MDSAX — This directory contains the MDSAX libraries and Swing example from Chapter 8.

IBM XML4J Version 2.0

The Java parser provided for this book, and against which all source code examples have been written is IBM's XML4J Version 2.0.

Push-Technologies, Inc.'s SpiritWave

SpiritWave is a pure-Java implementation of the Java Messaging Service (JMS) that supports both queues and topics.

Bluestone Software's Visual-XML

Bluestone Visual-XML is a development tool that helps developers build XML document handlers. It provides a visual representation of XML documents and allows the developer to define methods for transformation. This package can be found in the Bluestone sub-directory.

Extensibility's XML Authority

XML Authority is an XML schema development tool. It supports extracting metadata from number of popular sources including: databases, Java classes, COM objects, and LDAP servers.

WDDX SDK

WDDX is a proposed technology by Allaire Corporation to assist developers in moving structured data between applications over the Web.

License Agreement

Use of the software accompanying Enterprise Application Integration with XML and Java is subject to the terms of the License Agreement and Limited Warranty, found on the previous two pages.

Technical Support

Prentice Hall does not offer technical support for any of the programs on the CD-ROM. However, if the CD-ROM is damaged, you may obtain a replacement copy by sending an email that describes the problem to: disc_exchange@prenhall.com